Praise for

BETRAYAL

The Crisis in the Catholic Church

"What we are now calling the Catholic Church scandal began with a court document that could have been buried in a sea of legal papers had it not been for a team of reporters from the *Boston Globe*. . . . The *Globe*'s work, both in the stories that began appearing in January 2002 and in this book, is extraordinary."
— Sandi Dolbee, *San Diego Union-Tribune*

"Every detail of this sordid story has had to be dragged from the reluctant archdiocese, mostly by the dogged investigative reporting of the *Boston Globe*."
— Bill Keller, *New York Times*

"If the *Boston Globe* had not told the story of the church's horrific failures in Boston, the abuse would have gone right on. There would have been no crisis, no demand from the laity that the church cut out this cancer of irresponsibility, corruption, and sin, and no charter for the protection of children. The *Globe* did the church an enormous favor."
— Andrew Greeley, *Chicago Sun-Times*

"Only one newspaper, the *Boston Globe*, had the persistence and courage to tackle this story by forcing the Boston archdiocese to release internal documents that finally revealed the scope of the scandal."
— Peggy Noonan, *Wall Street Journal*

"This book is more than a religious and journalistic morality play for modern times. It's a classic example of what serious, long-form investigative reporting and dedicated community service by the press can accomplish."
— *Buffalo News*

"This is a watershed moment for the *Boston Globe*. They brought the Church to heel. Not only was it an outstanding piece of reporting, but a brave piece of publishing."

— Alex S. Jones, *American Journalism Review*

"The only reason that some of the truth has been revealed is because the *Boston Globe* got a judge to open documents that the Boston archdiocese fought to keep closed."

— *Milwaukee Journal Sentinel*

"It is hard to imagine any reader interested enough to pick up the book putting it down unfinished. *Betrayal* shows public-affairs journalism at its best."

— Steve Weinberg, *Denver Post*

"If journalism is the first draft of history, *Betrayal* gives present readers and future historians a good start."

— Alan Cochrum, *Fort Worth Star-Telegram*

"Although published in the summer, *Betrayal* is even more germane today because of the continuing upheaval in the Catholic Church and the abdication of Bernard Cardinal Law. *Betrayal* covers the whole gamut of rogue predatory priests."

— Dermot McEvoy, author of *Terrible Angel*

"An excellent account of [Cardinal] Law's troubles by the *Boston Globe* reporters who exposed them."

— Garry Wills, *New York Review of Books*

"A stunning account of the genesis of the Church's headline-grabbing sex-abuse scandal. . . . *Betrayal* is a must-read for anyone who has doubted the importance of this ongoing story."

— Michelle Bearden, *Tampa Tribune*

BETRAYAL

THE CRISIS IN THE CATHOLIC CHURCH

**THE FINDINGS OF THE
INVESTIGATION THAT INSPIRED
THE MAJOR MOTION PICTURE
*SPOTLIGHT***

Updated Edition

BY THE INVESTIGATIVE STAFF OF
THE *BOSTON GLOBE*

Matt Carroll   Michael Paulson
Kevin Cullen   Sacha Pfeiffer
Thomas Farragher   Michael Rezendes
Stephen Kurkjian   Walter V. Robinson

BACK BAY BOOKS

Little, Brown and Company

New York Boston London

Back Bay Books / Little, Brown and Company

Hachette Book Group

1290 Avenue of the Americas, New York, NY 10104

littlebrown.com

Originally published in hardcover by Little, Brown and Company, May 2002

First Back Bay paperback edition, April 2003

Updated Back Bay paperback edition, October 2015

Back Bay Books is an imprint of Little, Brown and Company, a division of Hachette Book Group, Inc. The Back Bay Books name and logo are trademarks of Hachette Book Group, Inc.

The publisher is not responsible for websites (or their content) that are not owned by the publisher.

The Hachette Speakers Bureau provides a wide range of authors for speaking events. To find out more, go to hachettespeakersbureau.com or call (866) 376-6591.

ISBN 978-0-316-07558-9 (hc) / 978-0-316-77675-2 (pb) / 978-0-316-27153-0 (updated pb)

LCCN 2015951503

10 9 8 7 6 5 4 3

RRD-C

Printed in the United States of America

Contents

"Betrayal hangs like a heavy cloud over the Church today."

Cardinal Bernard F. Law
Archbishop of Boston
Good Friday (March 29), 2002

Preface

A Statement from *Spotlight* Director Tom McCarthy and Screenwriter Josh Singer

The past ten years have been very unkind to the newspaper business, especially on the local level. Over a dozen metro dailies have gone out of print. Newspaper revenues in 2014 were less than half of what they were ten years earlier. And thousands of reporters have lost their jobs. Of course, there has been innovation online. Many would point out that there's more information available now than ever before, and, to that end, some would argue there is no longer a need for traditional investigative journalism.

We disagree.

The pages of this book contain the findings of the *Boston Globe* Spotlight Team—hard facts and even harder stories of priests, lawyers, and survivors that had been hidden for dozens of years. Taken together, they tell a larger narrative of corruption and concealment, of a scandal at the core of the Boston archdiocese, one of the most powerful institutions in New England. It was these findings that led to similar investigations in dozens of cities in the United States and around the world—all of which served to shed light on the larger issue of clergy sex abuse and the institutional cover-up that allowed it to persist, an issue that we are still grappling with today.

The reporting in the pages of this book truly rocked the world. Nothing could possibly add to the significance of that. But context is a useful tool. Insight into *how* a team of four journalists and their two primary editors broke the story might help the world appreciate the reporting in these pages that much more—and appreciate why there is still very much a need for traditional investigative journalism.

That is why we decided to tell the *Spotlight* story. Of course, you won't find that story in this book. To get there, we had to do our own digging. We had to investigate the *Globe*'s investigation, which, for us, shed new meaning on the *Globe* journalists' original findings. Learning how in-depth and difficult their task was only added to the power of the end work itself.

To uncover a news story like this one, to really expose the breadth and the depth of the corruption detailed in the pages of this book, a journalist needs time. Four excellent, experienced reporters and two senior editors at the *Globe* spent more than a year working full time, overtime, on the investigation. A journalist also needs resources. In addition to paying salaries and overhead, the *Globe* paid for the legal work necessary to sue for the sealed documents in the case of Father John Geoghan — documents that would eventually prove the church's complicity in the cover-up beyond a shadow of a doubt. And finally, in most cases, a journalist needs the backing of an institution, one with the strength to call other powerful institutions to heel, just as the *Globe* did in 2002.

We hope that our movie, along with the rerelease of this incredible documentation of the *Globe* Spotlight Team's reporting, might help further the argument for traditional investigative journalism, and put forth an argument for the institutions that allow the Robinsons and Rezendeses, the Pfeiffers and Carrolls, the Barons and Bradlees of the world, to keep doing their work. As Marty Baron says, we spend most of our time stumbling around in the dark. Thank goodness for Spotlight.

September 10, 2015

BETRAYAL

Introduction

In June 2001, Cardinal Bernard F. Law, the longtime Roman Catholic archbishop of Boston, used a routine court filing to make an extraordinary admission: seventeen years earlier he had given Rev. John J. Geoghan a plum job as parochial vicar of an affluent suburban parish, despite having been notified just two months previously that Geoghan was alleged to have molested seven boys.

The *Boston Globe* had reported on Geoghan's case before, notably in February 1997 when, citing interviews and Church records, the paper revealed that the priest had been placed on sick leave in 1980 after a woman told Church officials he had been molesting her sons. But Geoghan was returned to duty in 1981, and later was found to have molested children in two more parishes before being placed on sick leave again in 1995.

For the investigative staff of the *Globe*, however, Law's 2001 court filing was a turning point: a story about a priest who was accused of molesting children was now a story about a bishop who protected that priest. The document prompted an investigation by the *Globe*'s four-person investigative unit, the Spotlight Team, which set out to determine whether the Geoghan case was an anomaly or part of a pattern.

The troubling answer to that question — that dozens of Boston-area priests had molested minors, and in too many cases bishops had known about the abuse — was revealed in a series of stories published in early 2002 that triggered one of the most serious challenges to the Catholic Church's hegemony in modern times.

The *Globe*'s reporting, and the events it set off, led to the writing of a book published in 2002, *Betrayal,* the story of scores of priests who abused the children in their care, victims whose lives were shattered, bishops who failed to prevent the abuse, and laypeople who rose up in anger. This edition of *Betrayal*, published in 2015, has been updated with new information to coincide with the release of *Spotlight*, the major motion picture that chronicles the *Globe*'s investigation into the sexual abuse crisis. The movie is based on an original screenplay by Josh Singer and director Tom McCarthy.

"Since the mid-1990s, more than 130 people have come forward with horrific childhood tales about how former priest John J. Geoghan allegedly fondled or raped them during a three-decade spree through a half-dozen Greater Boston parishes," began the Spotlight Team's first article on the subject, published in January 2002. "Almost always, his victims were grammar school boys. One was just 4 years old."

Over the next year, the *Globe* ran more than six hundred stories about clergy sexual abuse. Though the problem had been known nationally and sporadically written about since the mid-1980s, the *Globe*'s reporting used the Church's own documents to demonstrate that high-ranking officials had for decades hidden the prevalence of the abuse problem and repeatedly put the welfare of abusive priests ahead of that of the children.

In the Geoghan case, a succession of two cardinals and many bishops over thirty-four years had failed to place children out of Geoghan's reach, sending the priest compassionate letters even as they moved him from parish to parish, leaving a trail of victims in his wake.

The first *Globe* stories struck a nerve. Catholics were furious and felt betrayed. Cardinal Law apologized, repeatedly, and in the ensuing days and weeks, he agreed to turn over the names of all priests, past and present, accused of sexually abusing minors, even though such reporting was not then required under Massachusetts law. He announced a zero-tolerance policy, vowing to oust any priest against whom a credible allegation was lodged, and promised new efforts to reach out to victims.

But the dam had burst. Many Catholics called for Law's resignation and began withholding contributions to the Church. State legislators passed a bill requiring clergy to report allegations of sexual abuse to secular authorities. Prosecutors began issuing arrest warrants for priests.

The story began, as all stories do, with a group of reporters trying to answer a set of questions. The *Globe*'s Spotlight Team—editor Walter V. Robinson and reporters Matt Carroll, Sacha Pfeiffer, and Michael Rezendes—set out to determine how much the Church had known about Geoghan's three decades of abuse in six parishes throughout the archdiocese.

Within a few days, however, the reporters discovered that Geoghan was merely the best-known example of a much deeper problem. The Archdiocese of Boston had secretly settled claims of abuse against multiple priests in recent years. Most of the claims had been resolved in private, with no public record. It was an agreeable arrangement: the Church got to keep the ugly truth under wraps; shame-filled victims, having no clue that there were so many others, were able to protect their privacy. Victims' lawyers received a third or more of the financial settlements without ever having to air their cases in court.

Even in the infrequent instances when lawsuits were filed, the reporters found that official records often had vanished. That was because judges had improperly agreed to impound the cases once they were settled, shielding from the public not only the outcomes but any traces that the suits had even been filed in the first place.

Reporters met another roadblock. In the scores of civil lawsuits pending against Geoghan, a judge had placed a confidentiality seal on all the documents produced in the case, including depositions and Geoghan's personnel records.

Martin Baron, who had just become editor of the *Globe*, decided that the newspaper should challenge the judge's confidentiality order on the grounds that the public interest in unsealing the documents outweighed the privacy concerns of the litigants. In August 2001, the newspaper's lawyers filed a motion seeking to unseal the Geoghan papers.

Superior Court Judge Constance M. Sweeney ruled in the *Globe*'s favor in November. The Church appealed the decision, but in December a state appeals court judge upheld Sweeney's ruling. The documents would be released sometime in January 2002.

On December 17, 2001, Wilson D. Rogers Jr., Cardinal Law's lawyer, sent the *Globe* a letter threatening to seek legal sanctions against the newspaper and its law firm if stories were published based on anything gleaned from confidential records in the suits. He warned that he would seek court-imposed sanctions if reporters even asked questions of clergy involved in the case.

But by this time the Spotlight Team had obtained the most explosive of the sealed documents. It also had determined through numerous interviews that in the past decade many priests in the Boston archdiocese had faced sexual abuse allegations credible enough that the Church had paid settlements to the victims—and had done so secretly. The team used the archdiocese's annual directories, which list where priests are assigned, as its compass. The reporters developed a database showing that scores of active priests had inexplicably been removed from parish assignments around the time the victims were receiving settlements. The scope of the abuse was far greater than previously known.

With Geoghan due to face his first criminal trial on sex abuse charges in January, the Spotlight Team put aside the secret settlements story in mid-December and began work on what was initially conceived as a three-thousand-word article that would set the stage for the first Geoghan trial.

But the previously sealed documents the *Globe* had found were extremely damaging to the archdiocese. The records included a 1984 warning to Law from one of his bishops that Geoghan remained a danger; a 1982 letter from a parishioner to Law's predecessor, Cardinal Humberto S. Medeiros, laying out Geoghan's abuses and demanding to know why he was still allowed to serve in a parish with children; and some of Geoghan's psychiatric records. The documents proved that the archdiocese had known of Geoghan's abuse of children for generations.

So the *Globe* decided to publish a two-part Spotlight series on the

Geoghan case on January 6 and 7, 2002. Law, who at the time was considered the most influential American Catholic prelate with the Vatican, declined to be interviewed for the articles. Then, in anticipation of Judge Sweeney's release of about ten thousand more pages of Geoghan court documents on January 25, the *Globe* obtained the files early and published excerpts and stories about them on January 24, adding rich detail and context to the initial series.

On January 31, the newspaper ran the overarching piece it had begun reporting the previous summer, revealing that over the past decade the Archdiocese of Boston had secretly settled cases in which at least seventy priests had been accused of sexual abuse. The story—based on court documents and records, a database, and interviews with attorneys and other sources involved in the cases—was a watershed, establishing that the Geoghan case was no aberration. The abuse was widespread and had gone unchecked for decades.

Soon, prodded by their local media, other dioceses around the country were also combing their files for past complaints and jousting with authorities about what to do with their accused priests. Many of the dioceses began to formulate new policies on how to deal with sexual abuse complaints, and the U.S. Conference of Catholic Bishops prepared to adopt a national policy for the first time.

As the crisis in the Church grew, the *Globe* doubled to eight the number of reporters assigned to the story full-time, adding projects writers Stephen Kurkjian, Thomas Farragher, and Kevin Cullen, as well as religion reporter Michael Paulson. Over time, other reporters contributed on an ad hoc basis.

This book builds on the extensive reporting the *Globe* has done on the clergy sexual abuse scandal. Some of the interviews and facts were previously reported in the newspaper, but much of the reporting is new, and the book was written from scratch. Interviews and research for the book also produced stories for the paper. Those articles included previously undisclosed instances of sexual abuse, the interplay between local prosecutors and the Boston archdiocese, and the expanding effort by Catholic laity to challenge the Church's hierarchy.

The clergy sexual abuse story is still unfolding—thirteen years after it broke wide open in 2002—and it will likely take years before all the facts are known and all the changes it set off are in place. This book, written from the epicenter of the scandal in Boston, examines the origins of the crisis and its causes, the behavior of abusive priests and its impact on victims, the role of key figures including Geoghan and Law, and the decline of deference among the faithful and how the Catholic Church might change as a result.

It is the story of a large number of priests who abused both the trust given them and the children in their care. It is the story of the bishops and the cardinals who hired, promoted, protected, and thanked those priests, despite overwhelming evidence of their abusive behavior. It is the story of a powerful, proud Church thrown into crisis by the misdeeds, mistakes, and misjudgments of its own clergy. It is the story of victims who suffered in silence for years before finding the voice to publicly challenge their Church. And it is the story of the desire of the Church's many faithful members to learn from the crisis and bring about change.

In the winter of 2002, when the initial reports about how the Catholic Church had handled priests who sexually abused children surfaced in the *Globe*, the stories seemed almost too horrible to be true. The extent of betrayal—of children's innocence, of parents' trust, of priestly vows, of bishops' responsibilities, of the Church's basic tenets—was breathtaking. Most shocking to everyday Catholics, and most damaging to the Church, was the incontrovertible evidence that Cardinal Law and other leaders of his archdiocese had engaged in a massive cover-up. Rather than protect its most vulnerable members, the Church had been putting them in harm's way.

Soon newspapers all over the United States and overseas began demanding answers from their local dioceses. Newly empowered victims stepped forward. Lawyers who once played by the Church's rules in secretly settling cases did a public about-face, declaring that those agreements were no longer in their clients' or the public's interest because the scope of the abuse had remained concealed.

Next, law enforcement officials, who along with their predecessors had been wary of going after the Church that many of them belonged to, demanded records so they could decide whether to prosecute priests whose only previous sanctions were transfers to new parishes, being stashed away in hospital chaplaincies, or, for the worst offenders, being placed on a bureaucratic shelf. Chastened Church leaders were confronted with overwhelming evidence that the Archdiocese of Boston placed a premium on protecting the Church's reputation at the expense of its victims.

Across the country, and across the Catholic world, priests implicated in abuse were pulled from assignments — 176 in the United States alone in the first four months of 2002. Bishops resigned in the United States, Poland, and Ireland. Even in Rome, where Vatican leaders had studiously avoided previous outbreaks of the scandal, Pope John Paul II used his annual Holy Thursday letter to priests to weigh in on the subject, although only to comfort good priests.

The Pope's fleeting reference to the scandal — using a vague Latin phrase, *"mysterium iniquitatis,"* to describe a crime he called a sin — failed to mention the victims at all, and thus offered little comfort to those whose lives had been upended by predator priests. To many, the Pope's statement seemed to be more evidence of an aloof, arrogant, out-of-touch hierarchy whose inability to see beyond its own needs had the effect of rubbing salt into raw, open wounds.

The following day, in his Good Friday letter, Cardinal Law touched on the theme of betrayal. "Betrayal hangs like a heavy cloud over the Church today," he wrote. "While we do not presume to judge anyone's relationship with God, there is no doubt that a betrayal of trust is at the heart of the evil in the sexual abuse of children by clergy. Priests should be trustworthy beyond any shadow of a doubt. When some have broken that trust, all of us suffer the consequences."

Public opinion polls detected a deepening sense of disillusionment among parishioners with Law's handling of the problem. By mid-April 2002, a *Globe*/WBZ-TV poll found that 65 percent of the Catholics in the archdiocese believed the cardinal should resign.

Many Catholics were already withholding money from the archdiocese, and now churchgoers turned their backs on the cardinal's Annual Appeal, which funds many Church programs. And an ambitious $350 million capital fundraising campaign virtually ground to a halt. There was renewed discussion about the wisdom of a priest-hood restricted to celibate men, and some wondered whether there was a link between the high incidence of sexual abuse of teenage boys and the high percentage of gay men in the priesthood.

After three months of mounting scandal, the Vatican seemed to awaken: the Pope summoned all the American cardinals to an extra-ordinary emergency meeting in April. At that session, John Paul changed his tune, and his tone. He said the sexual abuse of minors by priests was not only an "appalling sin" but a crime. The Pope also responded to complaints that the Holy See appeared indifferent to the suffering of victims. "To the victims and their families, wherever they may be, I express my profound sense of solidarity and concern," the frail eighty-one-year-old pontiff said.

While the cardinals' meeting on the crisis was remarkable, and unprecedented, it remained unclear how tangible and far-reaching the promised reforms would become. There were still many within the Vatican who viewed sexual abuse by clergy as a peculiarly American phenomenon.

The question of the Church failing to take the issue seriously had surfaced now and then since 1985, when the first big case exploded in Louisiana. But the Church had engaged in largely successful damage control, taking advantage of the widespread deference toward it to dismiss the scandals as anomalies being blown out of proportion by anti-Catholic elements in the news media, in collaboration with Catholic dissidents who wanted to discredit the hierarchy.

But the Church's ability to deflect the issue began to crumble in the face of internal documents in the Boston cases that showed Cardinal Law and his top aides were repeatedly warned about dangerous priests, yet continued to put the abusers back in circulation, in a position to attack children.

The Geoghan case became a potent symbol of the compassion and gentle treatment the Church afforded its own rogue priests at the expense of the victims. Geoghan was an incorrigible pedophile. Nearly two hundred people who say they were raped or fondled by Geoghan had filed claims against him and his supervisors by 2002. The priest calmly explained to therapists how he would single out his prey, the needy children of poor, single mothers—struggling women who were thrilled to have a man in their sons' lives, especially a priest. Occasionally complaints would arise, but Geoghan's superiors would simply move him to another parish and a fresh set of victims.

And it was not just Geoghan. Law, his bishops, and their predecessors had moved other abusive priests around like pawns on a chessboard too. Some were allowed to relocate out of state, foisted on other dioceses. If parishioners were in the dark about the predators cast into their midst, so too were some of the abusers' new pastors. In one case, in the process of arranging for an alleged child rapist named Rev. Paul Shanley to be transferred to a new parish in California, Cardinal Law's top deputy wrote a letter of assurance to Church officials in San Bernardino, vouching for the integrity of someone the Boston archdiocese knew had been accused of engaging in sexual abuse. Even after the archdiocese had reached financial settlements with some of Shanley's victims on the condition that they keep quiet, Cardinal Law wrote the priest a glowing retirement letter and said he would not object to Shanley's appointment to head a Church-run guest home in New York whose clientele included young people.

The problem in Boston was a microcosm of a festering sore on the body of the entire Church. If to some defenders it seemed like merely a brushfire, it was to others the greatest conflagration to face the Church in generations. It spread across the North American continent, stretched to Europe, and scandalized Australia and parts of Latin America.

Since the Louisiana case, most of those implicated were ordinary priests. But now the scandal quickly broadened, ensnaring not only the priests but the bishops and cardinals who protected them. A bishop in France was prosecuted criminally for failing to report pedophile priests to police, and in Wales a bishop was forced to resign because he protected abusive priests. In the spring of 2002, a Polish archbishop close to the Pope was forced to resign after being accused of sexually harassing seminarians. Three days later, Bishop Brendan Comiskey of Ireland resigned after admitting he had not done enough to control a priest whose rampant sexual abuse of minors led to the suicide of several victims and, ultimately, of the abusive priest himself.

But it was Boston that became the epicenter of the scandal—because the story broke there, because of the sheer number of priests implicated there, and because of the Catholic character of the city. More than 2 million of the 3.8 million people who lived in the metropolitan Boston area at the time were Catholic. It was the only major archdiocese in the United States where Catholics accounted for more than half the population. In no other major American city were Catholics more represented in police precincts, in courtrooms, in boardrooms. Nowhere else was the impact of the scandal more deeply felt. And nowhere else was the erosion of deference traditionally shown the Church more dramatic.

In 1992, when a scandal erupted over James R. Porter—a pedophile priest who attacked more than one hundred children in southeastern Massachusetts, outside the Boston archdiocese—most Catholics accepted Law's assurance that Porter's transgressions were not the fault of a caring Church but "an aberrant act" of one depraved man. He also said the Porter affair had been deliberately overblown because of anti-Catholic bias in the secular media. "By all means," the cardinal said at the time, "we call down God's power on the media, particularly the *Globe*."

The newspaper, founded by members of the Protestant Brahmin ascendancy that once ran Boston, had been accused of anti-Catholic bias before. But the documents about Geoghan unsealed by Judge Sweeney—showing the level to which the cardinal and his bishops went to conceal the pattern of abuse from the public eye—produced a sea change in attitudes among most Catholics. Rather than blame the messenger, they focused their anger on Church leaders. They wanted answers from their cardinal. And by the time he departed for the April 2002 meeting with the Pope and the other American cardinals in Rome, even Law wasn't blaming the media anymore. "The crisis of clergy sexual abuse of minors is not just a media-driven or public-perception concern in the United States, but a very serious issue undermining the mission of the Catholic Church," he said.

In the past, some politicians, police, prosecutors, and judges had enabled the cover-up of priestly misconduct, both great and small. But the scope of the archdiocese's actions on behalf of abusive priests emboldened those in law enforcement and politics to push aside a culture of deference that was more than a century in the making. The Massachusetts attorney general and five of the state's top prosecutors, all Catholic, demanded and eventually obtained Church records showing that more than ninety priests in the Boston archdiocese had been accused of sexual abuse by hundreds of victims over the previous forty years. That figure didn't include priests who had died. Almost all the cases were beyond the statute of limitations, meaning most could not be prosecuted. But whatever the archdiocese was able to dodge in a court of law bedeviled it in the court of public opinion.

Boston may be the quintessential American Catholic city, yet the scandal soon proved to be far more than a local story. It became an international story about how the rights of powerless individuals are brushed away in the interests of a powerful institution, about how mortals can damage an immortal faith.

The costs so far have been high. Donations to the Church have fallen. Many people have sworn off their faith, and more have sworn off the hierarchy. Harder to measure are the human costs to the victims. There was the eleven-year-old who, during confession, was asked by a priest whether he masturbated, then was asked for a demonstration; the thirteen-year-old who was seduced by his priest and, in an era of far less tolerance toward homosexuality, was left to wonder whether he was gay; and the boy who was handed train fare by a priest who had just anally raped him and left him bleeding.

If there are any heroes in this squalid tale, they are the victims, who found their voice, who found the courage, after years of suffering in silence and isolation, to step into the light and say, as one did, "This happened to me, and this is wrong."

1

Father Geoghan

He was a small, wiry man with a disarming smile that, from a distance, gave him the gentle bearing of a kindly uncle or a friendly neighborhood shopkeeper. It was hard to detect the darkness behind John Geoghan's bright eyes. At first glance, almost no one did.

Frank Leary certainly didn't see it. The fifth of six children being raised by a single mother on welfare, Leary was thirteen years old and had yet to learn his older brothers' tricks for ditching Mass on Sunday mornings when he first encountered Geoghan in the late spring of 1974. The priest's smiling face was already a fixture at the back of St. Andrew's Church in the Jamaica Plain section of Boston. After Mass, the parish priest would hug the mothers, shake hands with the fathers, and deliver soft pats to the backs of the children.

"He always had a big grin — it was as wide as his face," Leary recalled. "My mother liked him. He was very popular. He was like a little imp." Leary said hello to the priest, received his friendly tap across the shoulder blades, and didn't focus on Geoghan again until the summer.

The rectory groundskeeper was Leary's friend, and Leary helped out a couple times a week, raking freshly mowed grass or gathering hedge clippings in a wheelbarrow. It was taxing work under an August sun, and one afternoon Geoghan bounded down the short steps of the rectory, offering a tall, cool glass of lemonade. Leary thanked the priest but demurred. He didn't like lemonade. But the priest insisted, and sweetened the offer. He had a wonderful stamp collection that the boy might enjoy. Soon the priest and the boy were upstairs in Geoghan's room at the rectory.

Leary sat in a large leather chair in the middle of the room, and the priest handed him an oversized book that contained the stamp collection. The priest went to the back of the room, keeping up a constant, reassuring patter. The collection did not hold the boy's interest, but Geoghan pressed the matter. "He said, 'Here, I'll show you a few things.' And he had me get up and he sat down and I sat on his lap," said Leary. The priest placed his hand on Leary's knee and started turning pages that were a blur to the boy. Geoghan told him that his mother had suggested the visit. But still, Geoghan said, they should keep it a secret. All the while the priest's hand climbed farther up Leary's leg, until it reached under his cotton shorts and beneath his underwear.

"He was touching me, fondling me. I'm frozen. I didn't know what the hell was going on. He was talking constantly. He said, 'Shut the book. Close your eyes. We'll say the Hail Mary.' And that's what I did." But before the prayer was finished, the boy darted from the room, hurried down the stairs, and found himself shaking behind the church.

Within a week or so, it happened again. Leary was sweeping concrete next to the church when Geoghan walked up, put his arm around the teenager, and told him how special he was. The priest then ushered Leary back into the rectory, where, Leary later said, he saw a scowling nun standing at the foot of the stairs.

Geoghan swept past the nun and directed Leary to the same chair in which the first attack had occurred. The shades were drawn against the summertime brightness. At first, the priest stood behind him, placing his hands on Leary's shoulders. He asked the boy to begin reciting the most familiar prayers of the Catholic faith: the Our Father and the Hail Mary. "I'm praying and I've got my eyes closed. And he moves over to the chair and pulls my pants down one leg. And I couldn't move. I was frozen. He had his shoulder on my chest at this point. He was praying too. And I was saying prayers, following him. I'm shaking. I felt very, very strange. I couldn't do anything."

Geoghan moved down the young boy's body and began to perform oral sex on him. "I was trying to hold back the tears and keep saying my prayers and keep my eyes closed. I didn't see him do that. I remember being pushed back in my chair."

The assault did not last long. Perhaps only a minute, Leary estimated, before it was interrupted by a sudden commotion. "Geoghan stood straight up. The door flew open. And a priest with longish white hair started yelling at him. 'Jack, we told you not to do this up here! What the hell are you doing! Are you nuts?' He was yelling and screaming, and I just remember floating out of that chair."

Leary fled to a tree-shaded spot behind the school and tried to regain his composure. He sat for a while in a local cemetery, and when he finally went home, he went directly to his room. He didn't tell anyone about the assault for many years.

Geoghan had been a Catholic priest for a dozen years at the time Leary says Geoghan sexually assaulted him. As he moved through parishes in and around Boston — from the edges of the city to the tony suburbs beyond — he was known as "Father Jack" to the people in the pews. He baptized their babies. He celebrated their weddings. He prayed over their dead, sprinkling the caskets with holy water. On Saturday afternoons, he sat in the dark and, from behind a screen, listened to their sins and meted out their penance. On Sunday mornings, he delivered the word of God to them.

For faithful Catholic mothers, especially those struggling to raise a large family by themselves, Geoghan seemed a godsend. He was there on their doorsteps with an offer to help. He'd take their sons out for ice cream. He'd read to them at bedtime. He would pray with them beside their beds. He would tuck them in for the night.

And then, in the near darkness, their parish priest would fondle them in their nightclothes, pressing a finger to his lips and swearing them to secrecy.

"He looked like a little altar boy," said Maryetta Dussourd, who eagerly and proudly allowed Geoghan access to the small apartment where she lived with her daughter, three sons, and four of their cousins in Jamaica Plain. Geoghan was a calculating predator whose deceptive charm opened many doors.

As he sits today in oversized prison-issued clothing, John J. Geoghan is perhaps the nation's most conspicuous example of a sexually abusive member of the clergy, not just because of the stunning number of his victims — nearly two hundred have come forward so far — but because of the delicate and deceptive way the Church handled his sins. For more than two decades, even as two successive cardinals and dozens of Church officials in the Boston archdiocese learned that Geoghan could not control his compulsion to attack children, Geoghan found extraordinary solace in the Church's culture of secrecy.

"Yours has been an effective life of ministry, sadly impaired by illness. On behalf of those you have served well, and in my own name, I would like to thank you," Cardinal Bernard F. Law wrote to Geoghan in 1996, long after the priest's assaults had been detected. "I understand yours is a painful situation. The passion we share can indeed seem unbearable and unrelenting. We are our best selves when we respond in honesty and trust. God bless you, Jack."

Geoghan was one among many. And while the breadth of his assaults was vast, they were perhaps not as horrific as those committed by fellow priests who in some cases violently raped their young prey and then shooed them away as they resumed their priestly ministry. If it was a secret to the daily communicants and the congregations that filled the churches on Sunday mornings, it was common knowledge among Church leaders, who heard the anguished pleas from the mothers and fathers of children abused by priests. They promised to address the problem. They vowed they would not let it happen again. And then they did.

When Maryetta Dussourd discovered that Geoghan was molesting her boys — one of them just four years old — she found no solace from her friends or her church. Fellow parishioners shunned her. They accused her of provoking scandal. Church officials implored her to keep quiet. It was for the sake of the children, they said. Don't sue, they warned her. They told her that no one would believe her.

"Everything you have taught your child about God and safety and trust — it is destroyed," said Dussourd, whose claims against the Church were settled in a 1997 confidential agreement — like scores of others in which the victims received money and the Church obtained their silence.

Until January 2002, when this scandal erupted, priests were the men whose Roman collars conferred upon them the reflexive trust of parents who considered it an honor to have them in their homes. That was certainly how it had been with Geoghan. On warm summer days when he arrived without notice and offered to take their little boys out for ice cream cones, they swelled with pride and wished the priest well on his outing with their kids. When he showed up on their doorstep at night offering bedtime stories, they were certain that God had smiled on their children.

John J. Geoghan's priestly career nearly ended just as it was beginning.

When Monsignor John J. Murray, the rector of Cardinal O'Connell Seminary in Jamaica Plain, reviewed Geoghan's performance in the summer of 1954, he was not impressed. His faculty was concerned about Geoghan. They considered the nineteen-year-old seminarian decidedly immature, a characteristic not entirely evident in a casual setting. Further, they found Geoghan "feminine in his manner of speech and approach."

"Scholastically he is a problem," Murray concluded in a letter to a colleague. "To be sure he received passing grades in most subjects, but I still have serious doubts about his ability to do satisfactory work in future studies." As he considered whether to recommend Geoghan to superiors at St. John's Seminary in nearby Brighton, the next academic rung in a ladder that would lead to Geoghan's ordination, Murray opted to look on the bright side. "In his favor are the following good qualities: a very fervent spiritual life, industry, determination to succeed, happy disposition, obedience, docility, interest in and regard for others, and respected by his contemporaries. Perhaps maturity will bring to this young man the qualities he needs in order to be successful in his quest for the priesthood."

Perhaps. But the troubled Geoghan, in a pattern that would repeat itself for more than thirty years, would need help from on high. This time he found it from a monsignor he could call his own: his uncle.

Geoghan's father, whom he recalled as a kind and generous man, died when he was just five years old. And although he would later remember the funeral as spiritually uplifting, the death of his father struck the young boy hard: he wet his bed for two years as he struggled with the loss. Geoghan considered his mother a saintly woman who provided for him and his older sister a household of prayer and normalcy. It was, he said, a happy childhood. And in his mother's brother, Monsignor Mark H. Keohane, he found a father figure, role model, and protector. "The perfect substitute father," Geoghan said of his uncle, who would dress his young nephew in the vestments of a priest for festive neighborhood parades at the family's summer home in Scituate, a picture-postcard seaside community twenty-six miles south of Boston known locally as the Irish Riviera. It was a summer haunt for wealthy and influential Irish Americans, among them legendary former Boston mayor James Michael Curley.

Keohane was a formidable figure. Autocratic, old-school, domineering, and — some would say — mean. But Geoghan saw only his "great work and sacrifices." And when Geoghan again ran into trouble in the seminary, Keohane was there to run interference for his nephew.

In the summer of 1955, Geoghan failed to show up for a mandatory seminary summer camp. His superiors knew that Geoghan suffered from a "nervous condition," but they did not consider it severe enough to preclude his attendance. Besides, rules were rules. And Geoghan's decision to skip the camp without notifying his superiors imperiled his status as a seminarian. "If I do not receive a satisfactory explanation of your absence before Sunday I shall presume you have decided to withdraw from the seminary and I shall remove your name from our list of students," Rev. Thomas J. Riley, rector of St. John's Seminary, wrote to Geoghan at his home in the West Roxbury section of Boston in July 1955.

Geoghan didn't respond, but his uncle, using the letterhead of St. Bartholomew's parish in suburban Needham, where he had been the founding pastor since 1952, went to bat for his sister's boy. "I telephoned you at Brighton last week relative to John J. Geoghan, a seminarian who was unable to go to camp," Keohane wrote Riley. "He has been treating [sic] with a physician since he left Brighton, because of a nervous and depressed state. He had a letter written to you explaining his inability to attend camp, but the doctor advised against mailing it because of his depressed state. That is why I am writing. The doctor has the hopeful prognosis that within a few weeks he will respond to medication and rest so that he himself can write to you."

Riley's reply two days later from the seminary camp was tart. He accepted Keohane's explanation, but requested a doctor's report to confirm Geoghan's condition. "I need not remind you that the circumstances of John's absence from the camp raise considerable doubt as to his ability to adjust to the regimen of the seminary," Riley wrote. "Nor need I remind you how necessary it is for us to deal with matters such as this on a completely objective basis, since unauthorized concessions made to one student so easily set a precedent which would lead others to seek favors. We shall do everything within reason to help John settle his problem, but I think it must be admitted as a matter of principle that John is subject to the rule of the seminary and that his case should be dealt with in the same way as that of any other student."

Keohane did not like Riley's tone. "I resent your implication that I sought favors or preferment for John," he wrote back. He also complained that Geoghan, after three years in the seminary, "is now sick, unhappy, and appears to be wrestling with his soul."

Geoghan left the seminary for a couple of years to attend Holy Cross, the liberal-arts Jesuit college in Worcester, Massachusetts. Then, his soul-searching apparently settled, he reentered the seminary. In 1962 he took his vows and was ordained into the Catholic priesthood.

It is not clear whether Geoghan's tortuous life as a seminarian was because of sexual dysfunction, depression, or immaturity. He would later tell therapists that his home was free of physical, sexual, and verbal abuse. He considered himself a heterosexual who was frightened by the sexual feelings he first experienced at age eleven. When he fantasized about sex, he focused on girls. As a teenager, he dated in group settings. He considered masturbation a sin to be avoided. Despite his attraction to girls as an adolescent and young adult, Geoghan said he entered the priesthood as a virgin. "After ordination, Father Geoghan says he consciously repressed his enjoyment of the company of women for fear of conflict with his desire for celibacy," one therapist would later write. Tragically for hundreds of children and their families, Geoghan would seek the satisfaction of his sexual desires in the boys to whom he would enjoy so much unquestioned access.

Geoghan later acknowledged to his psychiatrist that it was soon after he was assigned to his first parish, Blessed Sacrament in Saugus, a blue-collar community north of Boston, that he grew sexually aroused in the company of boys. They would sit on his lap. He would fondle them over their clothing. There is no dispute that Geoghan abused children at Blessed Sacrament. The Archdiocese of Boston has settled claims on accusations that he did. For example, Church records note that in 1995 Geoghan admitted to molesting four boys from the same family while there. Geoghan focused on the three older boys — ages nine, ten, and eleven — and only "on rare occasions" on the seven-year-old. He said he was "careful never to touch the one girl in the family."

"It was not the intention of these innocent youth to arouse me," Geoghan said in a critique of one of his psychiatric evaluations. "They were just happy to have a father figure with their own father being so angry and distant from them. . . . I have deceived myself that these intimate actions were not wrong. In hindsight, I should have sought advice as to how to deal with children from dysfunctional families."

It's not clear whether Church officials knew about his earliest attacks at the time. A former priest, Anthony Benzevich, has said he saw Geoghan frequently escort young boys into his bedroom at the rectory. And Benzevich said he alerted Church higher-ups about it. But under questioning during a pretrial deposition in 2000, Benzevich — then represented by a lawyer for the Church — said his memory was foggy. He could not be certain that Geoghan brought boys into his room. He could not recall telling Church officials about it. Questioned later still by the *Boston Globe*, Benzevich said Geoghan liked to wrestle with young boys and dress them in priest's attire. Benzevich repeated his sworn assertion that he did not recall notifying superiors.

If the details of Geoghan's earliest assaults were sketchy, they acquired a sharp and stunning focus as he gained more experience as a priest and settled into rectory life. Geoghan doted on altar boys. He worked with first communicants. "We knew something wasn't right," one Church teacher said. "He just zeroed in on some kids." Geoghan paid particular attention to children from poorer families. "The children were just so affectionate, I got caught up in their acts of affection," Geoghan explained. "Children from middle-class families never acted like that toward me, so I never got so confused."

One priest, a former colleague of Geoghan, said he never had a chance to form a friendship with him because Geoghan was frequently out of the rectory while other priests were eating together, or reading, or otherwise socializing.

"I found him different, I must say. I mean, I just didn't know how to react to him. He was different," added Rev. Thomas W. Moriarty, who was pastor at St. Paul's Church in Hingham, south of Boston, where Geoghan served from 1967 to 1974. "Something is wrong. . . . Something is not right here, but you can't put your finger on it."

While he served with Moriarty in Hingham, Geoghan found time to befriend Joanne Mueller, a single mother of four boys who lived in Melrose, twenty-three miles away. Mueller's mother knew Geoghan from his days at Blessed Sacrament, and she introduced her daughter to the priest.

Soon Geoghan was a familiar figure in Mueller's home. As with some of his other victims, he took the boys for ice cream. He read them books at night. He helped get the boys in and out of the bathtub. Mueller would slip out for errands, and Geoghan would baby-sit for an hour here or an hour there. "He was our friend," Mueller said. If Geoghan disappeared upstairs into the boys' bedroom, she didn't give it a second thought.

One night in 1973, when Geoghan called asking to come over for a visit, the reaction of Mueller's third son, then seven or eight, surprised her. The boy did not want Geoghan in his home. He grew increasingly upset when his mother pressed him about his reluctance to see the priest she considered a valued friend.

"And then finally he broke out in tears . . . ," Mueller recalled. "He kept saying, 'No, no, no. I don't want him coming down.' He was insisting and I shouted back at him and I said, 'Why? What? What is it?' And he said, 'I don't want him touching my wee-wee.' I hate to be so blunt, but that's what he said."

Mueller was shocked. "I said, 'What? What do you mean? What are you saying?' You know, I didn't understand. And then the next thing he blurted out was, 'I don't want him doing that to my wee-wee.'

"And that I will never forget. Because it was dawning on me, just shock and horror, that, you know, he's saying this. And, I mean, this isn't just a normal thing he's saying, and for a kid to say that. So now it dawned on me. I mean, this is awful. I said, 'What?' And he literally threw himself on the floor and sobbed. He was completely hysterical."

Soon, so too was the entire Mueller household. Her five-year-old dissolved into tears. She summoned her two other boys, who were upstairs. When their mother asked for details about Geoghan's conduct, they stood speechless at first. And then they began to cry. Her oldest boy told her, "Father said we couldn't talk about it and tell you, never to tell you because it was a confessional."

Mueller was overwhelmed — Geoghan, at that very moment, was on his way to her home. It was raining. The weather was cool. She grabbed some jackets for the kids and headed for her local rectory, St. Mary's in Melrose, where she and her boys met with Rev. Paul E. Miceli, a parish priest who knew both Geoghan and Mueller's family.

Mueller said Miceli counseled her sons "to try to not think about this; to forget about it. 'Bad as it was,' he said, 'just try. Don't think about it. It will never happen again.' . . . He said, 'He will never be a priest again. It will never happen again.' He reassured me."

Miceli, until recently a member of Cardinal Law's cabinet, contradicted Mueller in a court deposition. He said he did not recall her name and had never received a visit of the sort she described. But Miceli acknowledged receiving a call from a woman saying Geoghan was spending too much time with her children. Miceli testified that the caller said nothing about sexual abuse. Nonetheless, Miceli said he drove to Geoghan's new parish in Jamaica Plain to relay the woman's concerns to Geoghan face-to-face.

After Hingham, Geoghan's next stop was St. Andrew's, in the Forest Hills section of Jamaica Plain, where he served from 1974 to 1980.

Jamaica Plain was where Maryetta Dussourd was raising her own four children — three boys and a girl — as well as her niece's four boys. In her hardscrabble neighborhood, she hoped there was a priest the children could look up to. Then she met Geoghan. He supervised the parish's altar boys and Boy Scout troop. Geoghan was eager to help her too. Before long, he was visiting her apartment almost every evening — for nearly two years. He routinely took the seven boys out for ice cream and put them to sleep at night.

Dussourd worked hard to please Geoghan. When the priest mentioned that his uncle the monsignor had taken away his teddy bear when he was growing up, she bought him a blue one for his fortieth birthday. The gift delighted him.

All that time, Geoghan was regularly molesting the seven boys in their bedrooms. In some cases, he performed oral sex on them. Other times, he fondled their genitals or forced them to fondle his — occasionally as he prayed. An archdiocesan memo dated December 30, 1994, and labeled "personal and confidential," said Geoghan would stay in the Dussourd home even when he was on a three-day retreat because he missed the children so much. He "would touch them while they were sleeping and waken them by playing with their penises."

Dussourd discovered what was happening after the children finally told her sister, Margaret Gallant. When Dussourd asked one of her sons to confirm the abuse, he told her about the time Geoghan asked him to stay overnight at the home of the priest's elderly mother. It was a night her son had never before spoken about — and never wanted to.

"Father Geoghan's mother had put him [Dussourd's son] in a bedroom across from Father Geoghan's," Dussourd said. "And [he said] that three times during the night Father Geoghan had gone over to his room, and that he was making him feel very uncomfortable and he asked to go home. . . . He said that Father Geoghan then brought him over into his bedroom, which was across the hall. . . . He sat him up on his bed and he started to touch him. . . . He was touching my son's genitals. He asked him to stop and he was crying. He was crying very loudly. . . . And he continued to ask him to take him home, which he didn't, and after the episode was done, he returned him to his room.

"My son further told me that the next morning when they went down to breakfast that his mother questioned both Father John Geoghan and my son as to why my son was crying. She said she thought she had heard my son several times through the night." When Dussourd asked her son why he never told her about the abuse, "he said because Father Geoghan told him that I would never believe him, that I loved the Church too much, that I wouldn't believe my own son."

Horrified, Dussourd complained to Rev. John E. Thomas, the pastor of St. Thomas Aquinas, a nearby parish. Thomas confronted Geoghan with the allegations and was taken aback when Geoghan casually admitted they were true. "He said, 'Yes, that's all true,'" said one Church official who asked not to be named. It was as if Geoghan had been asked "if he preferred chocolate or vanilla ice cream."

Thomas promptly drove to the chancery, the archdiocesan headquarters in Brighton, to notify Bishop Thomas V. Daily, administrator of the archdiocese. In Thomas's presence that Saturday afternoon, February 9, 1980, Daily telephoned Geoghan at St. Andrew's and, in a brief conversation, delivered a curt directive: "Go home," the official said.

Geoghan protested, saying there was no one else to celebrate the 4:00 P.M. Mass.

"I'll say the Mass myself," Daily insisted. "Go home."

Geoghan disappeared from the parish.

Several weeks later a contrite Thomas came to Dussourd's apartment. He told her that Geoghan had admitted to abusing the boys but had excused his behavior by telling the pastor, "It was only two families." Thomas later pleaded with Dussourd not to follow through on her threat to go public, she said. He cited the years Geoghan had spent studying for the priesthood, and the consequences for Geoghan if the accusations against him were publicized.

"Do you realize what you're taking from him?" Dussourd said Thomas asked her.

Geoghan spent the next year — from early 1980 to early 1981 — on sick leave, but living with his mother in West Roxbury. In February 1981, he was sent to his fifth parish, St. Brendan's, in the Dorchester section of Boston. And almost immediately, Geoghan was working with first communicants, befriending children and their parents, even taking some boys to his family's summer home in Scituate.

There, at the Geoghan family home on the Atlantic Ocean, parents would later discover, Geoghan's sexual attacks continued.

Church officials knew about Geoghan's pedophilia. He was shuttled from parish to parish to avoid public scandal. There were whispers in the rectories about his affliction. There were memos about his treatment. But the details about the predator priest — common knowledge to some of his colleagues — were a closely held secret to be kept from the parishioners who welcomed him into their homes.

When Rev. William C. Francis was asked in 2001 what he knew about Geoghan, he explained, "Well, when he was removed from St. Brendan's in Dorchester, there was talk that he had been fooling around with kids."

Francis's simple reply belied the explosive substance of the gossip in the rectories. Indeed, Geoghan's long history of treatment, denial, and recidivism had already begun by the late 1960s, and perhaps even earlier. A. W. Richard Sipe, a psychotherapist and former priest, said Geoghan received treatment for sex abuse at the Seton Institute in Baltimore, where Sipe then worked. That treatment occurred about the same time that Leonard Muzzi Jr. discovered Geoghan in his Hingham home at the bedside of his son. Geoghan's hands were under the blankets. Muzzi ordered Geoghan out of his house and told him never to return. But a few nights later, Geoghan was back sitting on Muzzi's couch with his three children.

That sort of brazen conduct was frequently reflected in Geoghan's discussions with those who evaluated and treated him at a series of inpatient treatment centers. The priest would admit to sexual abuse. But Geoghan was apparently unable to see why his sexual assaults would have a serious effect on his priestly career. He would advise a young boy on the eve of his first Holy Communion and then take him into his shower at home, where he would fondle the boy until he ejaculated. And Geoghan, who was also accused of fondling a young boy in the bleachers at Fenway Park while watching a Boston Red Sox game, had a ready explanation for the avalanche of allegations that built up against him over the years: It was the children's fault.

"While I was at St. Andrew's, many of the youngsters I was involved with were from troubled homes," he said. "I recalled these two boys and I remembered their home situation. Both were severely disturbed children under treatment at various hospitals and clinics, both admitting to sexual abuse at the hands of anyone: doctors, teachers, friends. Anyone! I don't think they were able to distinguish between normal and abnormal, good or bad, right or wrong."

And as the years wore on, the same could be said for Geoghan's superiors in the Church. The man whose uncle had helped smooth his path to the priesthood expected help from above. He would pick up the phone or write a letter, seeking an intercession. Rarely was he disappointed.

Rev. Francis H. Delaney, a pastor at one of the churches Geoghan served, deflected allegations against his associate pastor in 1979 by questioning the credibility of his accuser. Geoghan, Delaney maintained, was "an outstanding, dedicated priest who is doing superior work" and "a zealous man of prayer who consistently gives of himself in furthering the cause of Christ." This was the same Francis Delaney who, while living in the rectory with Geoghan, once asked his housekeeper about the young voices he heard upstairs. "And the housekeeper, whoever that was, said that Father Geoghan had some urchins up there letting them use the shower, so I confronted him on that and said, 'You know the rule.' And he denied it vehemently, but I had no proof," Delaney said.

Asked once why he had not acted more decisively after a parishioner accused Geoghan of assaulting her sons and nephews, Bishop Thomas V. Daily answered: "I am not a policeman. I am a shepherd."

In this ecclesiastical climate of dodged facts and phantom rules, Geoghan endured with the help of friendly physicians on whose medical blessings his superiors relied for evidence that he had exorcised the sexual demons that drove him toward his predatory practices. "I feel like a newly ordained priest!" Geoghan exulted in February 1981, after the doctors cleared him for return to his priestly duties. "Thank God for modern medicine and good doctors."

Oddly, in the summer of 1982, with suspicions again swirling around Geoghan, with his victims' relatives demanding his removal, the Church decided to give Geoghan a sought-after perk. They shipped him to a scholarly renewal program in Rome. And his brethren helped pick up the tab.

"I am happy to inform you that you will receive a grant of $2,000 to help you with your expenses," Cardinal Humberto S. Medeiros told Geoghan that August. "These funds will be sent to you when they become available as a result of the generosity of your fellow priests. It is my hope that the three months will provide the opportunity for the kind of renewal of mind, body and spirit that will enable you to return to parish work refreshed and strengthened in the Lord."

But it didn't work. When he returned from Rome, Geoghan's attacks continued, even as he assured a Church bishop that his sexual attraction to children had withered and that he had been chaste for five years.

Increasingly, Geoghan grew defensive and dismissive — annoyed, really — at any suggestion that he needed outside help. His sister, Catherine, just seventeen months his senior, offered a window into his increasingly circumscribed world. No one had ever been closer to John Geoghan than Catherine, a kindergarten teacher, who watched him grow from a little boy into a priest and would stand by him later as prosecutors closed in and handcuffs tightened around his wrists. Asked once whether her brother was upset about the molestation charges against him, she replied, "Of course he's upset, because they're all false charges." Her brother told her he had been unfairly targeted by "dysfunctional" families. And she believed him. After all, she said, she had seen them for herself. In the summer of 1998, after Geoghan's abuse had become headline news across the region, some of his victims showed up at the family's summer home in Scituate. "They came and sat on my patio and sat and waited," Catherine Geoghan said. "I had to call the police and have them leave. They just came and sat. . . . They told the police they weren't sitting there, they were just waiting for Father Geoghan. They moved onto the seawall. They put down their chairs, their water bottles, their drinks, their binoculars, their cameras. That's the kind of people you're dealing with."

In the decade between 1980 and 1990, Geoghan had received several clean bills of health that the Archdiocese of Boston used to justify assigning him to two parishes despite his extensive record of abuse. By the mid-1990s, however, as police and prosecutors began to circle, top diocesan officials had finally conceded that Geoghan was an incurable child molester — a thrice-diagnosed pedophile. "A pedophile, a liar, and a manipulator," Rev. Brian M. Flatley, a Boston archdiocese official, pronounced him.

Through it all, Geoghan, now an embarrassment the Church desperately sought to conceal, tried to work the priestly network he had assembled and relied on for more than thirty years. When his pastor in Weston announced plans to retire in the early summer of 1990, he immediately wrote the cardinal at the chancery, raising his hand for the job. His qualifications? "I have been six years in Weston. I know the people, the parish, and its problems. I am confident that I can build a vibrant Faith Community." He did not mention that by then he had been removed three times from parishes for molesting children.

The archdiocese turned him down. And when Geoghan sought the same promotion two years later, the posting went instead to a former Holy Cross and seminary classmate. The Church tried to let Geoghan down easy. "It is important that you not interpret this appointment by the cardinal in any negative way with reference to yourself," an aide to Law wrote Geoghan.

By early 1993, the Church had shunted Geoghan into a job as associate director of the Office for Senior Priests at a clergy retirement home in downtown Boston, while it fretted about his unsupervised access to children. Superiors were not pleased with his performance there. They considered his work habits lax, his judgment poor, and his manner "boyish."

Sure enough, alarm bells sounded on December 30, 1994. Geoghan had been accused of molesting boys in nearby Waltham. "There is a crisis," Flatley told Edward Messner, a psychiatrist at Massachusetts General Hospital. Messner's notes from that day convey the situation's gravity. "A priest had admitted abusing minors in the past and had been acting out again recently. . . . Police and the district attorney are involved. . . . The allegations mirror what has come up before." Six hours later Geoghan was sitting in therapy with Messner, beginning regular sessions in which Geoghan admitted to being "drawn by affection and intimacy with boys" and "pointed out that his misconduct occurred during a time of sexual exploration in this country."

Remarkably, Church officials' patience had yet to be exhausted. Cardinal Law wrote that he was sorry to learn of the new allegations against Geoghan, placing him on administrative leave and confining his pastoral duties to the celebration of Mass in private. He was quietly shipped off again for inpatient psychiatric evaluation.

This time, after a ten-day stay at the St. Luke Institute, a Catholic psychiatric hospital in Maryland, the diagnosis was far less optimistic than earlier judgments. "It is our clinical judgment that Father Geoghan has a long-standing and continuing problem with sexual attraction to prepubescent males," the evaluation read. "His recognition of the problem and his insight into it is limited." Therapists at St. Luke advised that Geoghan have no unsupervised contact with minor males and that he return for residential treatment. For his part, Geoghan found the staff confrontational, but while at St. Luke he admitted that he had "inappropriate sexual activity with prepubertal boys in the early 1960s," an admission that directly contradicted an earlier contention to therapists that he had not been sexually attracted to children before 1976.

In early 1995, steeling himself for the gathering storm of civil lawsuits against him, Geoghan and his sister struck a business deal. Just months after prosecutors began a criminal investigation, and a year before the first civil lawsuits were filed against him, Geoghan sold his sister his half-interest in two houses he owned with her to a real estate trust she controlled. The two homes, a large brick-and-stucco colonial in West Roxbury and the oceanfront home in Scituate, were once owned by the Geoghans' mother and their uncle the monsignor.

The two houses — in the family for a half century and together worth from $895,000 to $1.3 million — were now Catherine Geoghan's alone to control. And they were legally out of the reach of the people who claimed that her brother the priest had attacked them. "My mother said she didn't think anything should be left in my brother's name because he's so generous and so kind to everybody that he wouldn't have a cent," Catherine Geoghan said. "We wouldn't have a house over our heads because he was always helping people out. So she thought it was better if just my name was on it." Now, with Geoghan's legal trouble advancing, his mother's wish came true. The price Catherine paid for the homes was $1 each.

Increasingly isolated, increasingly desperate, Geoghan grew anxious and bitter. He had difficulty sleeping, and when sleep did come it was fitful. He gained weight. In some respects Geoghan considered himself "already dead," but he assured his therapist that while he was scared, anxious, and afraid, he was not suicidal.

"I have been falsely accused and feel alienated from my ministry and fellowship with my brother priests," he wrote to then Monsignor William F. Murphy after Murphy asked for his resignation as associate director of the Office for Senior Priests in late 1995. Geoghan refused Murphy's request, considering resignation tantamount to an admission of guilt, which he would not concede. "Where is there justice or due process?" he asked.

Geoghan, still mourning his "saintly" mother's 1994 death, expressed anger at God for the indignity that was visited upon her in her final days: her incontinence, her helplessness. He tried to buoy himself with a trip to Ireland with the then ninety-three-year-old Monsignor Keohane. He came home with gifts for his therapist. "He gave me a package of three nips of Bailey's Irish Cream," Messner recalled. "He was enthusiastic about his vacation in Ireland with his uncle, despite the pall over him."

"I enjoy a lot: family, friends, good food, good conversation, but I get tired easily," Geoghan said. He took up golf again. He helped his sister clean out her attic. He gathered salt marsh hay near his home in Scituate for use in his garden. When friends visited from Ireland, he played tour guide and showed them the cranberry bogs of Plymouth and the Hyannis Port compound on Cape Cod that was still home to the extended Kennedy family. He tried to focus his day by gardening, cooking, even cleaning his room at Regina Cleri, the residence for older priests. He even joined his uncle in the celebration of Mass there. And, he confided to his psychiatrist, he was still sexually attracted to boys.

Finally, Law had had enough. In January 1996 he removed Geoghan from his post at Regina Cleri, and weeks later he ordered the priest into a residential treatment center, writing, "I know that this is a difficult moment for you." Geoghan resisted. The Church wanted him to attend meetings of Sex and Love Addicts Anonymous. Geoghan refused. He insisted he wasn't tempted. The Church wasn't convinced. "I see no signs that Father Geoghan has taken the steps that addicted people seem to feel are essential to recovery," Flatley, who was handling Geoghan's case for the archdiocese, wrote. "He has not joined a group. He does not attend 12-step meetings. He has not been receiving ongoing counseling."

Indeed, Geoghan was digging in his heels. He believed inpatient counseling unnecessary and punitive. "I feel depressed, tired, and beaten — on the verge of death row," he said. "I feel condemned." He scrutinized Church law to determine his rights and found the bishops held all the power. He was at their mercy. He wondered about retreating to his family's home, where he would live with his sister. But in July 1996, a Waltham, Massachusetts, woman filed a lawsuit against him, alleging that he sexually abused her three sons after she asked him to counsel them and be the father figure she felt the boys needed after their father moved out.

This was the first time, after decades of abuse, that Geoghan's problem with children became public, and it provoked a hand-delivered letter from Law with an ultimatum. Geoghan could choose inpatient analysis in Maryland or at the Southdown Institute in Canada, but he must go. Geoghan again balked, but his elderly uncle counseled him that the priesthood was worth any price, and Geoghan agreed to pay it by going to the Canadian treatment facility. The day after he arrived he said he was doing fine.

By the end of the year, Geoghan's treatment in Canada and what was left of his active priesthood would be over. The archdiocese declared him "permanently disabled" and agreed to finance his retirement from its clergy medical fund. At age sixty-one, Geoghan looked forward to taking college courses in creative writing and computer science. "Thank you for the permissions granted me. I also appreciate the warmth of your letter," Geoghan wrote Law, acknowledging the cardinal's letter granting his retirement. "I am sure it was as difficult for you to write as it was for me to read."

As the Church opened its season of Advent in 1996 — a bright time of preparation for the celebration of Jesus' birth — Cardinal Law may well have believed he had heard the last of John J. Geoghan and the allegations against him.

But what he had heard was barely the beginning.

2

Cover-Up

When, precisely, Archbishop Bernard F. Law first became aware of the wayward John J. Geoghan is not known to anyone but Law himself. But what is certain is that in early September of 1984, less than six months after he arrived in Boston, Law received an urgent letter from Margaret Gallant informing him that Father Geoghan was a serial child molester.

"It is with deep regret that I impart the following information," she wrote on September 6.

There is a priest at St. Brendan's in Dorchester who has been known in the past to molest boys. The Cardinal [Medeiros] had sent father for treatments, and after returning to parish duties he maintained a low profile for quite a while. Lately, however, he has been seen in the company of many boys, to the extent of dropping them off at their homes as late as 9:30 P.M.

Writing in the voice of the devout Catholic that she was, Gallant spoke of her own sense of responsibility for Geoghan's sexual predations and the secrecy that had enshrouded his crimes. "My heart is broken over the whole situation and it is a burden to my conscience since I am trying to keep a lid on the anger of family members," she said. Chillingly, she added that she also harbored "a very real fear of the disgrace this would bring to the Church, to all good priests and finally, but most importantly, my fellow members in this Body of Christ who are left in the dark as to the danger their children are in, while I have knowledge of the truth."

Law's reply just two weeks later was terse and devoid of concern for the seven boys in Gallant's extended family who had allegedly been repeatedly molested by Geoghan. It was also decidedly vague. "The matter of your concern is being investigated and appropriate pastoral decisions will be made both for the priest and God's people," Law wrote.

But by then Law had already consulted with Bishop Thomas V. Daily — who had been Medeiros's chief deputy and was now Law's — and had removed Geoghan from St. Brendan's. Law defined Geoghan's status as "in between assignments," a term the archdiocese often used to describe problem priests. Law also had heard from the pastor at St. Brendan's, Rev. James H. Lane, who had been shocked by complaints that Geoghan was molesting children in the parish.

Before Law's arrival, Church leaders had taken steps that almost guaranteed that Geoghan's crimes would continue. For instance, Church officials had never told Lane about the earlier instances of sexual misbehavior by Geoghan. So when Geoghan arrived at St. Brendan's, in 1981, Lane and others in the parish had initially admired the new priest's eagerness to spend a lot of time with children. But over time, some parishioners had become suspicious.

"We knew something wasn't right," recalled a teacher in the parish who spoke often with Lane. "He just zeroed in on some kids." When Lane learned Geoghan was sexually molesting those children, he was so devastated that he broke down while trying to tell his teacher friend the news. "Father Lane was almost destroyed by this," the teacher said, speaking years later, after Lane's retirement.

But the next decision Law made only put more children at risk. Despite Geoghan's recidivism, Law's response was simply to sweep Geoghan and his troubles to another parish, from blue-collar St. Brendan's in Boston to St. Julia's in Weston, an upscale suburb off the high-technology Route 128 corridor. This time the church pastor, Monsignor Francis S. Rossiter, was told about Geoghan's background. But parishioners were left in the dark, even though many entrusted their children to Geoghan as altar boys, youngsters attending religious instruction, and members of a church youth group.

When he arrived in Boston in March of 1984, Archbishop Bernard Law seemed the perfect choice to lead the faithful in America's most Catholic major city. A Harvard man with no shortage of charisma, Law charmed Church leaders and thrilled the laity during an inaugural week of hope and celebration.

On a Monday night in Weymouth, a Boston suburb, Law was all but mobbed by an overflow crowd that waited several hours for him to say a rare seven-thirty Mass at Immaculate Conception Church. By four in the afternoon, nearly two thousand parishioners had crammed into all of the available seats, while three thousand more jammed the aisles and spilled outside into the cold evening air to await the new archbishop.

And Law did not disappoint. At fifty-two he had a shock of thick, silvery hair. And he had a politician's gift for addressing a large crowd while making each person feel he was speaking directly to them. "There's a magnetism I certainly have not witnessed before, almost of the Kennedy magnitude," said John Logue, an administrator at Catholic-affiliated Carney Hospital, who read one of the scripture lessons for the Mass that evening.

To be compared to the late John F. Kennedy, the slain scion of Boston's most celebrated political clan and the nation's first Roman Catholic president, was secular praise of the highest order. But Law was also quickly compared to the late Cardinal Richard Cushing, the popular prelate who had led the Boston archdiocese for twenty-six years, until 1970, and had become an internationally known figure for his role in the Second Vatican Council and his association with the Kennedy family.

There was plenty of subtext here too. While comparing Law favorably with two of the most beloved figures in the city's storied past, Boston Catholics were also implicitly saying that Law was not like his immediate predecessor, the late Cardinal Humberto S. Medeiros. Whereas Law appeared to connect easily with Church leaders and average parishioners, Medeiros had been humble to a fault, naturally shy and retiring in a city that expected wit and charm and a healthy dose of political savvy from its tribal chiefs. In that sense Boston Catholics were also hailing the new archbishop as one of their own. And Law reinforced that notion right away. A supporter of civil rights during an early stint as editor of a Catholic newspaper in Natchez, Mississippi, he let Boston Catholics know that he was also deeply conservative in other respects, and ready to toe the ecclesiastical line drawn by Pope John Paul II on a wide array of issues.

At one Saturday evening Mass, Law said, "I will call you who with me are the archdiocese to live out fully our profession of faith. . . . We cannot tolerate the false notion that it can be 'yes' in some aspects of our life and 'no' in others." Asked later about his stand on a proposed constitutional amendment to ban abortion, Law said there should be no doubt that "whatever breath I have will be expended in the cause of human life."

That apparent toughness was what inspired many to liken Law to Cushing. Still, Rev. A. Paul White, editor of the Boston archdiocesan newspaper, *The Pilot,* who had known both men, took exception to the comparison. "Both are forceful," White said, "but I see in Archbishop Law the charm and personality and the clarity and openness I didn't see in Cardinal Cushing."

If White or anyone else believed "clarity and openness" would be the touchstone of Law's tenure, they were terribly mistaken. Indeed, if Law had listened to one of his own bishops, Geoghan's crimes might have ended shortly after the priest arrived at St. Julia's — only eight months into Law's tenure and before he was elevated to cardinal. Less than a month after Geoghan started working at St. Julia's, Bishop John M. D'Arcy wrote to Law, challenging the wisdom of the assignment in light of Geoghan's "history of homosexual involvement with young boys." D'Arcy also reflected the common understanding among top bishops in the archdiocese that Geoghan's "recent abrupt departure from St. Brendan's, Dorchester may be related to this problem."

In the same letter, D'Arcy urged Law to restrict Geoghan to saying weekend Masses while undergoing treatment for his pedophilia. But

D'Arcy was promoted to bishop of the Fort Wayne–South Bend, Indiana, diocese and Geoghan was permitted to remain at St. Julia's, where he was free to select new victims from the stable of boys who helped him say Mass and deliver Holy Communion.

Yet the boys of St. Julia's were not enough to satisfy Geoghan's appetites. With unerring radar for the weak and the needy, Geoghan had long ago realized that children from poor families, especially those living in broken homes, were more vulnerable than children from wealthier two-parent families. The priest began hanging out at the Boys & Girls Club in nearby Waltham, a working-class suburb west of Boston not far from St. Julia's, and before long he was in trouble again.

In 1989, with more accusations leveled at Geoghan, Law removed the priest from St. Julia's and had him sent to the St. Luke Institute, in Maryland, which had developed a treatment program for priests with sexual disorders. After a three-week evaluation, doctors diagnosed Geoghan as a "homosexual pedophile, non-exclusive type" and characterized him as a "high risk." At that point Bishop Robert J. Banks, another Law deputy, told Geoghan he could no longer continue working as a priest. But after Geoghan spent three months at the Institute of Living, a Hartford, Connecticut, facility that also treated priests with sexual problems, Banks in effect negotiated a diagnosis more favorable to Geoghan and allowed the priest to return to St. Julia's.

From the time Law assigned Geoghan to St. Julia's parish in November of 1984 to the day Law finally removed him in January of 1993, Geoghan sexually molested many more children; more than thirty of them later filed claims against him.

Of course, the Church's habit of concealing Geoghan's activities was well established before Law arrived in Boston. And Law, in a column he would publish in *The Pilot* in July of 2001, insisted he had not attempted to hide Geoghan's crimes by moving him from one parish to another. "Never was there an effort on my part to shift a problem from one place to the next," Law wrote. "It has always been my contention that it is better to know a problem and to deal with it than to be kept in ignorance about it."

In the same column, Law attributed the decisions he did make about

Geoghan to a dearth of knowledge among Church officials and the larger society about the forces that motivate child molesters. "I only wish that the knowledge that we have today had been available to us earlier," Law said. "It is fair to say, however, that society has been on a learning curve with regard to the sexual abuse of minors. The Church, too, has been on a learning curve."

Yet Law's learning curve seemed to be remarkably flat. In 1981, when he was bishop of the Springfield–Cape Girardeau diocese in southern Missouri, Law had been told that a forty-three-year-old priest he had recently promoted to pastor had sexually molested the teenage son of a Springfield couple. In a move that would later emerge as a pattern, Law pulled Rev. Leonard R. Chambers from his ministry, ordered him to undergo treatment, and ten months later reassigned him to another parish. Years after Law left, Chambers was removed from the priesthood for violating an order that he not be alone with children.

After arriving in Boston, Law had also initially been one of the principal backers of a confidential 1985 report on clergy sexual abuse of minors written for the National Conference of Catholic Bishops (now the U.S. Conference of Catholic Bishops). The report was laced with clear and dire warnings — often in capital letters — about the incorrigible nature of priests who sexually molest youths, especially those who, like Geoghan, preferred prepubescent boys.

"The recidivism rate for pedophilia is second only to exhibitionism, particularly for homosexual pedophilia," the report said. "This is whether the person has received traditional psychiatric treatment or not." Indeed, the authors of the report — a trio of psychiatric, legal, and canon law experts — said, "Recidivism is so high with pedophilia and exhibitionism that all controlled studies have shown that traditional outpatient psychiatric or psychological models alone DO NOT WORK." Finally, as if to erase any and all doubt about these sexual disorders, a section on follow-up care declared pedophilia a "lifelong disease with NO HOPE AT THIS POINT IN TIME for cure."

The report was written by Rev. Thomas P. Doyle, a canon lawyer then stationed at the Vatican embassy in Washington; the late Michael R. Peterson, then a psychiatrist and director of the St. Luke Institute; and

F. Ray Mouton, a Louisiana attorney who was representing Rev. Gilbert Gauthé, who had been criminally charged with sexually molesting eleven boys in the Lafayette diocese.

Details of Rev. Gauthé's serial abuse of the children entrusted to his care began to trickle out on a sweltering night in June 1983, when a nine-year-old altar boy in the tiny village of Henry, Louisiana, told his mother, "God doesn't love me anymore." Alarmed, the boy's mother pressed for details and learned that her son had been sexually molested by the priest that she and her husband had often invited into their home.

When the boy's mother and father discovered that Gauthé had also abused their two older sons, they hired an attorney, Paul Hebert, who accompanied the boys' father to a meeting with Church officials, where they asked that Gauthé be removed from the parish. As described in Jason Berry's richly detailed 1992 book, *Lead Us Not into Temptation,* what they learned from Church leaders left them stunned: Gauthé had abused other children and the Church had known about it and allowed him to continue working as a parish priest. "We've known that Fr. Gauthé had a problem for some time but thought it had been resolved," said Monsignor Henri Alexandre Larroque, a top diocesan official. In fact, when Bishop Gerard L. Frey was later deposed he admitted knowing of allegations against Gauthé dating to 1974.

When Church officials confronted Gauthé about the new allegations, he confessed and was quietly sent to the House of Affirmation, a now-defunct Massachusetts facility for sexually abusive priests, located in the Worcester diocese. Its director, Rev. Thomas Kane, later settled a sexual misconduct lawsuit, although he admitted no wrongdoing.

Back in the village of Henry, parishioners at St. John the Evangelist Church were told that Gauthé had been removed "because of grievous misconduct . . . of an immoral nature." Despite the lack of specificity, parishioners divined the truth as the families of more of Gauthé's victims began coming forward.

In June of 1984, a year after the nine-year-old altar boy's bedtime confession, the Lafayette diocese secretly paid $4.2 million to nine of Gauthé's victims. At about the same time, the families of four additional victims filed lawsuits against Gauthé and the diocese. Still, the mounting accusations and growing knowledge of Gauthé's crimes were largely confined to village gossip and the hushed conversations of Church officials.

But in October, prosecutors indicted Gauthé on criminal charges that included rape and the possession of child pornography — photographs that Gauthé himself had taken of his victims. And Glenn Gastal, the father of a seven-year-old who was molested by Gauthé, became so outraged by what his son had suffered that he sought out reporters who had begun asking questions about Gauthé. The priest, Gastal said, had anally raped his son so viciously that the boy had had to be hospitalized. Gauthé entered a not guilty plea.

By late 1984 regional news organizations began reporting the Gauthé story. And in April, May, and June of the following year, Jason Berry, reporting for the *Times of Acadiana,* a local weekly, wrote definitively about Gauthé's abuses and the Church leadership that had shunted him from parish to parish to hide his crimes. Berry followed up with a piece in the *National Catholic Reporter,* which were followed by stories by the *New York Times* and the *Washington Post.* For the first time, America's Roman Catholic Church was roiled by the scandal of clergy sexual abuse of children.

In October 1985 Gauthé changed his plea to guilty on the criminal charges and was sentenced to twenty years in prison. A decade later he would be released and arrested again on charges he had molested a Texas boy. But the scandal in Lafayette didn't end with Gauthé's prison sentence. Gastal, the enraged parent, refused offers of a settlement and decided to sue the Church.

When his lawyer put him on the stand in a packed courtroom, with Bishop Frey and other Church officials in attendance, Gastal said that his son was so traumatized that he could no longer bear to be touched by his father. "After Gauthé, he kissed me only if I demanded it before he went to bed," Gastal said. Jurors, several of whom wept during Gastal's testimony, awarded him $1.2 million, although Gastal later settled for $1 million after the Church appealed.

Despite assurances by Church officials that the Gauthé case was merely an aberration, bishops in dioceses around the country worried about new allegations against their priests. And they worried about what seemed to be a growing willingness on the part of parishioners to speak out and take their accusations to court.

Rev. Doyle said that he and the other authors of the 1985 report on clergy sexual abuse, which was written on the authors' own initiative to address the bishops' concerns, relied on support from Cardinal John Krol, then archbishop of Philadelphia, and, primarily, Law. "I met him [Law] when he was a bishop down in Missouri and we hit it off," Doyle recalled. "I liked him because he seemed to be a thinker and not someone primarily concerned with Church politics." Doyle said that he and Law would chat whenever Law was in the capital for a meeting at the apostolic nunciature (the Vatican embassy), and that it was only natural for him to turn to Law after allegations that priests were sexually abusing minors began to be heard in dioceses across the country. "Law was definitely a supporter," Doyle said. "We never discussed any specifics from his experience in Boston, and he was in Boston when this was going down, because the issue was how do we get an action plan and how do we get the NCCB to do something?" But when the authors of the report tried to have it introduced at a 1985 bishops' meeting in Collegeville, Minnesota, Law suddenly withdrew his support. Doyle said Law never explained why.

At their meeting the bishops declined to formally take up the ninety-two-page report. Mark Chopko, the general counsel for the NCCB, would say years later he had read the report and concluded that it merely repeated information previously gathered by the bishops. He also said he objected to a proposal in the report that called for a national crisis intervention team with expertise in medicine, law, and public relations to respond to allegations of clergy sexual abuse. "My judgment is that there is no substitute for local experts," Chopko said. But by the early 1990s, few if any of the bishops in the nearly two hundred dioceses across the country had heeded the report's warnings about sexually abusive priests. In the meantime, Doyle lost his post at the nunciature. "I was too much of a maverick for them," he would say later. The politically adroit Law, meanwhile, had been elevated to cardinal.

Aside from its recommendations for the treatment of sexually abusive priests, Doyle's report also took on the legal issues that were beginning to confront bishops presented with allegations of clergy sexual misconduct. In particular the report urged bishops to take scrupulous care of clergy personnel records, warning that they could be subpoenaed in civil lawsuits. It also dismissed talk by Church officials that files containing documents about sexually abusive priests could be cleansed of incriminating information. "The idea of sanitizing or purging files of potentially damaging material has been brought up." But "this would be in contempt of court and an obstruction of justice if the files had already been subpoenaed by the courts," the report said. "Even if there had been no such subpoena, such actions could be construed as a violation of the law in the event of a class action suit." At the same time, the report also brushed aside a potentially more creative solution to the problems presented by incriminating documents: sending them to the apostolic nunciature in Washington, which enjoyed diplomatic immunity. "In all likelihood such action would ensure that the immunity of the Nunciature would be damaged or destroyed by the civil courts," the report concluded.

Still, the idea that bishops could use the Vatican embassy's diplomatic immunity to cleanse their files persisted. In a 1990 speech on pedophilia to the Midwest Canon Law Society, an organization of Church lawyers, Bishop A. James Quinn, himself an attorney and an auxiliary bishop of the Cleveland diocese, delivered a speech in which he appeared to recommend cloaking damaging records with diplomatic immunity. "If there's something there you really don't want people to see, you might send it off to the Apostolic Delegate, because they have immunity to protect something that is potentially dangerous, or that you consider to be dangerous," Quinn said.

Quinn's remarks were recorded and transcribed into a document obtained by Minnesota attorney Jeffrey R. Anderson and Cleveland attorney William M. Crosby for a 1993 clergy sexual abuse lawsuit against the Cleveland diocese. As part of the suit, Anderson and Crosby took a sworn deposition from Quinn in which he denied that his reference to "protecting something that is potentially dangerous" was to documents that could connect a priest to allegations of sexual misconduct. "Obviously not a pedophilia report," Quinn said, when asked what he had meant. "The use of the word 'dangerous' could be anything. It could be a confessional matter. It could be a matter, as we talked about this morning, that doesn't belong in the file." In a statement issued through the Cleveland diocese, Quinn also said his comment "was a single sentence taken out of context from a transcript that covered more than twenty pages." But as Anderson and Crosby noted in the deposition, the topic of Quinn's speech that day in 1990 was "NCCB Guidelines and Other Considerations in Pedophilia Cases."

In 1984 Anderson had represented a Minnesota man who sued the Archdiocese of St. Paul and Minneapolis and Rev. Thomas Adamson, claiming that Adamson had molested him when he was a boy. Anderson had discovered that the families of other abuse victims had been complaining about Adamson since at least 1963, when a fourteen-year-old boy had told two priests that Adamson had molested him. Documents turned over by Church officials during the lawsuit showed that priests had informed their bishop about some of the allegations but that little if anything had been done. On the contrary, despite the complaints against him, Adamson had been named principal of a parochial school, where he abused at least one additional boy.

Other alleged victims of Adamson learned about the case and stepped forward with new claims. Some reached monetary settlements with the archdiocese. But one former altar boy pressed forward. In 1990, a jury awarded him $3.6 million in compensatory and punitive damages — the first time a jury had ever awarded punitive damages against the Catholic Church in a clergy sexual abuse case. A judge later stripped away most of the punitive damages, but the victim was left with nearly $1 million, and the precedent remained.

As word of the Gauthé and the Adamson cases spread slowly across the country, victims of clergy sexual abuse began to understand that silence was not their only option. And attorneys began to focus on trying to hold Church authorities — traditionally protected by the First

Amendment's guarantee of freedom of religion, as well as by friendly judges and state legislatures — liable for the actions of their priests. Attorney Anderson, for example, would move on from the Adamson case to represent more than four hundred alleged victims of clergy sexual abuse, winning millions of dollars in judgments and settlements from several dioceses across the country. The result: still more victims stepping forward with claims of abuse, and more scandal for the Church.

The Archdiocese of Santa Fe, in New Mexico, was hit especially hard. In 1993 Archbishop Robert Sanchez stepped down after admitting he had had sex with several women. But his resignation came in the midst of a much larger scandal, involving dozens of priests accused of sexually molesting boys, that would leave the archdiocese financially hobbled. Many of the accusations of sexual misconduct were directed at priests who had come from other states to receive treatment for sexual disorders. The treatment was offered by the Servants of the Paraclete, a small Catholic religious order that had established a center in Jemez Springs, New Mexico, for priests suffering from alcoholism and others who had been accused of sexually abusing children. But the priests who filled the center's fifty beds patronized local restaurants, mingled with townspeople, and even took on weekend parish duties. Two of the center's former residents — both of them from Massachusetts — would become notorious. James Porter, of the Fall River diocese, would later be sentenced to a twenty-year term in a Massachusetts prison, and David A. Holley, a sexually troubled priest of the Worcester diocese who molested more children after he was reassigned to a New Mexico parish, was eventually sentenced to a 275-year prison term in New Mexico.

In the meantime, complaints against priests who had received treatment at the Jemez Springs center mounted steadily. The first lawsuit was filed in 1991. Four years later, abuse victims had filed some two hundred claims and driven the Santa Fe archdiocese to the edge of bankruptcy through a combination of settlements and judgments estimated at between $25 million and $50 million. In the end, the archdiocese was able to cling to solvency only after selling off Church property and appealing to parishioners for extra cash.

The Dallas diocese also faced bankruptcy, in 1997, when a jury seeking to send a pointed message to the Church awarded $119.6 million to the families of eleven youths sexually molested at All Saints Catholic Church from 1981 to 1992 by Rev. Rudolph Kos. It was the largest verdict ever awarded against the Catholic Church in America. Kos was later sentenced to life in prison. After the Church appealed the award and said it might bankrupt the diocese, the families of the victims eventually agreed to accept $31 million. Jurors said they were motivated by the knowledge that Church officials had brushed aside earlier allegations against Kos and by their belief that Kos's abuse had led one victim to commit suicide. The jury even took the unusual step of including with the award a message to Church authorities: "Please admit your guilt and allow these young men to get on with their lives." Later one juror explained the record award, saying, "We wanted to say that this must stop and never be allowed to happen again."

The first public scandal to put Cardinal Law on the defensive was the case of Father Porter, a serial child molester from the neighboring Diocese of Fall River. In 1992 more than one hundred people who claimed they'd been molested by Porter over fourteen years in a string of parishes across southeastern Massachusetts were stepping forward.

By then Porter had been retired for eighteen years and was living in Minnesota with a wife and four children. But because the statute of limitations is frozen when an alleged criminal leaves the state, he was tried and prosecuted in Massachusetts for the crimes he'd committed decades earlier. Within eighteen months, Porter pleaded guilty to forty-one counts of sexual assault and was sentenced to prison. The Fall River diocese agreed to pay more than $7 million to his victims.

While the claims against Porter mushroomed, families and friends of the victims were overwhelmed by a single question: How could Porter have molested so many children without getting caught and being punished? Two answers came from the victims themselves: the unquestioning deference of Catholic children to clergy, and a profound reluctance on the part of Church officials to investigate the complaints of the few parishioners courageous enough to question a priest. "We were taught they were Christ's representatives on earth, and that's a direct quote," said Fred Paine of Attleboro, one of Porter's victims. "A priest would walk in and nuns would bow."

Roderick MacLeish Jr., a Boston attorney who represented most of Porter's victims, said several priests in the diocese were told of Porter's crimes against children yet did nothing to stop him. In fact, the lawyer said, at least ten individuals had informed two priests in St. Mary's parish in North Attleboro that Porter, who was their assistant, was molesting young children. In some instances the two priests, Rev. Edward Booth and Rev. Armando Annunziato, had actually witnessed the abuse. In one case, Porter had taken a young boy named Paul Merry into a rectory office and had begun molesting him when Booth, the church pastor, happened to walk in. "Father Booth looked at Father Porter and then back at me, and then at Father Porter, who was zipping his fly," Merry recalled. "Then Father Booth shook his head and walked out the door. He didn't say a word." In another case, Porter was once again in the rectory office at St. Mary's, molesting an eleven-year-old named Peter Calderone. This time it was Annunziato who walked in. But like Booth, he merely looked at Porter and said, "It's getting late. It's time for everyone to go home."

Still, the complaints against Porter, even at that time, were either too serious or too numerous to be entirely ignored. Church officials responding to the accusations shuffled Porter from parish to parish in an effort to convince his victims that something had been done. Those officials included then-monsignor Medeiros, who would later approve similar reassignments for Father Geoghan after Medeiros had been installed as archbishop of Boston. Even Vatican officials under Pope Paul VI knew of Porter's obsessive sexual compulsion for children. In 1973, when Porter opted to leave the priesthood, he was remarkably candid about his condition when submitting his resignation papers. "I know in the past I used to hide behind a Roman collar, thinking that it would be a shield for me," he wrote. "Now there is no shield. I know that if I become familiar with children, people would immediately become suspicious. . . . In the lay life, I find out of necessity that I must cope with the problem or suffer the consequences." But the document was hidden away in Vatican files. And Porter's victims would keep their dark secret until 1992, when Frank Fitzpatrick, a victim who was also a private detective, located Porter in Minnesota and began the process of having criminal charges filed.

When news stories about Porter began appearing, Cardinal Law's first response was to declare the retired priest an "aberration," insisting that priests who sexually abused minors were the "rare exception." To victims he also appeared to evince an excess of sympathy for abusive priests. At a Mass for priests celebrating their twenty-fifth anniversary with the Boston archdiocese, Law said, "We would be less than the community of faith and love which we are called to be, however, were we not to attempt to respond both to victim and betrayer in truth, in love, and in reconciliation."

Behind the scenes, Law was hearing plenty of evidence, if he needed any, that Porter was anything but an aberration. As with the earlier publicized cases of clergy sexual abuse in Louisiana and Minnesota, news accounts of Porter's crimes were encouraging victims to step forward with further tales of sexual abuse committed by still more priests — and many of those victims were stepping forward in the Boston archdiocese.

Among them were Raymond Sinibaldi and Robert Anderton. Sinibaldi and Anderton were cousins who had grown up in Weymouth, south of Boston, where they were molested in the early 1960s by Rev. Ernest E. Tourigney, when Tourigney was a recently ordained priest at Immaculate Conception Church — the same church that would offer Law the enthusiastic welcome in 1984.

Like so many other victims of clergy sexual abuse, Sinibaldi and Anderton had for decades kept their stories secret. But after the Porter story broke, they realized Tourigney was still working, as copastor of a church in Revere, north of Boston, where he was spiritual director of its elementary and middle school. Worried that he might still be molesting children, they decided to confront the priest and report him to Law.

At their meeting with Tourigney in the parking lot of an area hotel,

Sinibaldi nearly lost his temper. "I believe you are worse than a purveyor of child pornography," he said, sneering. Concerned that he might attack Tourigney, Sinibaldi had written down the remainder of what he wanted to say: "A person who would wrap themselves in God and weave themselves into the very fabric of a family who came to know, love and trust him for the purpose of molesting their children is the incarnation of evil."

When they visited the chancery of the Boston archdiocese a few days later, Sinibaldi and Anderton had their tempers in check. But they also made it clear to Rev. John B. McCormack, then Law's top deputy for handling allegations of clergy sexual abuse, that they would tell their story to a television reporter if Law would not listen to them. Within days Sinibaldi and Anderton were seated at the long, deeply burnished mahogany table in the conference room of Law's residence, recounting the years of abuse they had suffered at the hands of Tourigney when they were between thirteen and sixteen years of age. Law appeared to listen attentively, but Sinibaldi and Anderton wanted more than a sympathetic ear. They wanted Law to remove Tourigney from his ministry and formulate an aggressive policy for ridding the archdiocese of all priests who had been credibly accused of molesting children.

Law did pull Tourigney from active ministry, and in the wake of the Porter case had already been moving quietly to put in place a policy for handling claims of clergy sexual abuse. As work on a first draft moved forward, two critical questions emerged: Should accused priests who receive treatment for their sexual disorders be allowed to return to parishes in the archdiocese, and should Church officials be required to report allegations of clergy sexual misconduct to state authorities?

Sinibaldi, who had worked with sex offenders at Bridgewater State Hospital, a facility for the criminally insane, wrote Law to recommend that Church officials report all allegations of sexual misconduct by priests. "The crime of sexual abuse of a minor is one of such heinous proportion that to withhold information about a known perpetrator is in and of itself criminal," Sinibaldi wrote. But when Law unveiled his new policy, in January 1993, Sinibaldi and Anderton were sorely disappointed. Although Law said that the archdiocese would offer to pay for counseling for the victims and that he would appoint a review board with lay members to examine allegations of clergy sexual abuse, he also said that in some cases he might permit priests who had been treated for sexual disorders to return to parish work. And he reserved for the archdiocese the primary responsibility for hearing and investigating all complaints of clergy sexual misconduct.

Under Massachusetts law, individuals working in two dozen professions, including physicians, social workers, and teachers, were required to report allegations of sexual misconduct with minors to the state's Department of Social Services, which could in turn refer the allegations to law enforcement authorities. In releasing his new policy, Law pledged that Church officials would report allegations of sexual misconduct in accordance with state law. But priests were not among those covered by the statute, and the Church had successfully fought off legislation to add clergy to the list of so-called mandated reporters. So it was largely a meaningless promise.

Feeling that the Church had once again betrayed them, Sinibaldi and Anderton hired Boston attorney MacLeish to file suit against the archdiocese and Tourigney. In 1995 each of the men received a settlement of $35,000. But Sinibaldi came to regret the outcome. "In the end they used us," he said. "They wanted to say they had worked with victims on the new policy, and they did say that. The problem is, they didn't hear anything we said." The other problem was that Sinibaldi and Anderton, like scores of victims who went to the archdiocese, signed confidentiality agreements — or gag orders — as a condition of receiving their settlement payments. In fact virtually all those who went to the Church with claims of sexual misconduct by priests received settlements before they filed suit, an arrangement that left no public record of the crime committed by the abusing priests. And the confidentiality agreements signed by the victims said the Church could get back its settlement payments if details of the abuse were ever divulged — further protection for abusive priests.

In short, the process led to an unholy alliance among Church officials, victims, and the attorneys. As a result, the archdiocese was able to conceal the crimes committed by its priests. Indeed, in his deposition in the Geoghan case, Bishop Daily said it was the policy of the archdiocese to avoid scandal where possible. Meanwhile, victims were spared embarrassment, while their attorneys collected their fees — generally a third of the settlement awards. Some lawyers called the payments "hush money"; others said they were a legitimate means of compensating victims while preserving their anonymity. But the process also helped to perpetuate the abuse. "Obviously, confidentiality agreements are good for the perpetrator and his or her enablers, since the secrecy allows for further wrongful acts to continue," said Mitchell Garabedian, an attorney who represented more than one hundred of Father Geoghan's victims.

To be sure, earlier Garabedian clients had settled in secret. But by late 2001, Garabedian had spent five years interviewing alleged victims of John Geoghan's sexual abuse, filing lawsuits, requesting Church records through the legal discovery process, and deposing Church officials under oath. Through it all, he compiled a body of evidence showing that cardinals, bishops, and other Church officials had been covering up for Geoghan for more than three decades. These documents were among those released at the request of the *Globe* by Judge Constance Sweeney in January of 2002, and they were at the heart of the lawsuits that were the flash point for the scandal that would engulf the Catholic Church.

Garabedian and his associate, William H. Gordon, had taken a novel approach when filing what would ultimately total eighty-four lawsuits on behalf of eighty-six plaintiffs. Other attorneys bringing clergy sexual abuse lawsuits had sued the Archdiocese of Boston. But like all nonprofit organizations in the state, the archdiocese is protected by a doctrine of charitable immunity that limits its liability to $20,000. Because of that cap, attorneys with sexual misconduct claims had often settled with the archdiocese for modest sums without even going to court, or shortly after filing suit.

But instead of suing the archdiocese, Garabedian sued Cardinal Law, five of Law's bishops, and several other Church officials, claiming that all of them knew of Geoghan's sexual misconduct and were therefore responsible for it. Garabedian even filed notice to depose Law.

The strategy paid off — at least initially. In March of 2002, after the *Globe* stories on Geoghan had appeared and before Law's scheduled deposition, Garabedian and attorneys for the archdiocese reached a settlement agreement hammered together by mediator Paul A. Finn. Under the agreement, the eighty-four lawsuits would be settled for between $15 million and $30 million, with the final amount to be determined by Finn and his associates, who would evaluate each claim and award an individual settlement to each plaintiff.

But the avalanche of disclosures about Geoghan and other priests that had begun in January produced a wave of new alleged victims — and potentially enormous liability for the archdiocese. At least five hundred people claiming they'd been sexually abused by priests retained lawyers in the first four months of 2002. And in May, with donations to the Church falling off rapidly, the archdiocese reneged on the deal — stunning victims and many faithful Catholics.

That the Geoghan revelations would produce a torrent of new claims should have come as no surprise to the Church. In the years immediately following the Porter case, there had been many new complaints. In fact, during the ten years after Porter's victims started coming forward, the Church quietly settled child molestation claims against at least seventy priests in the Boston archdiocese, with MacLeish representing many of the victims. In some cases, he said, Church officials eager to dispense with complaints quickly and quietly would refer the victims to him.

MacLeish also said later that he eventually grew to despise the settlements, because he knew that the confidentiality agreements that went with them helped keep clergy sexual abuse hidden. "It sickened me to see so many of these cases going by unnoticed," he said. And so after a year of urging clients to sign the agreements, MacLeish says, he told a reporter that his clients had made sexual abuse allegations against several priests who remained in active ministry. Still, Philip Saviano, a victim of clergy sexual abuse who hired MacLeish to represent him, criticized MacLeish and other lawyers for being too eager to have their clients settle their claims. Only through filing lawsuits, Saviano said, are victims likely to obtain Church records shedding light on precisely who had responsibility for the priests who abused them. Saviano, for instance, filed suit against the Worcester, Massachusetts, diocese in the early 1990s, claiming he was abused by Father Holley, the priest sentenced to prison in New Mexico, and received Church documents showing that six bishops in three states knew about Holley's record of abuse. Saviano also refused to sign a confidentiality agreement, although he might have paid a price for that decision. When Saviano settled, he received only $12,500 from the Worcester diocese, whereas two other victims who claimed abuse by Holley and agreed to stay silent each received more.

One of the most notable public statements issued to help the Boston archdiocese evade its responsibility for Geoghan was made by Law's attorney, Wilson D. Rogers Jr., in a July 2001 edition of *The Pilot*. "Each assignment of John Geoghan, subsequent to the first complaint of sexual misconduct, was incident to an independent medical evaluation advising that such assignment was appropriate and safe," Rogers wrote.

The cardinal echoed that statement in January 2002, when he attempted to contain the Geoghan scandal by apologizing for having reassigned the pedophile priest to parish work even though he knew Geoghan was a repeat child molester. In an extraordinary mea culpa, Law said it was "tragically incorrect" for him to have assigned Geoghan to St. Julia's parish in 1984. Yet he also seemed to be excusing his actions when he echoed Rogers's earlier statement in *The Pilot* and claimed his decision was based on "psychiatric assessments and medical opinions that such assignments were safe and reasonable."

At first glance the statements made by Law and his attorney appear to be supported by Church documents. For example, the documents show that in 1980, after Geoghan had casually admitted to a Boston pastor that he had sexually molested Maryetta Dussourd's seven sons and nephews, Church officials sent him to Dr. Robert W. Mullins for psychotherapy and to Dr. John H. Brennan for psychoanalysis. The records also show that in 1981, after Geoghan had admitted to molesting the Dussourd boys and had been removed from St. Andrew's parish, in

Boston's Jamaica Plain section, Brennan wrote to Bishop Daily to say he had met with Geoghan and that "it was mutually agreed that he was now able to resume priestly duties." In 1984, after Geoghan had been transferred to St. Brendan's parish in Dorchester, where he had molested still more children, Church officials once again sent him to Mullins and Brennan. Mullins, in a written evaluation, described Geoghan as "a longtime friend and patient" who had been removed from his parish due to "a rather unfortunate traumatic experience." And he recommended that Geoghan be allowed to return to "full pastoral activities without any need for specific restriction." Brennan, for his part, met with Geoghan again and, despite the priest's recidivism, gave him yet another favorable review. "No psychiatric contraindications or restrictions to his work," he wrote.

In fact neither Mullins nor Brennan had any expertise in evaluating sexually deviant behavior. Mullins, a neighbor and friend of the Geoghan family in Boston's West Roxbury section, was a family physician with no credentials in psychotherapy, psychology, or psychiatry. Indeed, a 1989 evaluation of Geoghan by the Institute of Living referred to Mullins's treatment of Geoghan as "friendly, paternal chats and not really psychotherapy." Brennan, for his part, was a certified psychiatrist but with no specialty in treating sexual disorders. And in 1977 he had been charged in a civil lawsuit with sexually molesting one of his patients. In 1980, at about the time he began treating Geoghan, the suit was settled and the woman was paid $100,000.

Moreover, neither Mullins nor Brennan could be said to have made an "independent" evaluation of Geoghan — the term used by Law's attorney. While Mullins's impartiality was compromised by his friendship with the Geoghan family, Brennan's was tainted by his relationship with the Church. At the time, Brennan was director of psychiatric education at St. Elizabeth's Hospital in Brighton, a Catholic institution, and was accepting patient referrals to his private practice from Rev. Fulgence Buonanno, a well-known Franciscan priest and a psychologist who worked at St. Anthony's Shrine, in downtown Boston.

Still, Church records show that Brennan was capable of delivering a harsh critique, though never in writing. In April of 1989, five years after

Geoghan had been reassigned to St. Julia's, and after more accusations that he had molested boys, Brennan delivered a dire message to Bishop Banks, who was jotting down notes of their telephone conversation. "You better clip his wings before there is an explosion," Brennan said. "You can't afford to have him in a parish." After that exchange, Banks asked Geoghan to resign from the priesthood, but he later changed his mind. And after he and Law had cleared Geoghan to return to St. Julia's, Brennan resurrected the sympathetic tone he had used in all of his written evaluations. "I have known Father Geoghan since February 1980," Brennan wrote in December of 1990. "There is no psychiatric contraindication to Fr. Geoghan's pastoral work at this time."

The Church's aversion to negative evaluations of Geoghan — and its preference for positive written assessments to coincide with new parish assignments — is underscored by several letters between Bishop Banks and officials at the Institute of Living that were written in 1989 after Geoghan had received treatment there. In a three-page evaluation written in November of that year, doctors Robert F. Swords and Vincent J. Stephens said psychological testing of Geoghan "showed an immature and impulsive nature" and an individual who "could be a high risk-taker." Their official diagnosis: an "atypical pedophile in remission." But Banks wrote back to say he was "disappointed and disturbed by the report" and insisted that he had been "assured that it would be all right to reassign Father Geoghan to pastoral ministry and that he would not present a risk for the parishioners whom he would serve." Underscoring his displeasure, Banks noted that Geoghan had already been allowed to return to St. Julia's and asked for an additional letter that "would express the assurance I was given orally about Father Geoghan's reassignment." Two weeks later, Banks got what he asked for. "We judge Father Geoghan to be clinically quite safe to resume his pastoral ministry after observation, evaluation, and treatment here for three months," Swords wrote. "The probability that he would sexually act out again is quite low." Yet within weeks of his 1989 return to St. Julia's, Geoghan lured a thirteen-year-old youngster to the rectory and molested him, according to a lawsuit filed in 2002.

By 1994, criminal authorities were finally investigating Geoghan. Their unusual appearance put the archdiocese in a state of crisis — and the crisis was spreading. Since the late 1980s Law and his deputies had been covering up the past sexual misdeeds of a growing number of priests. In 1996 the first of scores of civil lawsuits accusing Geoghan of sexually molesting children was filed, and two criminal investigations were under way. Two years later, in 1998, the church announced it had settled a dozen lawsuits against Geoghan for as much as $10 million. Then, with still more lawsuits being filed and investigators and police from two counties closing in, Cardinal Law finally defrocked Geoghan, removing his right to act as a priest. And he did so in a rarely used procedure that required the approval of Pope John Paul II and left Geoghan no opportunity for appeal. Law, in his first public acknowledgment of the dangers posed by a priest who had been on a sexual rampage through a half-dozen parishes over three decades, said, "I don't have the powers of incarceration but I do have the responsibility for the public exercise of ministry."

But by then it was too late.

3

The Predators

To Michael McCabe, an altar boy in training, the touch seemed innocent enough. It was the early 1960s. He knew little about sex or sexuality. It happened casually and nonchalantly. It never occurred to the boy to tell his parents. After all, he called Joseph Birmingham "Father."

"He'd come up behind you, rub your shoulders, make you calm, and then slip his hand beneath your underwear," said McCabe, who is now in his early fifties. "It didn't seem wrong, and that's what's so weird about it." Had McCabe's dad not sat his adolescent son down one day and given him the age-old talk fathers give their sons about the private things men and women do together, Michael McCabe might never have told anyone about Father Birmingham's wandering hands. When Howard McCabe raised the delicate issue of homosexuality, young Michael had informed his father that that was one aspect of sex he already knew something about. "My dad told me about how some boys touch other boys," Michael McCabe recalled, "and I said, 'Oh, hey, that's what Father Birmingham does to me.'" The touching, he told his father, happened in the sacristy, just off the altar, at Our Lady of Fatima parish in Sudbury, west of Boston. Michael was twelve or thirteen at the time.

Nearly forty years later, that faith-altering day remains vivid in his father's mind. "I was giving him my lecture on the birds and the bees, and when I got through I said, 'If you've got any questions, just ask me,'" Howard McCabe, who is now seventy-nine, recalled. "Finally he said, 'Jeez, Dad, Father Birmingham played with my penis.' And I said, 'You've got to be kidding.' I couldn't believe what he said, and I didn't know how to handle it." And so began the McCabe family's disturbing and, ultimately, shattering introduction to the troubled universe of priests who sexually abuse children.

Why some priests, and why some men in general, are sexually attracted to minors remains a much-debated and highly controversial issue, one cluttered with unanswered questions. But while the origins of the crisis remain uncertain, the reality that numerous priests have become abusers is not.

In the past fifteen years, an estimated fifteen hundred American priests have faced allegations of sexual abuse, according to Jason Berry, the reporter who documented Gilbert Gauthé's abuses and the author of *Lead Us Not into Temptation: Catholic Priests and the Sexual Abuse of Children,* an authoritative early examination of the issue. In the aftermath of the Geoghan disclosures in January 2002, the names of more than ninety priests alleged to have sexually abused minors were turned over to Massachusetts law enforcement officials by the Boston archdiocese alone. And eleven sitting priests were abruptly removed from their posts — eight of them after Church officials discovered credible allegations of sexual abuse in their files — even though Cardinal Law had publicly asserted weeks before that all such priests had been removed from their assignments. The other three were removed when new victims came forward for the first time. Law's decision to cooperate with prosecutors, made under pressure, spurred Church officials in other major American cities, including Philadelphia, Los Angeles, and New York, to share with authorities the names of allegedly abusive priests in their dioceses as well. As a result of reverberations from the Boston scandal, more than one hundred and seventy priests suspected of molesting minors had either resigned or been taken off duty in the early months of 2002, according to a nationwide survey of Catholic dioceses by the Associated Press.

For every name passed along to prosecutors, a secret Church file of some type existed in virtually every case. But the smattering of information released by dioceses across the nation underscored an alarming reality: repeat abusers such as Geoghan, Porter, Kos, and Gauthé, all of whom were convicted for their crimes, appear not to have been the aberrations some Church officials claimed they were. Serial molesters "are not as much of an anomaly as people would like to think," said A. W. Richard Sipe, a former priest and psychotherapist who specialized in treating priests who abuse children. The Geoghans and Porters of the priesthood, he said, are "extreme examples, in a way, because they're the ones who have gotten the notoriety. But there are many priests who have just never been reported."

In the case of McCabe's abuser, Joseph E. Birmingham, the abuses were reported, but the reports fell on deaf ears. Like Geoghan, Birmingham served as a priest for nearly three decades, from his ordination in 1960 until his death in 1989 at age fifty-five. Like Geoghan, he was rotated through six parishes, despite a string of complaints about his sexual compulsion. Like Geoghan, he allegedly accumulated dozens of victims even though high Church officials knew he was molesting children. And, like Geoghan, the number of Birmingham's alleged victims is large — as many as twenty-five alone from his third assignment at St. Michael's parish in Lowell, north of Boston, in the 1970s. But in Birmingham's case, the public evidence that the Church stood by and did nothing to stop him early in his career appears to be even stronger.

That the McCabes even reported the alleged molestation to Church authorities made them unusual. Shame, embarrassment, and, sometimes, warnings by their abusers kept many victims from disclosing the abuse. Others confided in family members who found it difficult to believe them.

Howard McCabe himself at first doubted his son's innocent admission and intended to follow the advice of a neighbor and keep the information secret. But he changed his mind when Michael told him that a grade-school friend, Peter Taylor, had also been molested by Birmingham, and Taylor's father, Frank, confirmed that his son had indeed been victimized. Once the shock wore off and the anger took hold, the men acted.

"He came pounding on my door, and he had fire in his eyes," Howard McCabe said, recalling the sight from almost four decades ago of Frank

Taylor quaking with anger on his front porch. "He was a big man, but an awful gentle man, and he wanted to kill Birmingham."

Stunned and chagrined, the two men contacted their local pastor, who arranged for them and their sons to meet with Church administrators at archdiocesan headquarters in Boston.

The chancery of the Boston archdiocese, located in the Brighton section of the city, made for an intimidating setting: mahogany tables, imposing Church officials. Among those gathered at the table was Monsignor Francis J. Sexton, a vice chancellor.

"I was scared to death," recalled Peter Taylor. "I was just a kid."

With Birmingham present, the two boys were ordered to repeat their complaints, in detail. Once they had described to the adults at the table what had happened to them, it was Birmingham's turn to speak.

He denied any wrongdoing.

"It was wicked embarrassing for a kid to have to tell this story in public," Michael McCabe said. "I couldn't believe they were making us do that, making us say this in front of him and making us look like liars. When we left I said to my dad, 'I told the truth, Dad. I really did.'"

The arduous experience seemed to have been worthwhile. Later the same day, their pastor paid a visit to the Taylor family's home, where the two men and their sons had gathered after the meeting. He had good news to relay: Birmingham, the pastor said, would be removed from Sudbury and sent to Salem, north of Boston, where he would be made chaplain of Salem Hospital and receive psychiatric treatment.

True to the pastor's word, Birmingham was transferred to Salem in 1964. Pleased and relieved, Howard McCabe felt his decision to notify the Church of the boys' complaints had been the correct one. But that sense of relief evaporated about a year later, when his son saw Birmingham skiing in New Hampshire with a busload of young boys on what appeared to be an official school outing. The thought that their complaints had been brushed aside by Church authorities was crushing to the men's faith. "It was devastating," Howard McCabe said.

"I left the Church," said Frank Taylor, now seventy-seven. "I never went back again."

The McCabes and Taylors would not be the last parents to take their concerns about Birmingham's sexual habits to the chancery. Over the course of the priest's career, at least seven people from at least two different parishes notified Boston archdiocesan officials of his alleged abuse. In his second assignment, a group of five Salem mothers also visited the chancery, in about 1970, to complain that Birmingham had molested several of their children, sometimes during confession. Their pleas too went unheeded.

It was several weeks after Birmingham had been transferred from St. James's parish in Salem to St. Michael's parish in Lowell that Judy Fairbank, Anne McDaid, Mary McGee, and Winifred Morton traveled together to the chancery to alert Church officials to the allegations. A fifth woman attended the meeting, but her son insisted that she not be named. They wanted to ensure that Birmingham's new pastor in Lowell would be notified of his history and that Birmingham would receive psychiatric care.

Until several of their sons told them that Birmingham had molested them, the women had believed that the priest's move to Lowell had been a routine transfer; they had even held a farewell party for him. But during their chancery meeting with Monsignor John Jennings, "We got no place," said McGee. "He was sitting there, pompous, and pacifying us. At the end of the meeting he said, 'You know, ladies, you have to be very careful of slander.'"

Distraught, McGee paid a visit to Rev. John B. McCormack, who was then serving as regional director of Catholic Charities in Salem, and who later became bishop of Manchester, New Hampshire. McCormack acknowledges that parents complained to him that Birmingham was molesting children and says he referred them to "the pastor of the parish who was responsible for Father Birmingham's ministry." But Birmingham remained a priest in Lowell and continued to victimize young boys such as David Lyko, who says he was fondled by Birmingham about a dozen times when he was nine or ten, and Olan Horne, who said he received a beating from Birmingham when he was fourteen or fifteen after resisting his advances.

In the spring of 2002, within weeks after Birmingham's abuse was revealed in Boston newspapers, more than forty of his alleged victims had come forward.

In March a former Salem man, James Hogan, filed a lawsuit against the Boston archdiocese and New Hampshire Bishop McCormack, alleging that in the 1960s McCormack — who was assigned to St. James's in Salem at the same time Birmingham was — saw Birmingham taking him to his rectory bedroom and did nothing to stop it. That lawsuit was later amended to include an additional thirty-nine alleged victims. McCormack has acknowledged that in about 1970 he was warned that Birmingham was molesting children. But he has denied that he ever saw Birmingham take boys into his rectory bedroom. Separately, Thomas Blanchette, formerly of Sudbury, alleged that Birmingham molested him and his four brothers — attacks that included attempted rape — at Our Lady of Fatima in the 1960s. And Paul Cultrera, a former altar boy who says Birmingham began molesting him in Salem when he was a high school freshman in 1963 or 1964, disclosed publicly that he had received a $60,000 settlement from the archdiocese in 1996.

After Birmingham was transferred to Lowell, he was brought into police headquarters in neighboring Chelmsford for questioning in a rape case. He was let go, but not before admitting he had molested children in the past, according to retired Chelmsford police chief Raymond P. McKeon. At the time, Birmingham insisted he was "cured," McKeon said. Birmingham also told him he had never been treated for abusing children and said his pastor in Lowell had not been told about his history of molestation.

The total number of children Birmingham abused is unknown. But during his three decades as a priest, Birmingham made a grand tour of parishes in the Boston archdiocese. After serving in Sudbury, Salem, and Lowell, he had yet another assignment at St. Columbkille's in Brighton — where he established a youth drop-in center — before he was promoted to pastor of St. Ann's in Gloucester in 1985. His last assignment before his death was at St. Brigid's in Lexington. He also served as juvenile-court chaplain at Brighton Municipal Court, and he frequently took teenage parishioners on out-of-state field trips; in his suit, Hogan alleges that Birmingham abused him during ski trips to Vermont and an eighth-grade trip to Arizona, Nevada, and California.

"What I know now is that I should have gone to the police," said McGee. "But I thought I'd go to the Church and I thought the Church would take care of it."

The air snapped with the chilly bite of late fall and the sun had barely begun to rise when Rev. Ronald H. Paquin roused the four teenage boys from their alcohol-soaked sleep and piled them in his Lincoln Continental for the long drive home.

The thirty-nine-year-old priest and his young companions, who ranged from thirteen to sixteen, were still drowsy, and they could feel the groggy aftereffects of the previous night. All five had stayed up drinking until one or two in the morning, so the predawn wakeup that cold morning on November 28, 1981, was an unwelcome jolt to their systems. Nevertheless, they wanted to get an early start back to Haverhill, a blue-collar community north of Boston, where Paquin was a curate at St. John the Baptist, the same parish where the four teenagers — James Francis, Joseph Bresnahan, Joseph Vaillancourt, and Christopher Hatch — served as altar boys.

Paquin had arranged the weekend outing at a private chalet in Bethlehem, New Hampshire, supposedly to reward the boys for their work launching a parish youth group. They originally planned to spend only one evening at the house, but because the boys had enjoyed the trip so much, Paquin later told a reporter, they decided to stay Friday night as well. More than two decades later, it remains unclear what Paquin had in mind when he crawled into Jimmy Francis's sleeping bag on one of those evenings, as one of the other boys saw him do, and how Jimmy reacted when he found the priest next to him in his bedding.

They are questions Francis never had a chance to answer. Tired from the night of drinking, Paquin fell asleep at the wheel twice on the ride home. The second time Paquin nodded off, on a stretch of highway on Interstate 93 in Tilton, New Hampshire, Francis grabbed the wheel in a futile attempt to keep the car from going off the road, according to one of the other boys. The heavy car rolled over, throwing Francis out of the vehicle and pinning him beneath the wreckage. Another of the four boys was seriously injured. Paquin and the remaining two escaped with minor injuries. Trapped under the car, Francis — a junior at Haverhill High School, an honor student, and an athlete — died of asphyxiation.

The fatal auto accident, which cost Harold and Sheila Francis their only son, resulted in no criminal charges. And twenty-one years later, Paquin insists he was sober when he lost control of the car, despite the account of one of the other boys, now a grown man, who described the night of drinking.

Had the archdiocese removed Paquin from the priesthood the first time it received a complaint about his behavior, it is unlikely that Jimmy Francis would have died on that New Hampshire highway.

Three years earlier, Robert P. Bartlett had complained to the pastor at St. Monica's in nearby Methuen, where Paquin was then assigned, that the priest had molested him and two other teenage boys. But Paquin was transferred to Haverhill in 1981 anyway, and it took the Boston archdiocese nine more years to remove him from there, a decision that came only after Church officials were told he had molested more children in Haverhill.

Sheila and Harold Francis filed a wrongful death lawsuit against the Boston archdiocese in April 2002 after learning from newspaper accounts that the archdiocese had known that Paquin had allegedly molested children before transferring the priest to the parish where he met their son. In the suit, they charged that the archdiocese had breached its duty to them by allowing Paquin, "a known pedophile who had engaged in predatory sex with minors in his parish, to remain a priest where he could continue to prey upon children to satisfy his unbridled sexual desires."

Paquin, who has admitted in interviews to molesting children, left a tragic imprint in each of the parishes to which he was assigned. Ordained in 1973, Paquin started his career at St. Monica's, where he was in charge of the altar boys, Boy Scouts, and Catholic Youth Organization, Church directories show. He began abusing young boys almost immediately. When he was transferred to Haverhill in 1981, Church officials were aware of his sexual compulsions.

In one distinct way, Paquin stands out from most other abusive priests: he acknowledges a long history of sexually deviant behavior. In an interview with a *Globe* reporter, he admitted abusing boys in Methuen and Haverhill for over fifteen years, until the Boston archdiocese removed him from active ministry in 1990. In what he offered as an explanation of sorts for his abusive behavior, Paquin said he was raped by a Catholic priest when he was growing up in Salem. "Sure, I fooled around. But I never raped anyone and I never felt gratified myself," Paquin said. His own psychiatrist, he said, told him he "had the sexuality of a thirteen-year-old. I was stuck as a thirteen-year-old. Whenever I felt pressure, I would hang around with the thirteen-year-old kids." From 1990 to 1998, Church directories list him as "unassigned," "awaiting assignment," or on "sick leave." He was assigned to Youville Hospital in Cambridge, Massachusetts, in 1999 and 2000, the same year he was laicized, which meant he could no longer perform any priestly duties.

To date, at least seven of Paquin's victims have won financial settlements from the Boston archdiocese. One of them is Bartlett, who said he was molested by Paquin numerous times over six years during the 1970s. Paquin insisted that he stopped abusing minors after he was removed from parish work in 1990, an assertion contradicted by one of his alleged victims, now in his midtwenties, who asked that he not be identified. That man, now married, filed a lawsuit against Paquin in March 2002 claiming that Paquin began to sexually abuse him soon after he became an altar boy at age eleven or twelve. It continued until 1993 or 1994, when he was seventeen or eighteen, he said.

The abuse had begun when the man was a young altar boy at St. John's in Haverhill, where he met Paquin, who was assigned there. "He immediately wanted to start being my friend," the man said of Paquin, who often took him shopping, bought him gifts, gave him money, and invited him to visit the church, where they would talk about religion. His father and stepmother were grateful that the priest had taken an interest in their son. A friendship blossomed, and the man came to regard Paquin as a father figure. "I really became an active part of church and his life," he said.

After about seven months, the man said, Paquin began to invite him on day trips to shopping outlets in Maine and, eventually, overnight trips to a camp in Kennebunkport. "We'd drink Corona, make lobster, eat ice cream," he recalled. Before long, their conversations during the ride up Interstate 95 took a sexual turn, as Paquin steered the topics to psychology, then Freud, then sex. Had he ever masturbated? Paquin would ask him. Had he ever had an erection? "He just started making this a part of our normal conversation," he said. "It was embarrassing at first, but he'd say, 'I know this is weird and embarrassing, but it's normal to talk about this, and it's good to feel comfortable with your sexuality,' and I'd listen to what he'd say. He'd say some good stuff, too — he'd talk about religion and faith and morals and being a good person. You couldn't dislike him."

During one visit to the camp, Paquin began talking about massage therapy, and then began massaging the boy's back and legs. "Next thing you know he's fondling me," the man said, "then physically bringing me to ejaculation. He was very gentle about it, and if he noticed me getting tense he'd back off. He'd say, 'Are you okay? This is completely normal.' He said it was just a good feeling. And that's how he pitched it: it's good to have an ejaculation, it's good to be comfortable with him." It was the man's first sexual experience.

Eventually, Paquin was regularly performing oral sex on him, often in a car in a Haverhill cemetery. Their sexual encounters also took place on numerous trips to Vermont, Maine, and other states, as well as Canada. Years later, when the man visited Paquin at Baldpate — a psychiatric facility in Georgetown, a rural community north of Boston — Paquin also tried to fondle him there. And the sexual activity continued when Paquin was sent to Our Lady's Hall, a well-maintained, sprawling brick mansion in Milton (an affluent suburb south of Boston) used by the Boston archdiocese to house depressed, alcoholic, and abusive priests. While claiming to offer treatment and rehabilitation, the facility provided

Paquin with additional opportunities to continue his abuse, giving him a private, unsupervised place to spend time with the young man.

The man estimated he visited the facility several dozen times during the two to three years Paquin lived there, sometimes entering through the front door, sometimes through a less visible side or basement door. Once they were in Paquin's room, Paquin often masturbated him and performed oral sex on him there, the man said. On two occasions, the man spent the night.

On one of the mornings after he slept over, he said, Paquin offered to make him breakfast — but asked him to stay in the bedroom while he prepared food downstairs. The facility did not require visitors to check in or out, or have any apparent supervision, the man said, and his presence there was never challenged by other priests. "No one questioned me," he said. "No one said, 'Who are you?'" The man was not aware at the time why Paquin was staying at either Baldpate or Our Lady's Hall because the priest told him only that he was living there until he received a new assignment.

It wasn't until he turned seventeen and began dating that he became "increasingly, increasingly uncomfortable" with Paquin's sexual interest in him. Before that point, he said of the sexual activity, "I was made to believe it was normal and natural, so it seemed normal and natural."

"I remember driving down 95 from a ski trip one time, and I flipped out, basically," the man recalled. "I said, 'Either you and I are going to stop doing this or I'm out of here.' He said, 'You're right, it will stop, give me time.' But a little while later, maybe a few months down the line, he said, 'Let's go away again.' And I had developed a trust in him, and I thought it was over, but somehow it ended up happening again." Finally, after meeting the woman who would eventually become his wife, "That's when I told him, 'I can't do this anymore,'" he said.

In January 2002 stories in the *Globe* and other papers disclosed Paquin's long history of sexual abuse. "I was just in shock," said the man, who said he was unaware that Paquin had molested other children. He confronted Paquin, who said he could not recall the number of children he had abused. "That was the turning point for me," the man said, and he retained a lawyer.

Looking back, he says he is embarrassed and ashamed that he lacked the emotional maturity to end the relationship sooner. He struggles to explain — to those who struggle to understand — why he maintained contact with a priest who initiated a sexual relationship with him. Paquin, he said, steered the relationship in a sexual direction gradually and carefully, cultivating an emotional relationship with him along the way. The boy was a sexual neophyte when he met the priest, and he believed the older man's assurances that sex was a natural evolution of their relationship. And, he explained simply, Paquin had become a close and trusted companion. "He was my best adult friend. I can safely say that I loved this guy — I really did. I said to myself, 'You know, he did teach me a lot about patience and kindness and religion and faith.' But you've got to weigh his good and his bad, and the bad is just too heavy. He's got this issue, this psychological problem, and it's the Church's responsibility." In May 2002, Paquin was arrested on one count of child rape in connection with the boy's complaint. He pleaded not guilty to the charge and was later indicted on three counts of child rape.

While the 1960s were an era of massive social upheaval for American society, they also marked a time of radical change for the Roman Catholic Church and its priesthood. And in Boston, no priest embodied that change more than Rev. Paul R. Shanley.

He radiated confidence and charisma. Tall, handsome, bright, and self-assured, Shanley was warm and gregarious, and his captivating personality attracted admirers among both his seminary classmates and, later, his parishioners. And he had a special appeal to young people.

In 1960, when he left St. John's Seminary as a newly ordained priest, Shanley sported a youthful, clean-cut look. Photos taken around the time of his ordination show an attractive, freshly shorn young man with a broad, easy smile. But within a few years, he had cultivated a far different image, one that mirrored the counterculture sensibility of the time. He grew his brown hair long, until it fell below his Roman collar, and wore bushy sideburns that snaked partway down his cheeks. Eventually, he stopped wearing his collar altogether, trading his traditional priestly attire for plaid shirts and blue jeans.

It wasn't only Shanley's unconventional dress and shaggy hairstyle that made him stand out. In the midst of the tumult of the decade in which he was ordained, Shanley frequently challenged Church teachings, particularly its condemnation of homosexuality, and clashed vocally and publicly with his superiors, including Cardinal Medeiros.

Shanley openly embraced ostracized minorities such as gays, lesbians, and transsexuals, and in the early 1970s created his "ministry to alienated youth" for runaways, drug abusers, drifters, and teenagers struggling with their sexual identity. His unique, unprecedented ministry earned him the unofficial titles of "street priest" and "hippie priest." His outspokenness won him hero status among many of Boston's alienated young people and placed him in frequent conflict with his superiors.

It was also what Shanley said in private that set him apart. And it was what he did behind closed doors that, four decades after his ordination, brought him far more notoriety than did his rebellious dress and preaching style.

In the parishes and counseling rooms where desperate and troubled young people sought his help, Shanley was a sexual predator, a skilled manipulator who used his power and authority to prey on those who came to him for guidance and support. Therapy sessions became the settings for molestation and rape.

The Boston archdiocese has paid at least five settlements to Shanley's victims, including a $40,000 payment in about 1993 to a man who notified Church officials that he had repeatedly been anally raped by Shanley around 1972, when he was twelve or thirteen. Another man received a $100,000 settlement in 1998 after reporting a four-year sexual relationship with Shanley that began in 1965, when he was in the fifth grade.

But the breadth of Shanley's criminal behavior, and the extent to which he was coddled and protected by top Church officials, remained hidden until a lawsuit filed in February 2002 by Gregory Ford — who alleges he was repeatedly raped by Shanley in the 1980s — forced the release of the archdiocese's confidential files on the priest. More than sixteen hundred pages of previously secret Church records made clear that, for more than a decade, Law and his deputies paid no heed to detailed 1967 allegations of misconduct against Shanley and reacted casually to repeated complaints that he had publicly endorsed sexual relations between men and boys.

Law and his subordinates were so unconcerned about Shanley's behavior that, in 1988, two decades after the detailed complaints about his aberrant behavior began to trickle into the archdiocese, an accusation that Shanley had initiated a sexually explicit conversation was ignored.

The man who made the complaint, speaking on condition of anonymity, said Shanley visited him unannounced at McLean Hospital, a psychiatric facility northwest of Boston, ostensibly to offer counseling. But what began as a "very pleasant conversation" suddenly became "very, very, very sexual," the man said. "It was so bizarre. He started telling me about friends of his who were into sadomasochism," the man recalled. "It became extremely graphic to the point of him describing what they did to each other and whips and one of them ejaculating over other people." Yet despite evidence in the chancery's files about the 1967 accusations and Shanley's bizarre sexual views, Law's deputy Bishop Robert Banks concluded in a memo that nothing could be done because Shanley denied that the incident occurred.

The Shanley record reveals Medeiros as similarly complicit. At a talk in Rochester, New York, in 1977, Shanley publicly asserted that he could think of no sexual act that caused "psychic" damage to children, including incest and bestiality, and argued that the child is often the seducer in man-boy sexual relationships. In a letter to Medeiros written shortly after that talk, an appalled New York Catholic vented her dismay at Shanley's remarks. No apparent action was taken.

Shanley's public advocacy of homosexuality eventually attracted the attention of Vatican officials, one of whom wrote to Medeiros requesting an explanation. In his February 1979 reply to Cardinal Franjo Seper in Rome, Medeiros called Shanley "a troubled priest." Two months later, Medeiros was alerted by a New York City lawyer that Shanley had been quoted making similar remarks in an interview about man-boy love with a publication called *Gaysweek*. The only action taken by Church officials was to remove Shanley from his street ministry and send him to a suburban parish.

In response, Church documents show that Shanley tried to blackmail Medeiros into reversing his decision, apparently by threatening to reveal to the media unspecified information about St. John's, the archdiocesan seminary. Instead of being disciplined or permanently removed from positions that put him in contact with young people, Shanley was transferred to St. John the Evangelist Church in Newton, a prosperous suburb west of Boston. In a mild rebuke of sorts, the reassignment was accompanied by an admonition: "It is understood that your ministry at Saint John Parish and elsewhere in this Archdiocese of Boston will be exercised in full conformity with the clear teachings of the Church as expressed in papal documents and other pronouncements of the Holy See, especially those regarding sexual ethics," Medeiros wrote in a letter to Shanley.

In Newton Shanley's career flourished. Despite his troubled track record, he was promoted to pastor six years later by Cardinal Law, then the newly arrived archbishop, in 1985. Four months after that, the archdiocese reacted nonchalantly when a woman alerted the chancery that Shanley gave another talk in Rochester in which he once again endorsed sexual relations between men and boys. In response to the second Rochester letter, Rev. McCormack wrote a friendly note to Shanley, a seminary classmate. In a letter signed "Fraternally in Christ" and containing little sense of urgency, McCormack wrote: "Would you care to comment on the remarks she made? You can either put them in writing or we could get together some day about it." The files contained no evidence that Shanley responded to the request.

The Shanley file also revealed that top Church officials had evidence of the priest's abusive behavior at least as early as the late 1960s. In one handwritten letter, a priest at the Shrine of Our Lady of La Salette in Attleboro, near the Rhode Island border, notified the archdiocese that a young boy had told him that Shanley had masturbated him at a cabin in the Blue Hills, a woodland reservation south of Boston. The letter reported that Shanley routinely brought teenagers to the cabin on weekends, and it provided names, telephone numbers, and addresses of other possible young victims. Church files contain no hint that the allegations were ever investigated. But with an arrogance that defined his persona, Shanley denied the charges in defiant letters in which he offered sarcastic assessments of his accusers and referred to his own "brilliance." In another letter, Shanley used a contemptuous adage to refer to a woman who had accused him of molesting a boy: "Put a Roman collar on a lamp-post and some woman will fall in love with it."

Shanley's diaries and occasional newsletters, undated but also in his files, showed that he contracted venereal disease and instructed teenagers on how to inject drugs. Yet despite Shanley's damning case file, Law gave him a glowing tribute when the priest retired in 1996. In a February 29 letter the cardinal declared, "Without doubt over all of these years of generous and zealous care, the lives and hearts of many people have been touched by your sharing of the Lord's Spirit. You are truly appreciated for all that you have done."

The total number of Shanley's victims may never be known, but his involvement with children predated his years as a priest. Before his first parish assignment at St. Patrick's Church in Stoneham, north of Boston, Shanley worked with retarded children, orphans, juvenile delinquents, and poor and black youngsters at numerous organizations in Massachusetts and New Hampshire, including Camp Fatima, the Cardinal's Home for Children, St. Francis Boys Home, the Catholic Boys Guidance Center, the Dorchester Settlement House, and Camp Dorchester. In Stoneham Shanley began a Friday night "Top Ten Club" for local youth at the town hall, which he transformed for the occasion into a disco with live music and psychedelic lighting. In Braintree, he ran teen folk masses that attracted scores of young people. He established a retreat house for youth workers on a ninety-five-acre farm in Weston, Vermont, and named it "Rivendell" after the idyllic valley in J. R. R. Tolkien's *The Hobbit*. He also served as chaplain at Boston State College and held appointments at Warwick House in Roxbury and Exodus Center in Milton, just south of Boston. Both involved close work with teenagers. From all those periods, victims have now come forward.

During much of the 1970s, while he ran his street ministry, Shanley lived independently in a private apartment in Boston's Back Bay, where he frequently invited teenage boys for so-called counseling sessions that routinely led to sexual encounters. That's where one teenage boy, who is now forty-two and spoke on condition of anonymity, first met Shanley. It was the summer of 1974, and the man, then fifteen, had just finished his freshman year at Boston College High School amid considerable confusion over his sexual identity. An acquaintance suggested he meet with Shanley to talk through his turbulent emotions.

Shortly into their first meeting, Shanley suggested that the man work on feeling more at ease with his sexuality. "He said, 'You should get comfortable with your body. You don't seem comfortable with your body. Have you played strip poker?'" the man recalled. Shanley then stripped naked and persuaded the man to do the same, inviting him to compare their bodies in front of a full-length mirror. The nudity led to sex, the first of many times in years to come. Shanley also arranged sexual liaisons for him with other older men. The man described his relationship with Shanley as "damaging, because oftentimes I wanted and needed to talk, and it was time for sex. I began to think sex was my worth because he was charming and handsome and respected, and that was his interest in me." It wasn't until 1982, feeling "used and angry," that he cut off the relationship for good, when Shanley was at the Newton parish. After Shanley's abuse was made public by the *Globe* in January 2002, the man retained a lawyer and filed a claim against the Church over his abuse.

After leaving Newton in 1990 for a "sabbatical" in California, Shanley was placed on paid sick leave and surfaced at St. Anne's parish in San Bernardino, his way paved by a letter from Bishop Banks asserting that Shanley was a priest in good standing in Boston. Shanley occasionally worked on weekends at St. Anne's and — unbeknownst to his colleagues there — spent his weekdays running the Cabana Club, a "clothing optional" gay motel in nearby Palm Springs, with another Boston priest who was then also on sick leave in California, Rev. John J. White. Shanley and White co-owned the property, even as they were receiving monthly payments from the Boston archdiocese.

In the mid-1990s, with the consent of the Boston archdiocese, Shanley was acting director of Leo House, the Church-run guest house in New York. As recently as 1997 — after the Boston archdiocese had already paid monetary settlements to several of Shanley's victims — Law did not object to Shanley's application to be director of the facility. Church files contain a draft of a letter written by Law recommending Shanley for the director's position, although New York Cardinal John O'Connor vetoed the idea and the letter was never sent. So Shanley returned to California, where he worked as a "senior civilian volunteer" for the San Diego Police Department.

Speaking in 1969 about the dangers that face runaways and street kids, Shanley seemed to dare the reporter interviewing him to scratch below the surface of his ministry. "Whom do you want to get these kids first? Professional counselors or the hustlers and the psychotics who prey on young people?" he asked. In the same interview, Shanley described the teenagers he worked with as "victims of violence, of disease, sexual deviates, and drugs."

Nearly thirty-five years after a sex abuse complaint was first made against him, Shanley finally attracted the attention of police. In early May of 2002, as many of his alleged victims came forward for the first time in the wake of newspaper accounts of his abusive past, Shanley was arrested in San Diego and pleaded not guilty to three counts of child rape dating to the 1980s. The charges were filed on behalf of Paul Busa, a former Newton man who alleged that Shanley abused him from 1983 to 1990, beginning when he was six. The seventy-one-year-old priest faced the prospect of spending the rest of his life in prison.

Like Shanley, who was one of his seminary classmates at St. John's, Rev. Bernard J. Lane was the subject of numerous sexual abuse allegations; the Boston archdiocese has settled at least six molestation complaints against him. And like Shanley, Lane sought positions throughout his career that put him in regular contact with children.

In 1969 he founded a treatment center for drug-using adolescents in

Malden, north of Boston, and organized retreats for youths at the churches where he worked as pastor. He was also a former chaplain at Malden Catholic High School. But most of the allegations against him stem from his tenure as director of Alpha Omega, a nonprofit center for troubled teenage boys in Littleton, Massachusetts, north of Boston, as well as a family-owned cabin in Barnstead, New Hampshire, described by some of his victims as a "bachelor pad" with mirrored ceilings.

As was the case with Paquin, many of Lane's alleged abuses appear to have been preventable. But state officials missed a chance to bring an early end to his actions. And once they stumbled upon evidence of inappropriate sexual behavior, the state and the Boston archdiocese decided it was better to transfer Lane to avoid public embarrassment — even though, at the time, the state could have launched a broader inquiry that might have led to criminal charges.

In the late 1970s Alpha Omega had two homes in Littleton, each housing fifteen boys between the ages of fourteen and seventeen with "serious acting-out problems," including drug or alcohol abuse and car theft. In 1976 or 1977 an evaluation team from the Massachusetts Department of Youth Services paid a visit to Alpha Omega for what was expected to be a routine inspection. But Lane refused to let the team in, saying it would be inappropriate for outsiders to observe the type of group therapy that took place there. When the team alerted its superior, John Isaacson, then the DYS assistant commissioner, he refused to intercede. Isaacson's decision, members of the team said in interviews with the *Globe*, was a serious lapse by the agency. "If we had been able to do the work we should have done at the time, there might have been some kids who weren't harmed," said Jean Bellow, one of the survey team members. Isaacson said he does not recall discussing Alpha Omega with the team but does not dispute the account by members. He also said he discounted the team's findings because he did not trust its judgment. Rebuffed, the team never returned. Not long after, in 1978, DYS received a complaint that Lane had fondled an Alpha Omega resident at his New Hampshire cottage.

Details of the accusation offered a glimpse of a troubled facility run by a troubled priest; according to one of Lane's accusers, boys at Alpha

Omega were encouraged to roll around on the floor in the nude. Questioned about the incident, Lane called it "therapeutic," according to Isaacson. The accusation led state officials to threaten to pull Alpha Omega's license for "unusual treatment practices," prompting Church officials to remove Lane from the facility the same year. State officials who were involved in the controversy said deference to the Church prevented the state from acting earlier.

Cornelius Coco, Alpha Omega's staff psychologist during the 1970s, didn't learn why Lane left Alpha Omega until allegations of his abusive behavior surfaced more than twenty years later, in early 2002. But he concedes that, in hindsight, there were telltale signs that all was not well at Alpha Omega. "There were occasions where Bernie would tell the staff that one of the boys had crawled into his bed, he had talked to the boy for a while, and then had sent him back to his own bed," said Coco. Yet after removing Lane from Littleton, the archdiocese assigned him to other churches in the Boston area, where he continued to have access to children: St. Peter's parish in Lowell; St. Maria Goretti's in Lynnfield; St. Charles's in Waltham, where he was in charge of altar boys and catechism classes; St. Anthony's in Cambridge; and Our Lady of Grace in Chelsea.

Like Geoghan, whose abuse was overlooked as he was shuttled from one parish to another, Lane continued to thrive as a priest despite evidence of his destructive behavior. Not until 1993, the year Law announced a new archdiocesan policy on sexual abuse that involved a review of the personnel files of all living priests, was Lane removed from Chelsea and placed on sick leave. After three years on sick leave, Lane became associate director of the Office of Senior Priests at Regina Cleri, the archdiocese's principal retirement home for priests in downtown Boston, from 1996 to 1998 — the same post previously held by Geoghan. Lane remained in that position until 1999, even though, by then, Church officials had settled the six allegations against him, all originating at Alpha Omega. Since Lane's alleged abuses at Alpha Omega became public in January 2002, more than a dozen victims have retained lawyers.

Lane, who is now retired and living in Barnstead, New Hampshire, has denied the accusations and referred all questions to his lawyer and nephew, Gerard F. Lane II, who acknowledged that the archdiocese settled three sex abuse cases against his uncle for incidents that happened during his tenure at Alpha Omega. But Gerard Lane said he believed there was no merit to the accusations; he claimed Wilson Rogers Jr., the archdiocese's lawyer, urged his uncle to settle the cases or more claimants would "come out of the woodwork."

One of the most striking aspects of the wave of clergy sex abuse complaints triggered by the revelations in Boston was this: the allegations knew no geographic bounds. It would have been troubling enough if the abuse had been limited to New England. But around the country, there had been other Shanleys, other Birminghams, other Lanes. From Maine to Florida to Los Angeles, new victims came forward to tell their stories, emboldened by other victims who had come forward before them. And in Arizona, just as the Geoghan case was attracting wide public attention, a case that had cast a spotlight on the Diocese of Tucson was coming to an end.

In January 2002 civil lawsuits filed against the diocese by eleven men alleging sexual abuse by four Arizona priests beginning in the 1960s were settled confidentially — for an amount some estimates placed at as much as $16 million. It was a case involving Church conduct that Lynne M. Cadigan, an attorney for the plaintiffs, called "the most outrageous pattern and practice of criminal concealment I've ever, ever seen in nineteen years of sex abuse litigation."

Among the revelations unearthed: several boys notified a Church official as early as 1976 that one of the accused priests, Monsignor Robert C. Trupia, had fondled them, yet Trupia remained in active ministry until 1992; two priests were brushed off in the late 1980s when they reported Trupia's abusive behavior to Church officials; the diocese knew Trupia had been banned from a California seminary in 1988 for arriving with unauthorized young male guests, yet promoted him twice in the sixteen years after the first complaint; and Trupia and another priest named in the suits, Rev. William T. Byrne, allegedly shared altar boys sexually at the Yuma, Arizona, parish where they served together in the 1970s.

The litany of damaging revelations seeped out of Tucson like a slow poison, prompting Arizona Church officials to hold a liturgy of healing for hundreds of parishioners after the settlement was reached. At the special service, held in February 2002, Bishop Manuel D. Moreno apologized for his role in the scandal, which had spurred the *Arizona Daily Star* to call on him to resign.

Among the eleven victims were Andrew and Arthur Menchaca, who were allegedly abused by both Trupia and Byrne in the 1970s when they were boys. Andrew Menchaca, now in his forties, said some of the abuse took place when Trupia offered to give him "private studies" in the rectory at St. Francis's Church in Yuma. With Byrne, who died of a brain tumor in 1991, the abuse also happened in the rectory, as well as during trips to Phoenix, Tucson, Los Angeles, and other cities the priest traveled to for his job as a military chaplain.

Like many victims, Menchaca had a choppy childhood. One of five siblings, he grew up in Yuma, a border town of migrant workers and deep poverty. His parents divorced when he was young, and his mother later remarried and had another child. Both Trupia and Byrne forged friendships with him, he said, that made him vulnerable to their manipulative ways. "Little boys with hormones think about what sex is, but they don't know anything about it," said Menchaca, "and then this is being done to you, and your body is reacting one way and your mind is reacting another. . . . You don't understand what's happening to your body and your life at this point. You know your orientation is toward a woman, but something like this is happening — somebody is telling me they desire my body, but it's not a woman. And your body responds physically."

The other priests named as defendants were Revs. Pedro Lucien Meunier de la Pierre and Michael J. Teta. Few facts were in dispute. Trupia, who now lives in Maryland, admitted he was a "loose cannon" who was "unfit for public ministry" when confronted with the abuse allegations by his superiors in 1992. Taking Trupia's statement as an admission of guilt, Moreno immediately suspended him from duty. But Moreno's seemingly swift action came more than sixteen years too late. Church officials first learned of Trupia's abuse in 1976, when Rev. Ted Oswald notified superiors that several boys at St. Francis's told him they had been fondled by Trupia. Monsignor John Anthony Oliver said he forwarded Oswald's report to then-Bishop Francis J. Green. But Oliver said he never questioned Trupia about the allegations. "It's not my responsibility to hear those things," Oliver testified, according to court records. "Personally, I don't care to know those things unless I have to."

And so Trupia continued to climb the ecclesiastical ladder. In 1976, the same year of the original complaints, Trupia was named head of the Tucson diocese's marriage tribunal and associate pastor of Our Mother of Sorrows Church in Tucson. In 1982, in his first year as bishop, Moreno was notified by an archbishop at a California seminary that Trupia had been seen there sleeping with a young man. In litigation years later, Church officials said there was no evidence that Trupia and his overnight guest "were doing anything other than sleeping."

In 1988 the same seminary alerted Moreno that Trupia had been banned from the facility for his habit of arriving with unauthorized young male guests. And a Tucson priest, Rev. Joseph Baker, said Moreno "got hostile" when he alerted him in 1989 to Trupia's habit of taking children into his bedroom. Another priest who raised similar concerns was told to "mind his own business," according to court records. That same year, Trupia won a scholarship to attend the Catholic University of America in Washington, D.C., to do doctoral work in Catholic canon law. No notice was sent to the university about his history of abuse. Yet even after Trupia's description of himself as a "loose cannon" prompted Moreno to suspend him in 1992, Moreno wrote the following year to the mother of one alleged victim and informed her that Trupia had denied any wrongdoing. And Moreno's eventual decision to investigate and suspend Trupia came only after the mother of one abuse victim notified Robert Sanchez, the archbishop of Santa Fe who oversaw Trupia's archdiocese, that Trupia had sexually abused her son, a former altar boy, in 1977. Sanchez himself resigned in 1993 after admitting he had had sexual relations with several women in the 1970s.

Meanwhile, Church officials never reported the accusations against Trupia to law enforcement officials. Nevertheless, the troubled priest finally attracted the attention of police investigators in 1988 and again in 1997. Both times Church officials failed to cooperate, refusing in 1997 to disclose Trupia's whereabouts to investigators even though he was on suspension and they were sending him checks. In 2001 Trupia was arrested in Yuma on seven counts of felony child molestation dating to 1973. But the charges were dropped because the criminal statute of limitations had expired.

How many Trupias were there? As long as dioceses across the country continued to keep abuse complaints confidential, the true number of abusive priests would remain unknown. Absent a policy of openness by Church officials from small-town parishes to the Vatican, the public was left to wonder whether the explosion of publicity about sexually deviant priests centered around a small minority of clergymen or only scraped at the surface of a much larger problem. Meanwhile, another issue loomed: how many victims were out there, scared, silent, and ashamed?

4

The Victims

For Peter Pollard, that moment from 1967 is indelibly imprinted in his memory. The sixteen-year-old altar boy and Rev. George Rosenkranz were alone in the church basement just after midnight on Easter Sunday morning, in the obvious early stages of a sexual encounter, when the pastor of the parish walked in on them.

Much like his peers were accustomed to doing, Monsignor William McCarthy pretended not to notice Pollard and Rosenkranz. And very much like the bishops and cardinals who have long known about the unchecked sexual yearnings of some of their priests, McCarthy sidestepped the opportunity to put a stop to it. As the Catholic Church has done for so long, McCarthy turned his back on the victim. "Could you put out the light when you are finished?" Monsignor McCarthy asked nonchalantly as he turned and walked away from Rosenkranz and his quarry.

Not long after the light was extinguished, Pollard descended into darkness. He had been an honor student at his high school in Marblehead, north of Boston, before Rosenkranz coaxed him into his first sexual experiences. But after that betrayal, his grades plummeted, his ambitions evaporated.

"I kissed a girl for the first time in the winter of 1967. I got *my* first kiss from Rosenkranz a few months earlier," Pollard recalled.

Pollard started college but stayed less than two months. He moved around the country, by his own description an itinerant hippie who took odd jobs so he could feed himself. After the sexual abuse by a priest he had trusted, he chose to live a celibate, ascetic life for several years. His withdrawal from the world around him was so complete that even when he encountered strangers at a bus stop, he opted to stand well behind them. It was nearly two decades before Pollard reclaimed his life, secured the education he had long postponed, started a family, and threw himself into a life's vocation — working with abused children.

By the time Pollard went to the Boston archdiocese in 1988 to complain about Rosenkranz, Monsignor McCarthy was long dead. But sitting in for McCarthy, with much of the same indifference, was Law's deputy Rev. John B. McCormack.

Pollard remembered McCormack saying that Rosenkranz had some "sexual issues," but they were not cause to remove him from parish work. Although Pollard informed McCormack that Rosenkranz, after the kissing and fondling, had asked him to masturbate for him, McCormack had a ready defense for his fellow priest. "He said some individuals growing up formed relationships with George Rosenkranz in which [Rosenkranz] might have expressed affection, and they might have interpreted these acts as sexual involvement," Pollard recalled. Besides, McCormack informed Pollard, Rosenkranz had denied the charges. "My experience is that if they are guilty, they admit it," the future bishop told the stunned Pollard. McCormack, he said, added that even if Pollard was telling the truth, the sexual activity was, in McCormack's view, consensual.

Only after other complaints against Rosenkranz surfaced three years later did the archdiocese quietly remove the priest from his parish and commission a nun to let Pollard know that his initial complaint had been handled "inappropriately." "From my perspective," said Pollard, "McCormack basically abused me again. For me, the emotional and spiritual scarring came from the betrayal, and my betrayal by [Cardinal] Law and McCormack was as damaging as what Rosenkranz did."

Finally, in April 2002, Pollard hired an attorney and sued the archdiocese and Rosenkranz. By then, Rosenkranz had left Massachusetts, and attempts to locate him were unavailing.

*   *   *

Pollard is not alone, but like so many others, he suffered privately for years because he thought he was. By the time he complained about Rosenkranz, he knew there were hundreds like him around the country, coaxed from the shadows in small clusters during scattered scandals involving priests that cropped up publicly beginning in the mid-1980s.

Now there are thousands. In the Boston archdiocese alone, more than five hundred people retained lawyers in the first four months of 2002 with claims that they were molested by priests when they were growing up.

Most victims, experts have long believed, will never come forward. But around the country, this scandal has prompted an unprecedented number of them to emerge from years of private darkness. As their numbers grow, the stigma attached to their experiences diminishes. In the first months of 2002, emboldened by the knowledge that the Church had hidden the extent of the abuse, more than two hundred victims of Boston-area priests contacted the *Globe*, most in confidence, to relate their stories. Hesitant at first, and often in tears, many said they now regret having kept the abuse a secret. They would never have dreamed of telling — or dared to tell — their devout parents. Some admitted that they have suffered in such profound silence that they have been unable to confide even in close friends, siblings, or spouses.

For some, men and women approaching middle age, the first people to hear about their experiences and the shame and guilt they had lived with for years were the faceless reporters who happened to take their phone calls. Others who contacted the *Globe* wanted the world to know what had happened to them and to talk about their childhood trauma.

"He took everything. He took my innocence. He took my spirituality. He took my purity," Timothy J. Lambert said of the priest who allegedly molested him — and his brother, he discovered years later — in a Queens, New York, parish, starting when he was in the sixth grade. "How bad is it when your first sexual experience happens when you are unwilling, a minor, it's a homosexual experience, and at the hands of a priest?" Lambert started drinking within days of the first molestation. "It's the way I medicated myself," he now says.

Lambert, the alleged victim of a priest, is a priest himself.

But he is an embittered priest — angry at the Brooklyn diocese, which he accuses of protecting the priest who allegedly molested him, Rev. Joseph P. Byrns, a Brooklyn pastor, and let down by his own New Jersey diocese, which he says ostracized him for not keeping his silence. Byrns and the Brooklyn diocese deny that Lambert was abused.

In Boston, the cardinal's advisers fear that mounting financial claims could bankrupt the archdiocese. But for most of the victims the issue is not money. It is the need to have their suffering acknowledged, they say, to have people understand what the Church has done to them. Some victims, like Patricia Dolan of Ipswich, on Boston's North Shore, have poured out their hearts because, like Pollard, they believe the Church has treated them coldly.

In the 1960s, Dolan's life was the Church. Her father worked three jobs to pay for his four daughters' parochial school educations. Seven days a week while she was in high school, Pat Dolan worked at the parish rectory in her hometown, answering phones, making spiritual bouquets, and assisting the parish's two priests. One of those priests repeatedly molested her, Dolan said, causing her to suffer panic attacks for years. Ever since then, the trauma has made it difficult for her to forge meaningful relationships, because of her inability to trust people.

In 1995 she finally went to the archdiocese, which agreed to pay for psychotherapy "as long as [she] needed it." But Dolan said the archdiocese has been needlessly callous toward her. Late in 2001, after a chancery official unsuccessfully tried to get her therapist to disclose the confidential results of her therapy sessions, she was notified that the payments would stop.

That was not the first time that she felt demeaned by the archdiocese. Dolan said that Sister Rita V. McCarthy, the chancery's former point person for abuse victims, once called her to say that she had been surprised to learn that the priest who molested her was past middle age when the abuse occurred. "He couldn't have done that much to you," McCarthy said, according to Dolan.

In testimonials like Dolan's, in the allegations now being made in scores of new lawsuits, and in the thousands of pages of Church documents that have been put on public display since January 2002, there is much for Catholics to digest. Among all the priests who dedicated themselves to healing souls and soothing hearts, some only pretended to do so. Their sexual misbehavior took a staggering toll on the victims, on the victims' loved ones, and on the Church: souls darkened, hearts broken, lives shattered, families disillusioned, faith abandoned, and the Church exposed to potentially catastrophic claims.

Years after their abuse, many victims say they have yet to recover from the trauma. Like Dolan, they have found it hard to establish or nourish close relationships. Or it has driven them to alcohol, drugs, or depression — or a life-threatening combination of the three.

One such victim is Patrick McSorley. He is still struggling to shake off the effects of his 1986 experience with former priest John J. Geoghan, whose serial pedophilia, well known to Law and other bishops at the time, has become the flash point for what is now a Churchwide scandal.

Following his usual modus operandi, the affable Geoghan befriended Catholic mothers, including McSorley's, whose lives were in crisis. His offers to help, often by taking the children for ice cream or praying with them at bedtime, were accepted without suspicion. For many families in such straits, the help of a priest was a blessing from God.

That is how McSorley, a twelve-year-old who lived in a Boston housing project, became a Geoghan victim. It was two years after Law, knowing about Geoghan's sexual attraction to young boys, had assigned Geoghan to an affluent parish in suburban Weston. From that base, with its intact, educated — and perhaps more vigilant — families, Geoghan revisited Boston's gritty neighborhoods in search of the more vulnerable.

Geoghan, who knew the McSorley family from his years at St. Andrew's in nearby Jamaica Plain, learned of the suicide of McSorley's alcoholic father and dropped by their apartment to offer his condolences. Geoghan offered to take Patrick out for ice cream.

"I felt a little funny about it," McSorley recalled. "I was twelve years old, and he was an old man." During the ride home, after the priest bought ice cream for his young charge, Geoghan consoled him. But then he patted McSorley's upper leg and slid his hand up toward his crotch. "I froze up," McSorley said. "I didn't know what to think. Then he put his hand on my genitals and started masturbating me. I was petrified.

"I was looking out the window the whole time, but I could see out of the corner of my eye that he had his private part out and was working it up and down." Gradually, the ice cream melted over his hand and down his arm as Geoghan continued to gratify himself and finally pulled the car over to the side of the road. "He made a moan like he ejaculated," McSorley remembered. Then Geoghan dropped McSorley off at home, but not before warning, "We're very good at keeping secrets."

When McSorley went indoors, his mother sensed something amiss and asked what was wrong. But the boy was tongue-tied. "I couldn't answer her. I remember my arm was all sticky from the ice cream. I didn't know how to tell anyone something like that," he said. Looking back, McSorley believes that if his molester was someone other than a priest, he might have done more to resist and might have been more willing to tell his mother. "I was at that preteen age when I knew right from wrong, but because it was a priest doing it, it set off a whole wave of confusion," he explained.

McSorley said he buried the memory of his encounter with Geoghan because of the trauma it caused him, and that it was the catalyst for the alcoholism and depression he has battled since. "I was actually going around to doctors asking them, 'Why am I so depressed?'" he said.

McSorley made the connection between his depression and his experience with Geoghan during a 1999 dinner with his girlfriend, his sister, and her husband. During dinner, his sister mentioned that a priest she had known in parochial school was being sued for molesting boys. "Things started to click right then, when she mentioned Father Geoghan," McSorley said. "I think I got up for a minute and had to go outside and get a breath of fresh air." When he returned to the table, he told the others what Geoghan had done to him.

"To find out later that the Catholic Church knew he was a child molester — every day it bothers me more and more," McSorley said.

Like others who were molested as children, McSorley is overprotective of his own children, particularly his three-year-old son. "I never let him away from me. I never let him away from my side," McSorley said.

"I don't trust anyone. If a priest can molest a little boy, anything can happen."

Thomas P. Fulchino was especially concerned about his children, ever mindful of that night in 1960 when he was twelve and was the last child left in his parochial school after an evening activity. Rev. James R. Porter, newly ordained, offered him a ride home.

But Porter started "being grabby." Frightened, Fulchino ran. "I ran up to the second floor, and that bastard, he got me then, and just, just got me down on the ground and was just going like a madman . . . just . . . now I understand this: he was humping me like a dog," Fulchino said.

Tom Fulchino finally pulled away and ran and hid under a desk in a dark classroom until Porter gave up trying to find him. Then he ran from the school and all the way home. For much of the time since then, he has been running from the memory.

In December 1992, Fulchino was one of more than one hundred people molested by Porter who received settlements from the Fall River diocese in southeastern Massachusetts. By then, Fulchino was a successful businessman with five children and a wife, who shared his caution about never leaving their children unattended with adults they do not know and trust.

Their caution extended even to St. Julia's in Weston, the parish where they worshiped and sent their children to Sunday school during the 1980s. It is the very parish where Law chose to transfer John Geoghan in 1984, the same parish from which Geoghan was removed for six months in 1989 and hospitalized for further treatment of his "affliction," as one Church document described it, and the same parish Geoghan was returned to after a diagnosis that his pedophilia was "in remission."

It was a brief remission.

On a Sunday morning weeks later, Geoghan was making his rounds of Sunday school classes, asking questions. Christopher T. Fulchino, a shy thirteen-year-old, fielded one of those questions and, to his everlasting regret, had the right answer. Mostly, Geoghan handed out quarters and candy for the right answer. But as Chris Fulchino recalled in a tremulous voice, Geoghan was fresh out of quarters and candy, so the priest said, according to Chris, "If you come over to the [rectory] during your break, I'll have milk and cookies with you, and we'll say Our Father. I was like, 'Hey, that's awesome!'"

In a dark room in the rectory, Geoghan was sitting in a lone red-velvet chair, with two glasses of milk and chocolate chip cookies on a plastic platter. He hoisted his unsuspecting guest onto his lap, and they said the Our Father. That was when Geoghan began to fondle the boy.

Father and son remembered the brute force of their attackers. "I thought I was going to die. I couldn't breathe," Tom Fulchino said of his struggle against Porter so long ago. From Chris, there was nearly an echo: "He squeezed me as tight as he could. I felt like I couldn't breathe, and I was gagging."

Like his father nearly three decades earlier, Chris squirmed free and ran. His dad had hidden under a desk; Chris hid behind the church until his unsuspecting father came to pick him up. And like Tom Fulchino in 1960, Chris Fulchino said nothing to his parents in 1989.

Since 1997, when Chris Fulchino told his parents what had happened, no one from the Fulchino family has set foot inside St. Julia's. When Chris is home from his job in Maine, he drives back roads in Weston to avoid passing the church. He refuses to enter any church at all. Often, he awakens from nightmares about Geoghan. Each time that happens, he takes a shower.

Like Chris Fulchino, few abuse victims told their parents, at least initially. Armand Landry, who is now eighty-six, said he was molested by his parish priest in Laconia, New Hampshire, in 1927, when he was twelve. Three quarters of a century later, Landry remembered the ride in the priest's car, where it happened, even the day — Saturday. "I never told my parents; they would have slapped your face," Landry said. "I was twelve years old or so. No one would believe you in those days. The priests were everything."

Even in recent years — though perhaps no longer — many Catholics have reacted in disbelief to the notion that a priest would molest a child. One woman was raped by a priest in a rectory closet in a parish in Lynn, north of Boston, in the 1960s when she was only nine. But she said she only summoned the courage to tell her mother what had happened to her five years ago. "My own mother didn't believe me. Her middle name is denial," the woman said. The archdiocesan nun who handled her case told her that her molester had left the priesthood to marry in the late 1960s, and now had a family and three children. "You wouldn't want to report him, because it would hurt his life," she said she was told. The archdiocese pays for her therapy, but the woman said the rape still affects her. For one thing, she said, "I have never worn anything but ugly underwear." And that, she said, is because the day she was raped, the priest "complimented me on my fancy underwear."

Until recently, a mountain constructed of these small secrets helped dioceses around the country hide the extent of the Church's problem. Children were too ashamed to tell their parents. If they did, guilt-ridden parents most often did nothing. To be sure, some went to their pastors but were usually asked to pray for the offender and say nothing — all for the good of the Church.

Even those who went to the chancery to insist that something be done about a molesting priest got little satisfaction for their efforts. At best, the priest was removed — and then promptly assigned to a new parish. In that respect, Geoghan was no anomaly among the scores of priests in the Boston archdiocese who are known to have abused children.

There are many reminders that to focus on the suffering of victims is to miss a larger universe of people who are also in pain — the parents of victims. Many blame themselves for entrusting their children to priests, for not detecting signs, now obvious in hindsight, that something was amiss.

Other parents feel an extra burden. They discovered at the time what was happening and now wish they had done more to end the careers of priests who abused their children and then went on to target others. Among those parents is Kenneth A. MacDonald. Now seventy-two and gravely ill with heart disease, he and his wife, Eileen, raised nine children in St. Gerard Majella parish in Canton, a suburb south of Boston.

Both parents taught Sunday school, Confraternity of Christian Doctrine, or CCD. Ken MacDonald was a lector at Mass and a member of the Parish Council.

In 1979, Rev. Peter R. Frost was one of St. Gerard's priests when Bryan MacDonald, the fifth of MacDonald's nine children, had a part-time job in the rectory. He was fourteen. The priest was thirty-nine. And one night, Frost got Bryan drunk and molested him.

"I was so shaken up, I told my cousin. He told my aunt and uncle, and they told Dad," Bryan said. Ken MacDonald remembered taking his son outside and drawing the truth out of him. "As soon as I found out, I felt like shooting Frost," he said. It never came to violence, but Ken MacDonald did something other parents rarely did — he confronted the priest.

"He was in the rectory. We went into his office. I was very upset. I told him, 'I [can't] believe this happened.' There was no denial. He admitted it. He said, 'I'm caught.' I asked him how he could have done it, and I got no answer," MacDonald said. Frost told MacDonald he was getting psychiatric help and led him to believe his superiors were helping him. From time to time, MacDonald remembered, "I spoke to Father Frost about it. I'd ask him, 'How's your problem going?' He'd say he was fine."

Several years later, the parents of another Canton teenager complained to St. Gerard's pastor when their son was also molested by Frost. According to the victim, they were assured Frost would get counseling. But instead of being put out of commission, Frost was transferred to St. Elizabeth's in nearby Milton in 1988. It was not until 1992 that the Boston archdiocese removed him from active ministry. Frost, now sixty-two, has been on "sick leave" ever since. The day Bryan MacDonald filed suit against Frost, the archdiocese admitted the priest had molested minors.

"It's bothered me all along. I let him get away with it. I ended up hiding his problem," Ken MacDonald said. "We had so much respect for priests." His wife Eileen interjected, "That's twenty-twenty hindsight. It was the Church that hid him."

*   *   *

Self-doubt, however undeserved, is a common denominator among parents of victims. For most, their children were grown and the priest long gone by the time they learned of the abuse. Among those who found out about it when it occurred, few were willing to confront the abuser, as MacDonald did.

For some other parents, the guilt is intermingled with feelings of deep betrayal. Unwittingly, they welcomed the Roman-collared predators into their families and gave them access to the children, often out of a reflexive Catholic conviction that there could be no better role model for them, especially the boys. In many Catholic homes, children were brought up to idolize priests. "God's men on Earth," their parents taught them.

In February 2002, the day before Law relieved Rev. Joseph L. Welsh because of allegations that he had molested children, members of one close-knit, devoutly Catholic family told the *Globe* that Welsh had been a de facto family member for three decades. He dined with them weekly, vacationed with them, and rarely missed a holiday dinner at their home. The family even named their youngest boy after him. Late last year, the family learned for the first time that as each son, including Welsh's namesake, had reached puberty, Welsh had sexually abused him.

Much the same fate befell a Maine family with such deep roots in the Church that the parents, Frank and Virginia Doherty, most often turned to the priests they knew for help in coping with the strains that raising three boys and a girl can bring to a marriage.

Frank Doherty was also a devoted alumnus of Cheverus High School in Portland. He was a friend to many of the Jesuits at the top-ranked Catholic high school, and he and Ginny were earnest in their practices and beliefs. They proudly sent their three sons to Cheverus.

Not surprisingly, when the Jesuit order transferred Rev. James R. Talbot from Boston College High School in Boston to Cheverus in 1980, the Doherty family formed a bond with a man who became their sons' soccer coach, and as Michael Doherty remembers, "the best teacher at Cheverus." Their home became Talbot's second home. They set aside a room, with a closetful of his clothes, for his frequent overnight stays.

"My wife bought his clothes for him so he could come over and take off his collar," Frank Doherty says. "She put cards in his jacket pockets to tell him what color went with what color." He had his mail delivered to their house. Even Talbot's mother was an occasional guest at the Dohertys'.

Talbot spent most holidays with the family. He celebrated family birthdays with them. And when Frank and Ginny Doherty experienced difficulty, they turned to Talbot. "When we had problems with the children we went to him, whether it was an issue of grades or sexuality. . . . We discussed those things with him as if he were a senior member of our family," Frank said. "I felt he had actually shared in the raising of my children. . . . That's how intimately close we were with him. He was as close as a brother to me."

Little did they know that Talbot had molested numerous boys during a decade at Boston College High School, according to claims about the priest that flooded in after some of his victims described in news articles in February how he molested them. What's more, documents obtained by the *Globe* contain strong hints that he was moved to Cheverus specifically because his superiors in Boston knew about his behavior.

The consequences of the decision to ship Talbot to Maine have been calamitous for the Dohertys. In 1984 and 1985, he repeatedly molested Michael, their youngest son, when he was fifteen and sixteen. For several years, Michael said nothing. But in the early 1990s, he shared some details of the abuse with his siblings.

His sister, Courtney Oland, then broke the dam. Concerned that Michael was severely affected by the abuse, and without telling anyone, she decided to act. When she mailed invitations to her 1995 wedding, she slipped a handwritten note into Talbot's invitation telling him not to dare show his face. She also told him not to return to her family's house. When mail still arrived at the home for Talbot, as it often did, she threw it away so her parents would think Talbot had stopped by to pick it up when they were out. Eventually, one of Michael's older brothers, Ryan, approached Talbot to ask why he'd stopped coming to their house. Talbot replied, "Ask your sister."

In 1998, Courtney wrote a letter to the Portland diocese notifying Church officials of the abuse. Talbot was quickly whisked out of Maine and sent for two years to a Maryland treatment center for priests who have sexually abused minors. She had to act, Courtney said, because "we were losing [Michael]. I said, 'This secret has to stop or we will lose him, or he will do something to himself.'"

Since 2000, the Jesuits have sequestered Talbot at their retirement home in Weston, Massachusetts. In 2001, Michael Doherty's lawsuit was settled by the Church. Nowadays, Michael said he has come to believe his sister's actions were wise. "I'll probably be healthier for it," he said.

Frank and Ginny Doherty no longer attend Mass. And the Cheverus community has turned its back on them, they feel, for the embarrassment that Michael's charges brought to the school.

"I don't want to be any other religion," Frank Doherty said. "I just can't go to church." The ordeal, he said, "destroyed not just our view of Catholicism, but our faith experience." Now, Frank said he has nowhere to turn when he needs help. "When everything else had shit the bed, you turned to the Church. Now what do you do?"

Like other parents, the Dohertys look back over those years and still blame themselves for not suspecting anything. "I feel so goddamn stupid, it's horrible," said Frank Doherty. "The ripple effect of what these men do and what this Church has done . . . is incredible. They've wrecked lives that weren't even in place when they did what they did."

The family remains disappointed by how coolly the Cheverus community has treated them, although they received several compassionate letters and phone calls after Talbot's alleged abuses in Boston were aired in the media. Cheverus, Ginny Doherty said bitterly, ostracized the family for telling the truth. "They talk about God, but I don't know who their God is."

If nothing else, the public attention to their case against Talbot has helped crack the layers of secrecy that have long cloaked, and even enabled, the Church's sexual predators.

"I think being silent is a sin," Ginny Doherty said. "There's never a healing if everybody's silent."

*   *   *

No serial child molester is likely to soon eclipse James Porter and John Geoghan in the public consciousness. More than three hundred of their victims have come forward since 1991 to accuse the two men of sexual abuse, and experts believe that is just a fraction of the number of children they molested. But Joseph Birmingham — the priest who abused, among others, Michael McCabe — isn't so far off. In late March 2002, with details about Birmingham's chronic urge to molest boys surfacing in the press, more than forty of his victims enlisted lawyers. And there is evidence that Birmingham molested many more children in the six parishes he served in after his ordination in 1960.

One of these children was Tom Blanchette. From his simple home on Martha's Vineyard, Blanchette stares at a wrinkled, black-and-white photograph and is transported back across forty years to a childhood in Sudbury, a pretty town west of Boston. He remembers how idyllic it was — until he was eleven, when Birmingham began molesting him.

The man whose happy image dominates the photograph Blanchette has saved for decades casts a dark shadow on his childhood memories. In the photo, Birmingham, then about thirty years old, stands smiling at a side altar at Our Lady of Fatima Church in Sudbury. In the background is a statue of the Blessed Virgin Mary. He is flanked by the officers of the Catholic Youth Organization; one of them is young Tommy Blanchette.

"He was gregarious, articulate. Very outgoing. He would always greet people with a booming, 'Hi! How are ya?' And by then, I had been having sex with this guy for two years — three or four times a week at that point," said Blanchette. "If a teacher's a pedophile, he's the best teacher. If a Little League coach is a pedophile, he's the best coach. If a Boy Scout leader is a pedophile, he's the best troop leader. And that's how it was with Father Birmingham."

Soon after the priest arrived in Sudbury, he became a frequent guest at the Blanchette home. As parents of seven boys and two girls, Blanchette's mother and father were happy to have the priest in their lives. What better role model for their sons? He even paid summertime visits to the family's Harwich Port cottage on Cape Cod. "It was like Bing Crosby in *The Bells of St. Mary's*," Blanchette recalled.

When Blanchette was about eleven years old, he was sick one evening, when Birmingham stopped by for a meal. The priest asked the Blanchettes' permission to check in on little Tommy, who was down the hall and under the covers in his first-floor bedroom. "He came in and said, 'What's the matter?' I told him I had the flu. And he offered to give me a stomach rub. The next thing I know, his hands are down my pajamas."

His part-time job mowing the parish lawn and washing floors kept him within easy grasp of Birmingham. Soon, he said, he was being repeatedly attacked, even as the priest remained a frequent dinner guest at his home. He said Birmingham attempted to anally rape him "but at eleven or twelve you can't accommodate that." The priest attempted to force the boy to perform oral sex on him. "But there was no way in hell I was going to do that," said Blanchette. But soon, in a sexual encounter he estimates repeated itself three hundred times, he found himself naked in Birmingham's bed. There was mutual masturbation. There was forced French kissing. "He would spread my thighs and insert his penis between [them]," said Blanchette.

Blanchette said he memorized the pattern on the wallpaper on Birmingham's walls. In his mind's eye, he can still see the Martha Washington bedspread across a four-poster, pineapple mahogany bed. There is a large oak desk against one wall. There is a chest of drawers. An air conditioner sits in the bottom of one window.

And always, there is one of Birmingham's shoes, jammed under the bedroom door — a safeguard Birmingham believed would guarantee privacy. "Afterward we would talk, but not about sex," said Blanchette. "It's very much the same modus operandi of a guy who rapes his wife. It's over, and you don't talk about it. I used to think this was unhealthy and not talking about it was unhealthy. I had the weirdest thoughts. He was always talking about vocations, saying sex is good but masturbation is bad. I thought, 'Is this a weird initiation to the priesthood?'"

The attacks occurred elsewhere too. They occurred so often in Birmingham's car that Blanchette vividly remembered details of the automobile — a 1963 black Ford Galaxy. It had a red interior and was a hardtop convertible, all the rage forty years ago.

By 1964, Birmingham was gone from Sudbury — whisked to his next parish in Salem after parents of some of his other victims went to the archdiocese to complain. Blanchette went on to a Catholic high school in Framingham, another Boston suburb, and attended college before joining the army in 1967.

Through it all, he never spoke of Birmingham's attacks. But in 1971, while home from the army, he was tossing back fifty-cent beers with some old buddies when Birmingham's name came up. "He queered me," one of Blanchette's boyhood friends declared. Blanchette was stunned. He told his friends that he too had been assaulted by Birmingham. And then, one by one, every young man at the table described abuse at the hands of their former parish priest. When Blanchette got home that evening, he called what amounted to an emergency family council. He revealed Birmingham's abuse. Four of his brothers said they too had been attacked. Blanchette's mother rushed for the telephone to report the assaults. But his father put a stop to it. "I think he was afraid if he got involved he would have gone up, got his .22, and killed the bastard," Blanchette said.

Tom Blanchette moved on with his life. He climbed the Matterhorn in Switzerland. In 1975, he crewed in a sailboat race from Newport to Bermuda. He went skydiving, sought out the thrills of white-water rafting, and skied down the faces of steep and icy mountains. In 1986 he was the number one salesman in the country for Monroe shock absorbers. After a long absence from church, he found religion again, this time as an Episcopalian. Yet he wondered about the effects of his years of abuse in Father Birmingham's bedroom.

"One of the things that I found was that I was short-fused. My cup was always ninety-five percent filled with anger," explained Blanchette. When anyone in authority — including a New Jersey state trooper who once pulled him over — used their power in a manner he thought excessive, Blanchette erupted. And like three of his four brothers who were also Birmingham victims, Blanchette, now fifty-four, has never married. He is in a relationship with a woman now and says he is happy. And he says he is no longer haunted by the memories of Father Birmingham. Like so few other victims, Blanchette confronted his tormentor.

In 1988, the year before the priest died, Blanchette made an unannounced visit to the rectory at St. Brigid's Church in Lexington, where he found Birmingham getting out of his car. Even as he wondered whether the priest ever worried about being punched or shot or stabbed by one of his victims, and despite all the abuse Blanchette had endured, he found himself shaking Birmingham's hand. The priest — heavier and his hair gone gray — reacted coolly.

"He was not physically intimidating anymore. I just walked up to him, and I said, 'Hi, I'm Tom Blanchette from Sudbury.' He said, 'Hi! How are ya?' And I said, 'I've been thinking about you, and I've been having some problems and I realize that some of those problems are a result of my relationship with you and I'd like to talk to you about that.'"

The priest put Blanchette off. He said he was leaving again for an appointment. He asked him to make an appointment, and Blanchette promised to call back. But he didn't. Six months later, Blanchette knocked on the rectory door at St. Brigid's. Birmingham answered the door, and soon the two men were seated in overstuffed chairs in a meeting room on the rectory's first floor. Blanchette remembers a German shepherd dozing nearby on the carpet.

"I said, 'You know, I realize that I'm responsible for being angry, but I think that has something to do with the abuse I got from you. You sexually abused me, my four brothers, and a litany of other guys.'" The priest, then in his mid-fifties, said he too had had a difficult life. His parents had died. He said he'd been very sick with a mysterious illness that defied diagnosis. But Blanchette pressed on. "With a sense of genuine righteousness I told him, 'What you did to us — and to me specifically — was wrong, and you had no right to do that.'" The priest stared unblinkingly into Blanchette's eyes, waiting but unprepared for what came next.

"'Having said that, it brings me to the real reason I've come here. The real reason I've come here is to ask you to forgive me for the hatred and resentment that I have felt toward you for the last twenty-five years.' When I said that, he stood up, and in what I would describe as a demonic voice, he said, 'Why are you asking me to forgive you?' And through tears I said, 'Because the Bible tells me to love my enemies and to pray for those who persecute me.'"

Blanchette said Birmingham collapsed as if he'd been punched in the chest. The priest dissolved into tears, and soon Blanchette too was crying. Blanchette began to take his leave but asked Birmingham if he could visit again. The priest explained that he was under tight restrictions at the rectory. He said he had been to a residential treatment center in Connecticut, and he returned there once a month. He was not allowed to leave the grounds except in the company of an adult.

Blanchette would not see the priest again until Tuesday, April 18, 1989, just hours before his death. Blanchette found his molester at Symmes Hospital in Arlington and discovered the priest — once robust and 215 pounds — was now an eighty-pound skeleton with skin. Morphine dripped into an IV in his arm. Oxygen was fed by a tube into his nostrils. His hair had been claimed by chemotherapy. The priest sat in a padded chair by his bed. His breathing was labored.

"I knelt down next to him and held his hand and began to pray. And as I did, he opened his eyes. I said, 'Father Birmingham, it's Tommy Blanchette from Sudbury.'"

He greeted Blanchette with a raspy and barely audible, "Hi. How are ya?"

"I said, 'Is it all right if I pray for you?' And he said, 'Yes.' And I began to pray, 'Dear Father, in the name of Jesus Christ, I ask you to heal Father Birmingham's body, mind, and soul.' I put my hand over his heart and said, 'Father, forgive him all his sins.'" Blanchette helped Birmingham into bed. It was about 10 P.M. He died the next morning.

The following Monday, Cardinal Law said Birmingham's funeral Mass. Blanchette sat in a pew midway down the church on the right side. He listened as a young man from another of Birmingham's parishes recalled him fondly in a eulogy.

It was at a reception in St. Brigid's basement immediately after the funeral that Blanchette saw the cardinal standing alone, eating a tiny sandwich and cradling a paper cup of hot coffee. "He had his back to me, and I went up to him and I told him I knew Father Birmingham. And he said, 'Very good. Very good. And you've maintained a friendship with him all these years?' And I said, 'No. But a few months ago I sought him out and had a long discussion.' The cardinal said, 'Wonderful. Wonderful.' I told him I prayed for him the night before he died, and he said, 'Wonderful. Wonderful.' And then I said, 'There's a lot of young men in the diocese who will be in need of counseling in the wake of their relationship with Father Birmingham.'"

"What are you driving at?" Law asked him, according to Blanchette.

Blanchette said he tried to be discreet because there were mourners close by. "I said Father Birmingham sexually molested me, my four brothers, and many, many boys in our parish. His facial expression dropped. He took me by the arm and said, 'Come with me.' And we walked into the middle of the hall so no one was within twenty feet."

When Blanchette was finished describing the abuse and his recent meeting with Birmingham, he said Law told him, " 'We need men like you in the Church, and you should come back to the Church.' He said, 'Bishop Banks is handling this, and I want you to make an appointment.'"

At one point, Blanchette said Law asked for permission to pray for him. "He laid his hands on my head for two or three minutes. And then he said this: 'I bind you by the power of the confessional never to speak about this to anyone else.' And that just burned me big time. . . . I didn't ask him to hear my confession. I went there to inform him."

When the *Globe* asked in 2002 about the discussion between the cardinal and Blanchette, Law said through a spokeswoman that he vaguely remembered it, but not with any precision. In any case, Law said in his statement to the *Globe* that he would be happy to meet with Blanchette. When Blanchette read Law's comments in the newspaper, he went to the chancery the next day, March 25.

Blanchette said he was shuttled around and finally got to speak briefly with Rev. John J. Connolly Jr., the cardinal's chief secretary. "He said, 'What can I do for you?' And I told him, I read in the paper that the cardinal would be happy to meet with me and I said I'd be happy to meet with him." Connolly said he would call him at his home on Martha's Vineyard that evening, Blanchette said. But he did not. And, a month later, he still hadn't. During that time, the archdiocese announced on several occasions that the cardinal was "continuing to meet" with victims. But not with Blanchette.

5

Explosion

For more than a decade, the Roman Catholic Church argued that serial predators such as John Geoghan and James Porter — both defrocked and imprisoned — were rotten apples, just like those anyone could find if they looked carefully among all accountants, postal workers, lawyers, or physicians.

That was the Church's reasoning.

And even as the *Boston Globe* reported in early January 2002 on the Church's detailed knowledge of Geoghan's horrific, persistent attacks, and how leaders of the Boston archdiocese worked vigorously to conceal them, officials insisted that Geoghan's conduct was an aberration. It was, they said, confined to a slender minority of men who wear Roman collars. But on January 31, 2002, the newspaper raised the stakes by reporting that the Boston archdiocese had secretly settled sexual abuse claims against at least seventy other priests over the past decade. The breadth of the problem was becoming startlingly, and publicly, apparent. In the next two months, the archdiocese would give to prosecutors the names of more than ninety priests who had been accused of abuse.

As dioceses across the country began to reexamine their policies concerning sexual misconduct by the clergy, new fissures were exposed. A chasm began to open between the faithful and those they had trusted to lead their Church.

As the scandal spread and gained momentum, Cardinal Law found himself on the cover of *Newsweek,* and the Church in crisis became grist for the echo chamber of talk radio and all-news cable stations. The image of TV reporters doing live shots from outside klieg-lit churches and rectories became a staple of the eleven o'clock news. Confidentiality deals, designed to contain the Church's scandal and maintain privacy for embarrassed victims, began to evaporate as those who had been attacked learned that the priests who had assaulted them had been put in positions where they could attack others too. There were stories about clergy sex abuse in virtually every state in the Union. The scandal reached Ireland, Mexico, Austria, France, Chile, Australia, and Poland, the homeland of the Pope.

A poll done for the *Washington Post,* ABC News, and Beliefnet.com showed that a growing majority of Catholics were critical of the way their Church was handling the crisis. Seven in ten called it a major problem that demanded immediate attention.

Hidden for so long, the financial price of the Church's negligence was astonishing. At least two dioceses said they had been pushed to the brink of bankruptcy after being abandoned by their insurance companies. In the past twenty years, according to some estimates, the cost to pay legal settlements to those victimized by the clergy was as much as $1.3 billion. Now the meter was running faster. Hundreds of people with fresh charges of abuse began to contact lawyers.

By April 2002, Cardinal Law was under siege and in seclusion in his mansion in Boston, where he was heckled by protesters, satirized by cartoonists, lampooned by late-night comics, and marginalized by a wide majority of his congregation that simply wanted him out. In mid-April, Law secretly flew to Rome, where he discussed resigning with the Pope.

Some Church leaders said the intense scrutiny of the practices of a highly secretive Church was a welcome salve. "A boil has been lanced, and I do feel strongly that this is a time of grace for us, as painful and difficult as this moment is," said Bishop William S. Skylstad of Spokane, Washington, vice president of the U.S. Conference of Catholic Bishops. "The fact is that the pain and the hurt were there, under the surface, for those who have been carrying this around for years, and opening this up helps us to minister to that situation as best we can, and begin the process of healing and reconciliation."

By late April, 176 priests from twenty-eight states and the District of Columbia had resigned or been removed in cases of sexual abuse, according to a survey by the Associated Press. The Vatican, which at first seemed to minimize the crisis as a peculiarly American problem, had heard enough. In a historic step, Pope John Paul II summoned all American cardinals to the Vatican to discuss the crisis that had shaken the two-thousand-year-old Church. The scandal that began in Boston had spread so fast and so far that even the frail Pope, who had consigned the happenings to oblique references tucked deep into lengthy papal messages, was forced to make it the focus of his attention.

The *Boston Globe*'s report on January 31, 2002, was a watershed.

It laid bare the depth of the scandal. It badly damaged the few-bad-apples theory. And it accelerated the wave of stories building around the country that would crash fiercely against the Church's ancient foundation.

"Under an extraordinary cloak of secrecy, the Archdiocese of Boston in the last 10 years has quietly settled child molestation claims against at least 70 priests," the story began. "In the public arena alone, the *Globe* found court records and other documents that identify 19 present and former priests as accused pedophiles. Four have been convicted of criminal charges of sex abuse, including former priest John J. Geoghan. Two others face criminal charges. But those public cases represent just a fraction of the priests whose cases have been disposed of in private negotiations that never brought the parties near a courthouse, according to interviews with many of the attorneys involved."

The report punctuated six months of work that began in the summer of 2001. The record showed that within six months of his arrival in Boston in 1984, Law knew about allegations that Geoghan had been attacking boys.

The Church's efforts to contain the scandal were so pervasive that even one of the priests whose abuse of children resulted in confidentiality settlements said he was troubled by a Church that successfully hid his problem and those of so many other priests. "What they were protecting was their notion that the Church is a perfect society," the priest said. "If the archdiocese really wanted to protect its other priests from scandal, they would have gotten those of us who abused children out of there much earlier."

By early February, Law had twice reassured the public that the archdiocese had removed all priests known to have sexually molested minors from any assignments. "There is no priest known to us to have been guilty of the sexual abuse of a minor holding any position in this archdiocese," Law said. Under questioning from reporters, Law repeated his assertion three times. And then finally, and with an edge to his voice, he promised: "There is no priest, or former priest, working in this archdiocese in any assignment whom we know to have been responsible for sexual abuse. I hope you get that straight."

Law's promise didn't last for long. Eight days after his statement, parishioners in two suburban Boston churches were stunned when their pastors were removed after the archdiocese found evidence that both men had been accused of sexually abusing children in the past. Five days after that, six more priests were removed after the archdiocese combed its personnel files going back forty years. Stunned parishioners walked into their churches, receiving the news through tears and disbelief.

"It's a shock to see your parish priest's picture in the newspaper with a story like this," said one parishioner, a prominent Boston businessman. "I mean, I took Communion from the guy." By May, eleven priests had been forced from assignments after Law's assurance that the Church had rid itself of problem priests. In March, a former vice chancellor of the archdiocese was ousted over similar accusations. By then, Boston's widening scandal was the talk of the nation.

Scottish bagpipes wailed. An Irish harp echoed lyrically. And more than two hundred deacons and priests paraded behind colorful banners to welcome a new bishop to Palm Beach in January 1999.

Anthony J. O'Connell, a son of County Clare on Ireland's west coast, had arrived, replacing Bishop Keith Symons, driven out after admitting sexual misconduct with young boys early in his forty-year priesthood. It was a time of hope and joy and prayer in Florida, a time of renewal. "It is an awesome responsibility that God entrusts to us the mission of Jesus Christ," a buoyant O'Connell told the faithful at his installation at the Cathedral of St. Ignatius. But even as he stood there before a congregation of twelve hundred and watched the smoke of sweet incense fill the crowded church, the newly arrived bishop harbored a dark secret.

"It always hung over me," O'Connell would later confess. What the Palm Beach congregation did not know on that winter's day in 1999 was that their new shepherd, who promised to repair the breach, was guilty of sexual abuse himself.

In the 1970s, when O'Connell was rector of St. Thomas Aquinas Seminary in Hannibal, Missouri, a seminary student named Christopher Dixon sought him out for counseling. Dixon, who is gay, said he was struggling with his sexual orientation. He was feeling guilt and shame. He told O'Connell, who was his school counselor, about an earlier molestation by a priest.

"We would talk for endless hours about my acceptance of who I am, my body," Dixon said. "He engendered a lot of trust. With a view to trying to [help me] accept my body, he took me to bed with him, naked, and rubbed his body up against mine. I thought, Well, this man is a man of God and how can he be wrong? But I just knew something was wrong, or I wouldn't have been feeling so sickly and nervous." Dixon said O'Connell fondled him three or four times over two years.

Some twenty years after that sexual contact, Dixon wrote to O'Connell, who by then was in Tennessee. In the twenty-fifth year of O'Connell's priesthood, the Pope had elevated him to be Knoxville's bishop. Dixon wanted O'Connell to get treatment and make restitution. The 1995 letter sounded alarm bells, and Church officials found their solution in a remedy that was already a familiar, if secret, fixture in the Church in Boston: they made a secret settlement. The Jefferson City diocese did not admit to Dixon's allegation, but they paid him $125,000 in 1996, and he promised to drop further claims against the diocese.

Dixon said he decided to break the confidentiality deal and call the *St. Louis Post-Dispatch* after reading about other victims who had stepped forward because of the Boston scandal; he felt safer in a crowd. "I do not want these men in a position where they can continue to do what they've done," Dixon said. Just hours after the St. Louis newspaper broke the story in Missouri, O'Connell, sixty-three, a popular and well-traveled bishop in Florida, announced his resignation. As he quit, he was flanked by many of the same priests and deacons who three years earlier had welcomed him as the leader of 350,000 Catholics in five Florida counties. A day earlier, O'Connell had joined nine other Florida bishops in issuing a statement that denounced sexual abuse as "criminal and sinful." Now he was pleading guilty to that abuse himself. He made his confession standing in the same cathedral where his Florida ministry had begun.

"I want to apologize as sincerely and as abjectly as I possibly can," said O'Connell, the lilting accent of his native County Clare still firm in his voice. "I am truly and deeply sorry for the pain and hurt and anger and confusion, as it will result from all of this. I have been loved since I came to this diocese, been loved far more than any human being could ever deserve to be loved. I certainly have worked hard in the diocese. That's the only way I know to work is to work hard. God has given me a lot of abilities and great gifts, and I can truthfully say I have used those gifts very fully.

"My heart bleeds for Chris Dixon. I have not heard anything from him since the time settlement was made. . . . My understanding was that he made the settlement with the diocese. He signed off. He asked for confidentiality for his own reasons. And I thought that brought all of that to a conclusion. It always hung over me. I don't think I've ever preached without being conscious of it and especially in these recent times." O'Connell called his conduct stupid and foolish and the result of trying to help Dixon work through personal issues. But he still seemed to diminish the seriousness of his conduct, lying naked with a youthful seminarian. "There was nothing in the relationship that was anything other than touches," O'Connell said. "There was nothing beyond that. Nothing of any sexual nature beyond that. So in the ordinary understanding of sexual activity — no, there wasn't — and I certainly want to make sure my people know that. It still doesn't change the naïveté and stupidity and misguidancy. Would I change all of that? I would change it in a minute, for his sake as well as for mine."

O'Connell's fast fall stunned and embarrassed the congregation he once led. Rev. Brian King of St. Juliana's in West Palm Beach had been a seminary student who worked as a driver for O'Connell's predecessor. He said he could understand suspicions that the cover-up of O'Connell's abuse was not an isolated event. "Given the fact that the bishop of this diocese — the second bishop, another bishop of this diocese — this has happened to him, they're all going to wonder, what's happening in this diocese that people are covering up? What's going on?" King told the *Palm Beach Post*.

Ordained in May 1990, Dixon has since left the priesthood. He remembers thinking that O'Connell was one of the brightest people he had ever met. "I don't feel like a victim now," Dixon said. "But this is bittersweet. Had this been taken care of appropriately years ago, we wouldn't have to be going through this now."

And within weeks, Dixon did not stand alone. Three more men stepped forward and charged that O'Connell had sexually abused them too.

O'Connell was Palm Beach's third bishop. Its second was Symons, the cleric forced out in June 1999 after acknowledging his own sexual misconduct. Its founding bishop was a man named Thomas Vose Daily — the same man accused of being one of the principal architects of the cover-up of John Geoghan's sexual assaults on children in Boston.

Bishop Daily preaches from New York now as leader of the Brooklyn diocese, the nation's fifth largest. From his pulpit there, he has expressed regret about the way he handled Geoghan in Boston, even as he confronted fresh accusations that he ignored sex abuse as the spiritual leader of 1.6 million Catholics in Brooklyn and Queens.

Daily, a native of Belmont, Massachusetts, was ordained in 1952. In the early 1960s, he worked for five years in the missions of Peru as a member of the Society of Saint James the Apostle. He returned to Boston and gradually worked his way up the rungs of the Boston archdiocese. When Cardinal Medeiros died in 1983, Daily ran the diocese until Law was appointed Medeiros's successor. Daily was a guardian of the archdiocesan secret personnel files that were kept under lock and key at the chancery.

In 1979, it was Daily who, when alerted about one instance of Geoghan's attacks, took charge. He oversaw a speedy, hands-off investigation. Without questioning the mother who reported the abuse of her son, Daily wrote to Geoghan to tell the pedophile priest that he had been cleared. Daily said a police chaplain had investigated and found the charges "irresponsible, totally false, [and] made by a woman who is well known and without credence in the community."

The bishop later said he believed at the time, incorrectly, that priests had immunity from civil and criminal prosecution for sexual abuse. To Daily, Geoghan was not a criminal or a rapist — he was a lost sheep. "I am a pastor who has to go after the Lord's sheep and find them and bring them back into the fold and give them the kind of guidance and discipline them in such a way that they will come back," Daily said. "I'm not a detective."

At seventy-four, as he said a Mass celebrating the fiftieth anniversary of his priesthood, the news from Boston shadowed him in New York. "He's such a good guy. It's tough to see this happening, especially now, with an anniversary of this import," the bishop's spokesman said. But as he fended off questions about his tenure in Massachusetts, Daily faced new charges raised in a *Globe* article that he had brushed aside sexual abuse allegations in New York four years earlier.

Rev. Timothy J. Lambert, a forty-four-year-old clergyman on a leave of absence, made the allegations in a 1998 meeting with diocesan leaders. His attorney repeated them a year later in an eight-page letter to Daily. The letter described Lambert's charges against a priest who had become a welcome figure in his home, where Lambert's mother struggled to raise four sons and a daughter on her own. Her husband, an alcoholic, had left the family. Lambert, a troubled teenager, yearned for a father figure's affection. "That set up the perfect situation for a predator," claimed the letter, which identified the accused priest as Rev. Joseph P. Byrns, a pastor at Brooklyn's St. Rose of Lima Church. "Fr. Byrns knew that many of his sexual needs would be satisfied by this young boy as long as he successfully groomed him with pseudo-affection and gifts, which represented to this child the love no other male figure, particularly his father, had ever given him."

Byrns admitted he had known the Lambert family since 1969, but he denied the accusations. "There's nothing to the story," Byrns said. And Byrns's bishop, Daily, backed him to the hilt. The bishop said he had reviewed the allegations. He blessed Byrns's reputation as solid, concluded that Byrns was innocent, and ruled the case closed.

Lambert called the "investigation" a fraud. He doubted that any diocesan investigator ever interviewed any of the counselors he had consulted about his abuse, or any member of his family. "They didn't investigate anything," Lambert said.

Daily's aversion to vigorous investigation meant that in the early days of the crisis, Brooklyn was not among the many dioceses around the nation that examined dusty personnel files and handed over to authorities the names of priests who had been accused of sexual abuse. This despite the Brooklyn district attorney's plea that "if there are any allegations, we want them sent over to us." And this despite the view of New York's newly elected mayor, Michael Bloomberg, who, when asked at a city hall press conference whether the Church should hand over information about clergy sexual abuse, did not hesitate to proclaim, "There's no reason, based on occupation, why any group should not have to obey the law. Period."

Daily defended his handling of the complaints against Byrns but said he regretted how he handled the Geoghan case in Boston. He insisted that most victims prefer secrecy to a public airing of allegations of sexual abuse. "We feel that we have a policy . . . and we feel that we've been responsible. And we're sticking with that policy." (When the bishop invited victims to contact his staff, Lambert replied acidly, "That's the last place I'd go.") And through it all, Daily dug in. He said he would not release the names of alleged sex abusers. "Some of these guys are dead," he said. "A man's got a right to his reputation even when he's dead."

By early April, however, Daily's defiance began to crumble. His aides were meeting with prosecutors from Queens and Brooklyn, and within days Daily was being accused of ignoring repeated warnings about a priest's after-hours parties with teenage boys in a rectory in Queens in the early 1990s. In June 2000, that priest was arrested on sodomy charges. *Newsday* reported that Rev. John McVernon said he had notified Daily four separate times that he was concerned about the priest's conduct. "I told Daily, 'There are things that are going on in the rectory that give me pause.' He listened attentively. Nothing changed after that first visit," McVernon said. The charges were later dropped, and records in the case were sealed.

After McVernon's first meeting with Daily in the early 1990s, he said he told Daily about the priest's conduct three more times. "Every year, I would tell him the same story," he said. "Nothing happened." Daily's spokesman said the priest was placed on administrative leave after his arrest. And he remains there today.

The *New York Times* supplied still further details about Daily's loose attention to allegations of clergy sexual abuse. The newspaper reported that in 1991 Daily had provided a bishop in Venezuela a glowing recommendation for Rev. Enrique Diaz Jimenez even as a sixty-count indictment was pending against Diaz in Queens on child abuse charges. Daily wrote that Diaz was "experiencing a very difficult situation" in New York because of the criminal case against him, but played down the priest's trouble with sexual abuse. A spokesman for Daily said that the bishop correctly praised Diaz's work as a priest during his official three-year assignment in New York, and said it was not fair to make a connection between the recommendation and "accusations that came out about his behavior years later." Later that year, after pleading guilty to three counts of sexual abuse in the case, Father Diaz was deported to Venezuela. There he was later accused of sexually abusing eighteen boys preparing for their first Holy Communion.

By the spring Daily could no longer dig in his heels against prosecutors. The Diocese of Brooklyn announced in mid-April that it would give prosecutors the names of priests accused of sexual abuse going back twenty years and also report any future accusations to authorities.

"As in the past, we will cooperate with them in any investigations they may wish to pursue," Daily said. It was the kind of spin that the man from Belmont had learned at the Archdiocese of Boston — the kind of skills that were appreciated by those he had left behind there. When *The Tablet*, the official newspaper of the Brooklyn diocese, printed a special edition commemorating Daily's twenty-five years as bishop in early 2000, it had solicited a greeting from Boston. Law, Daily's old boss, had kind words for his former chief lieutenant. "As a proud native Bostonian, he was invaluable to me. He not only knew the territory inside out, but, more importantly, he knew the 'players,'" Law wrote.

Thomas Daily was not the only New York prelate haunted by his past work in the parishes of New England.

Installed as the twelfth leader of the Archdiocese of New York in 2000, Cardinal Edward M. Egan succeeded Cardinal John J. O'Connor, who died of brain cancer after sixteen years as the nation's most high-profile prelate. By the time Egan left Connecticut for his new home on Madison Avenue, where he is spiritual leader of 2.4 million Roman Catholics — the nation's third-largest diocese — he had acquired a reputation as a conservative bishop who hewed closely to the Church's teachings against abortion and birth control.

The Chicago native seemed perfectly suited for his new job in New York. As a canon lawyer, he spent two decades at the Vatican advising Popes Paul VI and John Paul II. He spent two years as an auxiliary bishop overseeing Catholic schools in New York. Like O'Connor, who had come to New York from Scranton, Pennsylvania, Egan had gained the bulk of his experience in a relatively small and obscure see. "I don't feel like a boss," he said on the eve of his installation at St. Patrick's Cathedral. "But give me a little time and I will."

On March 17, 2002, Egan was buffeted by a *Hartford Courant* report that when he served as the bishop of Bridgeport, Connecticut, he allowed priests who faced accusations of molesting children to remain in their positions for years. One of those priests admitted that in order to prevent ejaculation, he once bit his teenage victim while performing oral sex on him. Egan initially greeted the allegations with a stony silence. Within days, he denounced the actions of pedophile priests as an "abomination." He urged victims to report their attacks to authorities. He insisted that he had acted appropriately. But the cardinal stubbornly resisted making any promise that the Church would report every case of sexual misconduct.

Like Cardinal Law, his colleague in Boston, Egan endured withering criticism from those who said he sacrificed the safety of children to the Church's desperate desire to avert scandal. "Egan, among the highest-ranking cardinals in America, did not act decisively in Diocese of Bridgeport cases," the *Connecticut Post* said in an editorial. "These were crimes that should have been brought to the attention of law enforcement officials and prosecutors." The paper called for Egan to resign, while the Diocese of Bridgeport began a review of the personnel files of priests dating back to the founding of the archdiocese nearly half a century ago.

The *Hartford Courant's* scathing piece was based on sealed court records, transcripts of pretrial depositions, personnel files, and internal Church memos that portrayed Egan as a laissez-faire administrator, slow to investigate charges of abuse and quick to dismiss those who accused his priests of assault. In a previously undisclosed 1999 deposition, for example, Egan suggested that twelve former altar boys and parishioners who charged they had been molested, raped, or beaten by the same priest may have been making it all up. "Allegations are allegations," Egan had said, and regarding the complaints against priests he concluded, "Very few have even come close to having anyone prove anything."

In his deposition, obtained by the *Courant*, Egan appeared feisty and dismissive about the accusations against diocesan priests. In one exchange with a lawyer, regarding sexual abuse by Rev. Laurence Brett, a Bridgeport priest who admitted attacking children across the nation in the 1960s, Egan displayed little sympathy for the victims of abuse. In 1991, after checking into the priest's history, Egan had decided that

Brett, by then a school chaplain in Baltimore, could remain under the auspices of the Bridgeport diocese. Egan said the priest had "made a good impression" on him.

The lawyers had questions about how Egan handled Brett's case. Egan parsed the lawyers' words closely:

Q: "[Brett] admits apparently that he had oral sex with this young boy and that he actually bit his penis and advised the boy to go to confession elsewhere?"

Egan: "Well, I think you're not exactly right. . . . It seemed to me that the gentleman in question was an eighteen-year-old student at Sacred Heart University."

Q: "Are you aware of the fact that in December of 1964 an individual under twenty-one years of age was a minor in the state of Connecticut?"

Egan: "My problem, my clarification, had to do with the expression 'a young boy' about an eighteen-year-old."

Q: "A young — all right, a minor, is that better then?"

Egan: "Fine."

Within days of the *Courant*'s report, Egan defended his actions in Connecticut as appropriate. He said he had routinely referred priests accused of assault for inpatient psychiatric care. "If the conclusions were favorable, he was returned to ministry, in some cases with restrictions, so as to be doubly careful. If they were not favorable, he was not allowed to function as a priest," he said.

As had been its practice elsewhere, the Church had successfully fought to keep the records of the largest clergy sexual abuse scandal in Connecticut history from public view. But once exposed, the Bridgeport details became essential reading by parishioners just an hour away in New York City. For example, a 1990 memo showed that one diocesan official worried about "a developing pattern of accusations" against a Norwalk priest who allegedly fondled young boys, but Egan did not suspend or dismiss the priest, Rev. Charles Carr. Five years later a law-

Rev. Paul R. Shanley publicly preached the benefits of man-boy love. In private, he allegedly sexually molested young, vulnerable boys.

PHOTO BY THE *BOSTON GLOBE*

The late Rev. Joseph Birmingham allegedly sexually molested scores of youths, with church leaders doing little to stop him early in his nearly thirty-year career.

ARCHDIOCESE OF BOSTON PHOTO

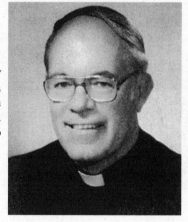

Rev. Ronald H. Paquin's car accident ended in the death of a sixteen-year-old youth he had allegedly abused the previous night. Before the accident, the archdiocese had allegedly been told of previous sexual abuse by Paquin.

ARCHDIOCESE OF BOSTON PHOTO

John J. Geoghan (left), a former priest, has been accused of molesting an estimated two hundred Boston-area children. Two cardinals transferred him from parish to parish, despite knowing of the allegations. In January 2002, he and his attorney, Geoffrey Packard, listened as Geoghan was convicted of abusing one young boy. Geoghan was sentenced to 9–10 years in prison.

PHOTO BY KEVIN WISNIEWSKI FOR THE *BOSTON GLOBE*

Catherine Geoghan, John J. Geoghan's older sister, loyally stayed by her brother's side during his trial. His friend Father John Casey with them in the Middlesex Superior Courtroom during a break from jury selection for Geoghan's trial.

PHOTO BY JOHN BLANDING FOR THE *BOSTON GLOBE*

Bishop Anthony J. O'Connell offered his resignation after he admitted to touching a young seminarian a quarter century earlier.

LANNIS WATERS/ *PALM BEACH POST*

Bishop Brendan Comiskey, of Wexford, Ireland, announced his resignation in April 2002 after being accused of protecting a sexually abusive priest.
DAVID SLEATOR/*IRISH TIMES*

Boston Cardinal Bernard F. Law mismanaged priests, including John J. Geoghan, who sexually abused children. The fallout was widespread outrage and an international scandal for the Roman Catholic Church. In January 2002 he addressed the media at a special press conference at his residence about the sex scandal.
PHOTO BY DAVID L. RYAN FOR THE *BOSTON GLOBE*

Cardinal Law after Mass at the Cathedral of the Holy Cross in Boston.
PHOTO BY MATTHEW J. LEE FOR THE *BOSTON GLOBE*

New York Cardinal Edward Egan, the *Hartford Courant* reported, allowed several sexually abusive priests to stay in their positions while he headed the Bridgeport, Connecticut, diocese.
AP/WIDE WORLD PHOTOS

Pope John Paul II, in his Easter 2002 letter, decried "the sins of some of our brothers." In April he summoned the U.S. cardinals to the Vatican for an emergency meeting, where he called the sexual abuse of children by priests a "crime."

AFP PHOTO/ALESSANDRO BIANCHI

Massachusetts Attorney General Tom Reilly, third from left, held a press conference after meeting with Boston archdiocese lawyers. District attorneys, from left to right: Dan Conley, Kevin Burke, Tim Cruz, Bill Keating, Martha Coakley, and Geline Williams, executive director of the Massachusetts D.A. Association.

PHOTO BY JONATHAN WIGGS FOR THE *BOSTON GLOBE*

As Cardinal Bernard Law celebrated Good Friday services, March 29, 2002, in the Cathedral of the Holy Cross, demonstrators outside called for his resignation.

Lay Catholics met in the basement of St. John the Evangelist Church in Wellesley, Massachusetts, in April 2002 to discuss the crisis rocking their Church.

Tom Blanchette (front left) with other Catholic Youth Organization members and Rev. Joseph Birmingham at Our Lady of Fatima Church in the early 1960s.
PHOTO COURTESY OF TOM BLANCHETTE

Patrick McSorley was allegedly molested by Geoghan after McSorley's father committed suicide.
PHOTO BY SARAH BREZINSKY FOR THE *BOSTON GLOBE*

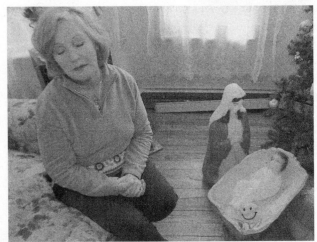

Maryetta Dussourd's three young sons and four nephews were allegedly molested at bedtime by Geoghan, sometimes as he said their evening prayers with them.
PHOTO BY PAT GREENHOUSE FOR THE *BOSTON GLOBE*

Margaret Gallant, Maryetta Dussourd's sister and a devout Catholic, wrote to Cardinal Medeiros in 1982 about how angry she was when Geoghan, who allegedly molested seven of her young relatives, was not removed from parish work.

PHOTO COURTESY OF
MARYETTA DUSSOURD

James Hogan was among the men who came forward to accuse the late Rev. Joseph Birmingham of sexual abuse. Cardinal Law and other church officials were charged with covering up Birmingham's actions in the suit.

AP/WIDE WORLD PHOTOS

The Pope delivering his address on sex abuse to the leaders of the American Catholic Church in his private library at the Vatican in April 2002. Cardinal Law is fifth from left.

AP/WIDE WORLD PHOTOS

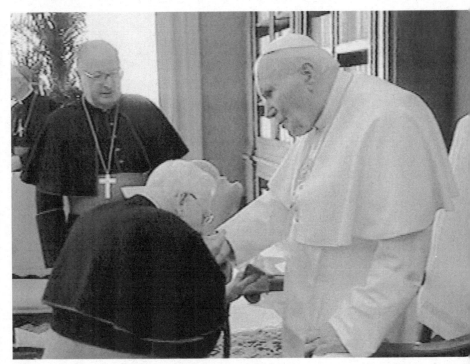

Cardinal Law kissing the Pope's ring at the extraordinary meeting called by the Pope at the Vatican in April. AP/WIDE WORLD PHOTOS

suit was filed and Egan finally acted, removing Carr, only to reinstate him in 1999 as a part-time nursing home chaplain in Danbury. (Carr would ultimately be defrocked by Egan's successor in Connecticut, Bishop William E. Lori.)

Egan's belief that it should be left up to the Church to determine which allegations of abuse should be forwarded to authorities did not sit well with Manhattan district attorney Robert M. Morgenthau. "Responsible officials in all religious institutions who have information about child abuse should make certain that information is brought to the attention of law enforcement," the prosecutor said. "I would expect the Archdiocese of New York to make available to my office all allegations of child abuse, including past allegations."

As pressure on Egan increased, his hand was finally forced. Within a few weeks, Egan gave Morgenthau a list of cases involving priests accused of sexual misconduct over the past thirty-five years, and the cardinal later removed six of his diocesan priests because of past allegations of abuse. Still, additional, fresh reports arrived from Connecticut about priest sexual abuse that occurred on Egan's watch. The seventy-year-old cardinal — a press-wary man who displayed little of the warm showmanship of his predecessor — was content for a time to let his words from the pulpit suffice. "With war and terrorism and sexual abuse on our mind, we all know that we are all sinners and we are all expected by our God to do penance," he said in his 2002 Palm Sunday sermon. "Acts have been committed against our children by those who were chosen and ordained to care for all with total self-sacrifice and the utmost of respect. The cry that comes from all of our hearts is that we never want to even think again that such a horror may be visited upon any of our young people, their parents, their loved ones, through the body of Jesus Christ, his Church. That cry goes from my heart as well."

But on April 20, the day before he departed to meet Pope John Paul II in Rome to discuss the sexual abuse crisis with the other American cardinals, Egan offered an apology that was decidedly conditional. "Over the past fifteen years, in both Bridgeport and New York, I consistently sought and acted upon the best independent advice available to me from medical experts and behavioral scientists," the cardinal said in a letter read throughout his archdiocese. "It is clear that today we have a much better understanding of this problem. If in hindsight we also discover that mistakes may have been made as regards prompt removal of priests and assistance to victims, I am deeply sorry." Egan promised to "do everything in my power to ensure, as much as is humanly possible, that such abuse by clergy will never happen again. You should expect nothing less of me, and the other leaders of our Church."

Even before Pope John Paul II summoned American cardinals to the Vatican in the spring of 2002 for an emergency meeting on the sex scandal, the crisis had spread throughout the United States and overseas. The criticism that it provoked was remarkably free of accusations of Catholic bashing.

"We spend our time monitoring and fighting anti-Catholicism wherever it exists in American society, but I have always had a disdain for intellectual dishonesty, and if I sat on the sidelines, I'd have to be accused of that myself," said William Donohue, president of the Catholic League for Religious and Civil Rights. "I don't know of a single Catholic priest or layman who isn't furious about the sex abuse scandal in terms of the tolerance they [the hierarchy] have had for intolerable behavior, and the way they've played musical chairs with these miscreant priests. I've never seen such anger." That anger, it seemed, was everywhere. In city after city, as officials reviewed personnel files and rewrote policies regarding sexual abuse by clergy, more priests stood accused. Scores were removed.

It happened first in Philadelphia, where in February the seventh-largest archdiocese in the nation, with 1.4 million Catholics, said it had found "credible evidence" that thirty-five priests sexually abused about fifty children dating back to 1950. Several priests still in their jobs were dismissed after Church leaders looked at personnel records. "In light of what happened in Boston, we reviewed our files and allegations from the past. We want to do better," an archdiocesan spokeswoman said. Within days, some prosecutors urged Philadelphia Church leaders to hand over the names of priests who had assaulted kids. The archdiocese balked. It noted that the statute of limitations for all the alleged abuses had expired and said it would withhold the names. By late April, District Attorney Lynne M. Abraham announced that she was convening a grand jury to investigate. She said Philadelphia would probe "all allegations involving priests, whether they are dead, dismissed, or retired."

In Cleveland, when Rev. Donald Rooney was called by his superiors at the archdiocese in early April to discuss allegations that he had sexually abused a young girl in 1980, he never showed up for the meeting. Instead, authorities said the forty-eight-year-old priest drove to a drugstore parking lot and shot himself in the head with a 9 mm handgun. Rooney left behind a one-sentence note. It instructed those who found his body on how to locate his sister.

On Long Island, just east of New York City, Thomas J. Spota, the Suffolk County district attorney, announced in mid-April that he was convening a special grand jury to look into abuse accusations. Spota suggested the Church was covering up cases.

In Cincinnati, Archbishop Daniel Pilarczyk became the first American prelate to receive a grand jury subpoena in a battle over Church records about child molestation complaints. Prosecutors subpoenaed Pilarczyk in late April, but he was spared from testifying after the Church released the requested information. Hamilton County prosecutor Michael K. Allen, a Catholic, did not say what the Church's information entailed, but he noted that he was keeping Pilarczyk's summons active. That meant, he said, that the archbishop could face the grand jury at a later time.

In Washington, D.C., Rev. Percival D'Silva, associate pastor of an influential Roman Catholic church in the nation's capital, looked northward to Boston and said from the pulpit: "Cardinal Law is not above the law. . . . I must be honest. . . . He should have the common sense and even the guts to say, 'I resign.' He has to go." His words were greeted by a standing ovation.

In Detroit, Church officials acknowledged that about a dozen priests in the metropolitan area had been removed from active ministry in the past fourteen years because of credible allegations of sex molestation against minors. Two priests left parishes in the spring of 2002. The archdiocese has been criticized for failing in the past to turn over accused priests to prosecutors. Cardinal Adam Maida asked his congregation's forgiveness.

In Los Angeles, the nation's largest archdiocese, Cardinal Roger Mahony admitted that he had made a mistake when he transferred a priest accused of assaulting children to a chaplain's post at Cedars-Sinai Medical Center fourteen years earlier without giving hospital officers details of the allegations against him, and publicly apologized to children who had been attacked by priests. He announced a zero-tolerance policy on sexual abuse: No priest credibly accused would ever return to parish work or retain any position with the archdiocese, he promised. And he fired eight priests, most of them retired, who had been accused of abuse.

For some, this was too little, too late. In 1998 Mahony himself had been at the center of a sensational clergy sexual abuse trial involving two brothers who lived near the industrial city of Stockton in California's Central Valley. They had allegedly been abused by a priest for years until they were in their late teens. The brothers won $7.6 million in damages after a jury heard testimony from a psychiatrist that Mahony, then Stockton's bishop but not a defendant in the suit, knew the priest was a pedophile and a risk to children. But Mahony then shipped the priest to another parish, where he abused others for years. At the trial, Mahony insisted he was not aware of the allegations against the priest. In late April, Mahony was sued under a federal racketeering law usually reserved for organized-crime figures, as two sets of brothers charged that they were abused as children by a Los Angeles diocesan priest.

The scandal also spread abroad.

By late March, a prominent Polish archbishop with ties to the Pope had resigned. Archbishop Juliusz Paetz of Poznan was accused of making sexual advances to young clerics. He denied it, but said he was leaving "for the good of the Church." Paetz, sixty-seven, was trained in Rome at two prestigious colleges and worked closely with Popes Paul VI, John Paul I, and John Paul II. He was a member of John Paul II's household staff before the pontiff sent him back to Poland as bishop of

Lomza in 1982. Fellow priests had accused Paetz of paying night visits to the lodgings of seminarians, cuddling up to young clerics in public, and using an underground tunnel to pay unannounced visits to their dormitories. "Not everyone understood my genuine openness and spontaneity toward people," Paetz said. "There was a misinterpretation of my words and gestures."

Then, in early April, a senior prelate in Ireland was gone. Bishop Brendan Comiskey, the bishop of Ferns in Ireland's southeast, became the first known member of the Roman Catholic hierarchy to resign voluntarily because of his mismanagement of a priest who had sexually abused children. Comiskey had been under fire for years for his handling of a pedophile priest, Rev. Sean Fortune. In 1999 Fortune had killed himself after he was charged with abusing boys, and Comiskey's resignation came on the eve of the airing in Ireland of a British Broadcasting Corporation documentary about some of Fortune's victims. "I did my best," Comiskey said outside his office in Wexford, reading a statement that shocked a nation where more than 90 percent of the 3.6 million people are Catholic. "Clearly that was not good enough. . . . As bishop I should be a binding force among people and priests within the ministry of Christ. I had hoped that I could bring about reconciliation between the diocese and those who were abused. Such, I hope, might be part of the healing. I now recognize that I am not the person who can best achieve these aims of unity and reconciliation. My continuation in office could indeed be an obstacle to healing."

In Mexico, whose 90 million Catholics make up the religion's second-largest congregation after Brazil, Cardinal Norberto Rivera of Mexico City rebuffed the nation's conference of bishops, which had maintained that charges of sexual abuse by priests should be dealt with internally. Bishop Sergio Obeso of Japala had argued that abusive priests should not be handed over to police, saying, "Dirty laundry is best washed at home." That position was assailed in the Mexican press and derided by Mexican judicial officials, who equated any move to stifle the reporting of abuse with cover-up and disaster. Rivera agreed. The cardinal said priests who abuse children deserve no special treatment. "They should be denounced to the corresponding authorities and justice must be done," Rivera announced in a sermon on national television. "No one should have immunity or privileges or be above the law."

In the United States, the impact of the scandal and the Church's struggle to cope with it were dramatically underscored by a series of Cardinal Mahony's confidential e-mails that were leaked to Los Angeles radio station KFI, which made copies available to the *Los Angeles Times*. The archdiocese's emergency appeal to a court to block their publication failed when a superior court judge ruled that the U.S. Constitution did not allow him to keep the cardinal's correspondence out of the pages of one of the nation's largest newspapers.

In one e-mail, dated March 27, Mahony was frustrated by his aides' failure to hand over to the police some of the names of the priests he had fired. The cardinal took to his computer to warn that he could be subpoenaed by a grand jury. The e-mail was entitled "Our Big Mistake." It was sent at seven o'clock on a Wednesday morning to Sister Judith Murphy, the archdiocese's general counsel.

Mahony, the nation's youngest cardinal, wrote:

Sr. Judy,

As the drum beats continue from every side for us to release the "names," I must still point to what I consider our greatest tactical mistake of the past few weeks.

If I recall, of the 8 priests involved, 5 had already been reported to local law enforcement agencies. That leaves 3.

Mahony's e-mail recounted how Murphy had resisted Mahony's suggestion that she consult with police about the other three priests. He said he had run out of patience and ordered immediate action. The tone of the electronic conversation underscored the gravity of the crisis that was by then the talk of the nation.

If we don't, today, "consult" with the Det. about those 3 names, I can guarantee you that I will get hauled into a Grand Jury proceeding and I will be forced to give all the names, etc.

I must now insist that this matter is no longer open for discussion. You must consult with the Det. about those 3 cases.

Mahony had reason to worry. Two days before, Los Angeles chief of police Bernard Parks had demanded to know the names. Mahony was frustrated that the archdiocese's lawyers were not forthcoming:

I'm not sure you grasp the gravity of the situation and where this is heading — not only with the media, but with the law enforcement and legal folks.

... If we don't take immediate, aggressive action here — the consequences for the [archdiocese] are going to be incredible: charges of cover-up, concealing criminals, etc., etc.

PLEASE make this task your highest priority this morning! I have reached the point where if I cannot guarantee that all 8 have been appropriately reported, then I will have to call the Det. and do it myself — today.

There is no middle ground on this one; we are losing the battle because we are somehow "hiding" those 3. The best way is to "consult" with the Det. about them, and let them decide what needs to be done next.

Thanks for listening. This public media pressure will never stop until we can announce that those few priests have all been reported to the appropriate authorities over the years.

+RMM

The archdiocese ultimately turned the priests' names over to the police, and Mahony became a leading voice for reform among American prelates. But when he and the other American cardinals met at the Vatican with the Pope, they did not, as Mahony had hoped, have a serious debate about priestly celibacy. The cardinals could not even agree on the details of a zero-tolerance policy under which any priest who sexually abused a child would face instant removal. Instead, the princes of the Church embraced a set of very traditional tenets: Priests and bishops should be holier. Pastors should reprimand people who spread dissent. Seminaries should more carefully screen applicants.

In the end, all the cardinals could muster was a single acknowledgment of the bishops' role, saying in a letter to priests, "We regret episcopal oversight has not been able to preserve the Church from this scandal."

As summer approached, that scandal turned violent and, in one case, deadly.

In the same week in mid-May, a man shot a Catholic priest in Baltimore who he said had sexually abused him nearly a decade before. It marked the first time since the scandal broke in January that an alleged victim had responded with such violence. Days later, a priest from Bridgeport, Connecticut, committed suicide at a Catholic psychiatric hospital in Silver Spring, Maryland. He was found hanged in St. Luke Institute seventeen days after he was removed from his parish when several men accused him of molesting them two decades ago.

6

The Decline of Deference

When Daniel F. Conley was growing up in the Hyde Park section of Boston, it was not uncommon for some of the nuns to smack children who stepped out of line. And if they did, kids wouldn't say anything when they got home, because they feared their parents would smack them again. If the nuns hit you, it was thought, you deserved it.

It was a different time. If the police pulled over a weaving car and saw that the driver was wearing a Roman collar, usually they would either drive him home or let him go with a warning: "Be careful, Father."

But that was then. In March 2002 Dan Conley, the district attorney for Suffolk County, Massachusetts, opened a file on his desk and saw that the target of a criminal investigation generated by allegations of sexual abuse was Monsignor Frederick J. Ryan — his religion teacher at Catholic Memorial High School approximately thirty years earlier.

Conley, the chief prosecutor in Boston, is a devout Catholic. He is pained by what is happening to his Church. But unlike some previous generations of law enforcement officials, who turned a blind eye to their Church's crimes and misdemeanors, Conley's reaction to the file he had before him was a no-brainer. He picked up the phone and called his colleague, Martha Coakley, the district attorney in neighboring Middlesex County, to ask her to handle the case, to avoid any appearance of conflict of interest.

Given the predominance of Irish Catholics in Massachusetts law enforcement circles, it's not surprising there had been little appetite to prosecute priests for anything, including the sexual abuse of children. Until recent years most Boston cops still had the map of Ireland on their face. Even when Ralph G. Martin II, Conley's predecessor, became the first African American to hold the post of district attorney in Boston in 1992, he inherited a roster of lawyers that read like the Dublin phone book.

It was the same in politics, where the names that dominated city hall and the State House, and those who represented the city and state in Washington, were Curley, McCormack, O'Neill, Flynn, and, most famously, Kennedy. When John F. Kennedy became the first Catholic to be elected president, one of the first people he invited to his inauguration was Boston's Cardinal Richard J. Cushing. Three years later Cushing flew from Boston to Washington to preside over the assassinated president's funeral.

The deference that politicians, police, and prosecutors showed the Catholic Church (to which most of them belonged) mirrored a deference shown in the wider society. But the extent of the sexual abuse that spilled out after the Geoghan case, especially the Church's efforts to buy the silence of the victims, shook to the core even the most devout Catholics in law enforcement and politics. A culture of deference that had taken more than a century to evolve seemed to erode in a matter of weeks. In other parts of the United States, there was a similar change in the way secular power viewed Church authorities. On Long Island, in Cincinnati, and in Philadelphia, district attorneys convened grand juries to investigate the role Church officials may have played in the scandal.

Many ordinary people said the newfound willingness of some prosecutors to hold the Church more accountable still showed deference because most still seemed unwilling to haul priests and bishops before grand juries to try to build criminal cases against them for harboring child molesters. But most prosecutors said they simply didn't have the laws to use.

The shift in attitudes toward the Church among secular authorities was nationwide, but it was most dramatic in Boston. The children, grandchildren, and great-grandchildren of immigrants who would never dream of challenging anything a priest did now demanded not just answers from their Church leaders but accountability. Even as Cardinal Law struggled to maintain his grip on power inside the Church, outside forces were building against him and other officials who never before had to worry about such pressure. The First Amendment, guaranteeing a separation of church and state, had always served as a deterrent to secular authorities probing too deeply into Church affairs. Local custom made it even more taboo for secular power brokers to throw their weight around with the Church. Cardinal Law could rightly say that by hiding the sexual abuse of priests from public view, he was doing no more than what his predecessors did. But that no longer cut him any slack with prosecutors and politicians, whose outrage at the Church's conduct was rising as their deference waned.

"I remember reading the first Spotlight reports and just getting furious," recalled Massachusetts Attorney General Thomas F. Reilly, the state's top prosecutor. "I found myself yelling out loud, 'My God, this is about children!'"

Reilly's parents had come from Ireland and were deeply devoted to the Church. Like many Irish immigrants who settled in Springfield, the third-largest city in Massachusetts, one hundred miles west of Boston, his mother hailed from Dingle, a picturesque harbor town in County Kerry. His father worked for the Springfield Department of Public Works but had grown up in a small village in County Mayo, where the priest was the most important person. Reilly's parents set a devout tone for his three brothers and two sisters. Even when he was teenager, Reilly was expected to be home at 7 P.M. "We knelt down and said the Rosary, as a family, every night," the attorney general recalled.

Reilly said his experiences with the nuns who taught him and with the priests who counseled him were only positive. The Sisters of St. Joseph who were his teachers at Cathedral High School had more confidence in him than he had in himself. His mother and a parish priest collaborated to get Reilly into St. Francis Xavier University in Nova Scotia.

When, as a young prosecutor, Reilly found himself building a case against a priest who had sexually abused a child in a Boston suburb, he looked at it as an aberration. "I guess I thought about it in the context of it being representative of all segments of society, that occasionally you'd find someone who would engage in that kind of behavior," he said. When the extent of the abuse committed by James Porter became known in 1992, Reilly said he was shocked but "gave the Church the benefit of the doubt. Cardinal Law said he had created a new policy so that allegations like this would be aggressively dealt with. At the time, I believed him. I had no reason not to."

Martha Coakley, who succeeded Reilly as the district attorney in Middlesex County after he was elected attorney general, was less inclined to give the Church the benefit of the doubt. From an early age, she saw inequity in her Church, especially in the way it treated the half of the faithful who were female. She noticed at a young age that women weren't on the altar. There were no sports for girls at her Catholic school, either.

Coakley grew up in North Adams, an old mill town tucked into the northwestern corner of Massachusetts. In North Adams, parishes were laid out along ethnic lines: St. Joseph's was the Irish parish, Notre Dame was French, St. Anthony's was Italian. Coakley went to Mass at St. Joseph's Church and to class at St. Joseph's School. Her father was a daily communicant and a leader of the local St. Vincent de Paul Society, which helped the poor. Her two sisters went to Catholic colleges. She sang in the choir. "In general, I have fond memories of my growing up in the Church," Coakley said.

The idea of priests sexually abusing children didn't even enter her consciousness until she was in her thirties. By that time, in the early 1990s, Coakley was a prosecutor and had been transferred, "kicking and screaming," to head a child sexual abuse unit.

Coakley said the incredulity with which the public greeted evidence suggesting that the Church had a large number of sexual predators in its clergy stems from societal ignorance about sexual abuse. "People expect the guy to be drooling, lurking around in a trench coat. But when I started doing these cases, it became obvious that most abusers are caretakers, respectable people who use that respectability as a cover to carry out their abuse. There was an aura around priests that protected them, and that protection extended to sexual abusers. The incredibly backward lifestyle of these men contributed to the problem. You have single men, moving from parish to parish, with no family of their own. It was a formula for disaster."

Like Reilly, Coakley was initially encouraged by Cardinal Law's response to the Porter case, and in 1993, as that case drew national attention, she began preparing for her first big sexual abuse trial. It involved a priest named Rev. Paul Manning, and it was a messy case. The eleven-year-old alleged victim, a Puerto Rican boy who spoke poor English and whose mother was very religious, recanted his allegations and would not testify against Manning. But another priest, Rev. Paul Sughrue, did come forward, and what he had to say was as disturbing as it was incriminating. Sughrue claimed that one night he had returned to the rectory at St. Charles's Church in Woburn, just north of Boston, and heard "five distinct screams" from a child. "They were horrifying," Sughrue later testified. "They were pain-filled screams. They demanded attention."

Sughrue said he went upstairs and, peering from a second-floor landing into Manning's third-floor study, saw two pairs of bare legs intertwined. A child was sitting on top of Manning, moving rhythmically, up and down. Sughrue said he was disturbed by what he saw but was also conflicted over what to do. He eventually contacted the chancery, where officials waited a month before contacting police about the allegations.

Because the victim refused to testify, Coakley knew the case would be difficult to win. But Sughrue's testimony was compelling and, in the Boston area at least, unprecedented — a priest breaking ranks to point a finger at another priest.

But it wasn't just a reluctant victim that Coakley had to contend with. Manning's parishioners stood by him. More than one hundred of them attended his arraignment. Dozens came to the courtroom each day of the trial. They said they were showing their faith in their priest. Coakley said they were intimidating the jury, just as the victim had been intimidated into recanting.

Parishioners seemed less upset about the substance of the allegations than the fact that Sughrue was making them. Coakley said the defense was a case study in exploiting a culture that was instinctively deferential to the Church in general and to priests in particular. An FBI agent testified for Manning as a character witness. Manning's lawyer, Eileen Donoghue, the mayor of Lowell, an old mill city north of Boston, portrayed Manning as a hardworking, caring priest whose fluency in Spanish made him especially beloved among Hispanics. Donoghue said Manning had taken the boy under his wing. She said there was no sexual contact between the boy and his priest, just "horseplay." If it seemed odd that a fifty-three-year-old priest would have an eleven-year-old boy in his third-floor study at night, Donoghue said the boy spent a lot of time in the rectory "because his family is poor."

After fifteen hours of deliberations over three days, the jury acquitted Manning, saying prosecutors had not convinced them of his guilt beyond a reasonable doubt. Despite the acquittal, the archdiocese removed him from parish work. As frustrated as Coakley was with the unquestioning loyalty Manning's parishioners showed him, she was encouraged by the archdiocese's cooperation with the prosecution and its decision to ensure that the priest did not have access to children anymore. Sughrue was subsequently promoted to pastor of another parish.

Coakley's actions did not win her the political gains Manning accused her of seeking with his prosecution. Quite the opposite: people accused her of being disrespectful to the Church. A *Lowell Sun* columnist berated her, and closer to home, the mother of one of her best friends said it was outrageous that she had prosecuted a priest. "They were still untouchables in many people's opinions," Coakley said.

But Coakley said attitudes began to change as the cases mounted. In 1994 Rev. John Hanlon was convicted of raping altar boys in Hingham, south of Boston. An unrepentant Hanlon was sentenced to three life terms in prison.

Coakley said attitudes have changed dramatically in the eight years since she unsuccessfully prosecuted Manning. "No way today would you get the level of intimidation that occurred in that case," she said. "And I think juries today are more willing to convict."

Judges are more willing to mete out severe punishment too. When a Middlesex County jury in February 2002 convicted Geoghan of squeezing the buttocks of a ten-year-old boy at a public swimming pool, the indecent-assault charge involved was one of the less egregious acts of abuse he had carried out over the years. But Judge Sandra Hamlin stunned some legal observers by handing down a ten-year sentence, the maximum allowed. Hamlin said she did so because she believed Geoghan would always pose a threat to children.

Hamlin's giving Geoghan the maximum was a far cry from 1984, when Judge Walter Steele sentenced Rev. Eugene M. O'Sullivan, the first priest in Massachusetts to be convicted of sexual abuse. The prosecutor, George Murphy, asked for three to five years after O'Sullivan admitted he had anally raped a thirteen-year-old altar boy. Judge Steele gave the priest probation on the condition he not be allowed to work with children. The Boston archdiocese ignored the judge, and the following year Cardinal Law shipped O'Sullivan off to a new diocese in New Jersey, where he served in four parishes over the next seven years.

Even in 1991, when prosecutors in western Massachusetts went to get a search warrant for the home of Rev. Richard Lavigne, a serial predator who later pleaded guilty to molesting three boys, a judge refused to give them a warrant, saying it would be outrageous for police to search the home of a priest. Despite committing a litany of abuse far worse than what Geoghan was convicted of, Lavigne got just ten years' probation when he was sentenced in 1992. "I think he would have gotten a much longer sentence today," said David Angier, who prosecuted Lavigne.

Judges, many of them Catholic, were complicit in the secrecy that kept the extent of the abuse hidden from public view. Between 1992 and 1996, for example, a group of judges sitting in Boston chose to impound all the records in five lawsuits involving three priests who molested children, because they reasoned that, as one judge put it, "the particulars of the controversy" ought to be kept from the public. In one case, a judge impounded all the records even though the victim testified that he only wanted his identity kept from public view. But well before then, the Church realized that its special treatment was in jeopardy nationwide: the 1985 confidential report on sexual abuse by priests warned, "Our dependence in the past on Roman Catholic judges and attorneys protecting the Diocese and clerics is GONE."

In January 2002 that report's prediction came true in the person of Suffolk County Superior Court Judge Constance M. Sweeney. She was the judge who had heard arguments in September 2001 on a *Globe* motion to lift an order that had shielded from public view all the damaging records in the lawsuits against Geoghan. Church lawyers were confident that Sweeney would not agree to make the records public.

At fifty-two, Sweeney had sixteen years on the bench — the same number of years she had spent in Catholic schools in her youth. After attending Catholic grammar school and high school in her native Springfield, Sweeney went to college at Newton College of the Sacred Heart. But in November 2001 Sweeney decided that the public's right to know overshadowed the Church's right to keep the documents secret. The cardinal's lawyers, staggered by the ruling, appealed her decision. It was upheld.

As the deadline for release of the documents approached, the lawyers worked feverishly to settle the lawsuits, believing a settlement would obviate the need to make the documents public. But during a January 2002 court hearing, Sweeney made it clear to the cardinal's lawyers that she was intent on having her decision carried out. The public, she said, had a right to see the documents. A week later nearly ten thousand pages of documents became public.

Coakley is encouraged by the change in attitudes, but wary too. "Of course, the pendulum can swing too far the other way also," she said. "First the attitude was, no priest could do this. Then it was, well, some might do it, but not my pastor. There is a danger of cynicism becoming so bad that too many will presume that all priests are like that, and that's not fair either. My feeling about priests is like my feeling about cops. Most are good. But if there are bad ones, I'll go after them. And the few bad ones are making everybody else look bad."

If many people give prosecutors credit for getting tough on the Church, many others can't understand why leaders like Cardinal Law have not been charged with being an accessory to the crimes of pedophiles such as Geoghan, especially because Law put Geoghan and others in positions to molest children, even after being warned about their sexual attraction to children.

Some prominent legal analysts, including Joseph di Genova, the former U.S. attorney in Washington, D.C., contend that Catholic prosecutors in and around Boston are still too deferential to the Church to bring criminal charges against those who put abusive priests in positions to victimize children. It is a charge many prosecutors bristle at. "That's baloney, and that's outrageous to say about me and any of my colleagues," Coakley said. "If we had the statutes, we'd prosecute anybody, including the cardinal. But the statutes are not there. We looked. Civil law provides for remedies for negligent supervision. But in Massachusetts, there are no criminal law provisions in this area." And there were other constraints too. "Remember, these people didn't come to law enforcement, and neither did their lawyers. They chose to settle this civilly, and enter into confidentiality agreements. I think the plaintiff lawyers bear some responsibility on that level, but that's the route they chose."

Reilly has also pointed out that accessory and conspiracy laws didn't seem to apply to the cardinal and other Church leaders who transferred known sexual predators, because they didn't share the predators' criminal intent. But Reilly has not ruled out bringing charges against Law and other Church leaders, and said his office was trying to determine if the state's broadly construed civil rights law was applicable. And though some lawyers have filed civil suits, citing the federal racketeering law, none has yet been successful. Others have urged federal prosecutors to use the racketeering law to charge those who move abusive priests around, but U.S. attorneys' offices have stayed clear of the issue.

Some, including di Genova, accuse prosecutors of hanging back and going after the hierarchy only after they saw public opinion was squarely behind doing so. Still others, including Stephen Gillers, a professor of legal ethics at New York University, said Coakley had compromised herself by taking a volunteer position on Law's Commission for the Protection of Children, which Law formed in response to the scandal. "She's in a position to be advising the Church hierarchy as she's investigating members of the clergy that could include the Church hierarchy, and those two roles simply do not mix," said Gillers. But in May 2002, after Rev. Paul Shanley was indicted by Coakley's office, arrested in San Diego, and extradited to face trial in Massachusetts, Coakley quit the cardinal's commission.

Coakley is dismissive of proposed legislation that would make it easier to criminally charge someone who knowingly moves a sexual predator to a job that gives him access to children. "I'm very conservative when it comes to creating new laws in the midst of an emotional period like this," she said. She believes that attitudes have changed so dramatically, and the Church's interests are so threatened by the kind of secrecy it employed to cover up sexual abuse, that it is virtually impossible for the situation ever to repeat itself. "We can't let the Church figure out who to report and who not to report. We're going to have mandatory reporting for the Church, and that is why I don't think you're going to see a new generation of victims."

Kevin Burke, the district attorney in Essex County, which covers Massachusetts's North Shore, also played a key role in forcing the Archdiocese of Boston to take the issue of sexual abuse by priests more seriously. And like the other prosecutors who dogged the cardinal, Burke was raised in a devoutly Catholic home. He grew up in Malden, a blue-collar city just north of Boston, then moved to Beverly, on the North Shore, when he was ten. His grandparents were Irish immigrants, and his grandmother was a daily communicant.

"My grandfather was in the old IRA, and he was anticlerical because the Church was against the rebels, so while I came from a fairly typical Irish Catholic family, where there was great deference shown to the Church and to priests, my grandfather's anticlericalism was also something I was aware of growing up," he said. For example, his grandfather pulled one of Burke's uncles out of parochial school after a nun belted the boy. "That wasn't done back then, openly challenging the Church's authority. The nuns could belt you all they wanted and the vast majority of Catholics didn't dare object, but my grandfather did," he said.

Burke's father made his children attend Mass every day during Lent. As a child, Burke looked upon priests "as separate from the rest of us, as special people, as holy people deserving our respect. But as you get older, you realize that priests have all the shortcomings of other people. I can't tell you exactly when it struck me, but at some point as a kid I realized that there were priests who were unkind, who would humiliate other kids, and that changed me."

Burke also recalled being irked by a growing realization of inequity. "All the nuns I knew were poor as church mice. And I'd see priests driving around in Cadillacs. I remember reading a story about how nuns didn't have full health insurance and was just infuriated by the injustice in that."

After he was first elected district attorney in 1978, Burke went to meet with a local monsignor to discuss a case of abuse. "He was a nice man," Burke recalled. "He invited me to lunch, and the setting in the rectory was stunning. We sat down to a fully set table, with fine china and crisp, white linen. Whenever the monsignor wanted anything, he would ring a little silver bell and this old housekeeper would come shuffling in, like a servant. Every time I tried to engage the monsignor in some serious discussion, he would pick up that bell and ring it, and the little old woman would come in to deal with his every whim. And so I'm sitting there, not only stunned at the level, the position in life, that they held themselves at, but how we in the Church allowed them to do this, that no one was saying, 'Hey, this is wrong. These guys shouldn't be living like this while the nuns don't have health insurance.' But what I realized that day, as the monsignor kept ringing that bell, was how distant, how aloof, how detached the hierarchy of the Church had become. They lived separate lives, completely disconnected from the lives of the laity, and we had allowed it to happen."

Eventually, Burke's office began negotiating with the archdiocese when allegations against priests surfaced. He wasn't impressed. "The archdiocese was probably the most arrogant crowd our office ever dealt with," Burke said. "If you were Catholic, as I am and many of my assistants are, it was implied that you were somehow threatening or being disrespectful to the faith by going after sexual abuse."

When, in 2000, Burke's office brought charges against Christopher Reardon, a Church lay worker who eventually pleaded guilty to raping and molesting more than twenty children, "the Church was less than forthcoming, to put it mildly," said Burke. "But what really struck me, in communications with the archdiocese, was that there was never any concern shown for the victims. Not the slightest nod of concern for these young people whose lives were turned upside down by this abuse. In hindsight, it's striking and shocking that Church leaders failed to meet their moral responsibility. We have an archdiocese that is now cooperative. But they were feeling out the public opinion effects of what they were doing. They weren't sorry for what happened to those kids. They were sorry that they got caught. I don't think the cardinal and the rest of the hierarchy ever really got that they were dealing with kids here. I don't think they even see that today. They see them as adults coming forward, not as the kids to whom this despicable stuff was done."

The failure, or inability, of the Church's hierarchy to sincerely sympathize with the victims of sexual abuse was evidence to Burke that the bishops — like the bell-ringing monsignor — were completely out of touch. Attorney General Reilly came to the same conclusion as he read Cardinal Law's fawning "God bless you, Jack" letter to Geoghan. "The cardinal didn't send letters like that to the victims," Reilly said bitterly.

Indeed, Reilly said he was left profoundly shaken by the extent to which Law and the archdiocese coddled abusive priests while treating victims as a nuisance. "What really offended me was knowing how the Church had been harsh on and intolerant of people who had done things which, by comparison, paled in significance. Look at the way the Church treats divorced Catholics, like pariahs, not allowed to remarry in the Church. Look how intolerant and tough they were on gay people." Reilly remembered reading two years earlier about Sister Jeannette Normandin, a seventy-two-year-old nun who was ousted from the Jesuit Urban Center at the Church of the Immaculate Conception in Boston's South End because she had baptized two boys. Canon law says that only priests or ordained deacons — always and only men — can perform baptisms, and there was no second chance for Sister Normandin. "This was a nun who gave her life to the Church," Reilly said. "And then look how they treated priests who raped children. We throw this word *abuse* around, and it's a nice, inoffensive word. In many of these cases, it wasn't abuse. It was rape. They were raping children. Where's the indignation? Where's the moral outrage? The intolerance and the hypocrisy of the Church lies at the heart of a lot of this. All of this came to a slow boil for me. To be covering up for those who rape children while being so judgmental of others, the hypocrisy is just breathtaking."

Reilly did more than get mad. He fired legal shots across the Church's bow, forcing the cardinal and the archdiocese to dramatically and repeatedly alter course. After the initial *Globe* reports, the cardinal held a televised press conference at which he apologized for his past mistakes and promised to report any future allegations against priests to the authorities. Reilly and Burke shook their head as they watched.

"No way, that's not enough," Burke said to himself, and Reilly said the cardinal's response reminded him of what he had said in 1992 in response to the Porter case. "He was basically saying, 'Trust us, give us the benefit of the doubt, we'll create a commission to make sure this doesn't happen again.' Well, we tried that. It didn't work. My attitude changed dramatically. It became, 'That's enough. You had your chance. You didn't do what you said you'd do. You allowed predators to prey on children.'

"Everybody was on notice after Father Porter. And I trusted them after Father Manning. But I don't feel that way now. They have to be changed. They can't change themselves."

A week after the cardinal insisted that there were no sexually abusive priests still working, Reilly and Burke went public in the *Globe*, saying the cardinal's postdated zero-tolerance policy wasn't sufficient. They said prosecutors, elected and accountable to the public, should be deciding the culpability of sexually abusive priests — not the cardinal, not the Church. They said retroactive reporting of sexual abuse might allow them to bring criminal cases against more priests.

"When it comes to any evidence, they should report any priest or member of the Church. Let prosecutors make decisions on whether they are actionable," said Reilly. "Given what's happened here, the Church should err on the side of complete disclosure on the issue of the abuse of children. There shouldn't be a free pass on anything when it comes to the sexual abuse of children."

Within a week, Cardinal Law held a second press conference and said, in light of Reilly's and Burke's comments, he had changed his mind and would turn over to the authorities the names of priests against whom credible allegations of sexual abuse had been made.

"I'd like to take credit for creating some profound, pivotal moment in holding the Church accountable, but really it was just a reaction created by life experience and moral outrage," said Burke. "I've seen so many kids abused over the years. I've watched videotapes of kids who were abused, and you see the pain, you see the anguish. The paradigm of child sexual abuse changed in the 1980s. It wasn't until we had a videotape of a police officer sexually abusing his own daughter that people would believe a cop could do something like that. The next step, in believing anyone is capable of this stuff, was with priests.

"The Geoghan documents were the most stunning set of documents, when it comes to secondary responsibility, I have ever read. They showed that if someone had met their moral responsibility, let alone whether they had a legal responsibility, hundreds of people would not be suffering today. I wouldn't say Tom and I speaking out made us profiles in courage as much as a reflection of the deference in society that has been eroded."

"Almost every day, somebody comes up to me and says, 'Keep doing what you're doing.'" said Reilly. "I was out one day and a guy came up to me, asked me if I'm the attorney general. He said, 'I'm about the same age as you. A priest abused me, and I never told anyone about it. It ate me up inside all these years. Things have got to change. Keep it up. Make them change.' It was very moving. You wonder how many victims are out there, and what it's been like for them all these years, suffering in silence."

The Geoghan documents also convinced Reilly and other prosecutors that the Church could not be trusted when Cardinal Law initially announced that as far as he knew, there were no active priests against whom there were credible allegations. In fact, Law later removed eleven priests, five of them pastors, because of accusations of sexual abuse.

Acting on the cardinal's orders, the archdiocese's lawyers turned over to Boston-area prosecutors the names of every living priest accused of sexual abuse. But as soon as the prosecutors got the names, they realized that the records were effectively useless. Without the names of the victims, and without the full case files on the priests, including witness statements, prosecutors could not evaluate whether any of the priests should be subject to prosecution. For nearly a month, however, the archdiocese ignored prosecutors' requests for more information.

Finally, Reilly and the five district attorneys whose jurisdictions cover the archdiocese decided to play hardball. They sent a letter to the archdiocese's lawyer that contained a thinly veiled threat to haul Church leaders before a grand jury if they didn't voluntarily turn over more information. The letter also called on the archdiocese to release victims from the terms of the confidentiality agreements the Church has used as a condition of settling private claims and civil lawsuits against abusive priests.

Less than twenty-four hours after Law's lawyer received the letter, the cardinal authorized turning over the names of victims and waiving the confidentiality agreements. Of the allegations leveled at hundreds of living priests across the country, only a handful were liable for prosecution because the statute of limitations had expired in so many cases. But the inability of prosecutors to bring charges was hardly a vindication of the Church.

Norfolk County District Attorney William R. Keating and Plymouth County District Attorney Timothy Cruz convened grand juries to try to pry more information out of the Church. It was a tough slog. Keating was frustrated that the statute of limitations had prevented him from mounting prosecutions against priests. Because of the Church's secrecy, he said, "the lives of many innocent victims were ruined, and people who are nothing more than common criminals cannot be brought to justice."

*   *   *

It wasn't just prosecutors who had decided that the old world order had become obsolete. The deference shown the Church by politicians had also done much to create a system whereby serial predators such as Geoghan could rape dozens of children with impunity, shielded by an archdiocese that had a strong incentive, and was completely within its legal rights, to hide the abuse from public view.

Reilly said the refusal of Massachusetts lawmakers — nearly three-quarters of whom were Catholics — to include clergy in a bill (which became law in 1983) requiring police officers, teachers, doctors, social workers, and other caregivers to report suspected child abuse was a disastrous mistake. As late as August 2001, the Massachusetts Catholic Conference, the public policy arm of the Boston archdiocese, was arguing that any bill that would include clergy as mandatory reporters of abuse would destroy the relationship between priest and parishioner.

"That is an example of deference creating a system that put children at risk," said Reilly. The legislature, he said, simply didn't want to take the heat for passing a law that implicitly suggested the Catholic Church needed the threat of criminal sanctions to do the right thing when confronted with allegations about child abuse.

"The policy the Church had, in terms of hushing things up, was completely consistent with a secret, authoritarian institution. As things were reported, they were dealt with secretly. I think it was a very conscious decision by the Church to handle things the way they did. It was not an oversight, not a lapse in judgment. It was consistent with the institution. . . . You're talking about changing a culture, and that is never easy. But if we had included clergy in mandatory reporting, it would have saved the Church from what it's going through now," Reilly added.

On May 3 Acting Governor Jane Swift, a Catholic, signed into law a bill requiring clergy to report any suspected cases of child abuse.

"Hopefully, this legislation will prevent this tragedy from happening to others. Our responsibility and our loyalty are to our children above all else," Swift said at the State House.

The same day, Rev. Paul Shanley waived extradition from California to face child rape charges in Massachusetts.

*   *   *

Marian Walsh was Cardinal Law's favorite lawmaker. A state senator from West Roxbury, an overwhelmingly middle-class Catholic enclave in Boston of single-family homes and well-kept lawns, Walsh is what they call "lace-curtain Irish" — those who have assimilated and made it.

The odyssey of Walsh's family, from poverty in Ireland to affluence and accomplishment in America, is a prototype for the American Dream, and for Catholic Americans. Her grandparents arrived in the United States with little more than a steamer trunk. Within two years of getting off the boat, her maternal grandfather, John Kelly, was fighting in the trenches for the U.S. Army in World War I. He returned to Boston and got a job as a policeman, only to lose it when he took part in the great Boston police strike of 1919. He went to work as a carpenter for the transit authority and raised nine kids, all of them baptized at Sacred Heart Church in the Roslindale section of Boston. The Church was the focal point of the community. It educated the children. It set the moral tone. It helped give the new arrivals a stake in the New World.

Walsh's paternal grandparents had arrived from Ireland with no money, either. But her grandmother, Delia O'Reilly, was a shrewd Galway woman who read the *Wall Street Journal* religiously. She had no formal education, but she took the money she made renting rooms out in the family's sprawling house and speculated in the stock market. Her hunches were impeccable, as was her timing: she cashed in her stock to pay for her son Francis's first semester at Boston College in September 1929, a month before the crash.

Francis Xavier Walsh, the son of a blacksmith, took the trolley out to Boston College every day. After graduation, he got into Tufts Medical School and became an obstetrician. He married Mary Elizabeth Kelly, a teacher who had obtained two master's degrees from Catholic universities. Like their immigrant parents, they had nine children. The Catholic Church was central to everything the family did and achieved. "My dad was taught by Jesuits and he conducted himself like a Jesuit," Marian Walsh recalled, sitting in her office in the Massachusetts State House on Boston's Beacon Hill. "He believed very much in social justice." He was also a daily communicant. "He walked the walk and talked the talk," she said. "Their faith was important to my parents as a couple. They went on retreats. They tried hard to live their lives according to the basic tenets of the Church, and my parents sacrificed a lot for the Church."

Walsh's aunt was a nun, and Walsh herself seriously considered entering a convent. Instead, after graduating from Newton College of the Sacred Heart, she enrolled in Harvard Divinity School. It was the first time she had stepped outside the comforting cocoon of growing up Catholic in Boston. "It was good for me because, for the first time, I was a minority," she said. "Harvard Divinity had a Protestant ethos. It was weird, but exciting."

Still, Walsh emerged from her studies more committed than ever to her Catholicism. After she decided she didn't want to be a nun, her parents were consoled by the fact that she chose a profession that was second only to the holy vocations in status among the Boston Irish: politics.

Walsh had long been an admirer of Cardinal Law, especially for his outspoken opposition to abortion and his work for the poor. It was a mutual admiration society. Law liked her, perhaps because no other legislator's voting record held so closely to the positions the cardinal advocated. Although some Catholic legislators were opposed to abortion, Walsh was one of the few who also sided with the cardinal in opposing the death penalty. "The cardinal and I saw eye to eye on everything legislatively," she acknowledged.

But in January 2002 she was furious when she read of what she called Law's dishonesty in handling Geoghan and other sexually abusive priests. "I never thought that a leading facilitator for child abuse would be the Church, where the Church would supply the victims and hide the perpetrators. I understand why pedophiles do what they do. I still can't understand, I still can't appreciate, how the Church could do this, how sophisticated and how diabolical this was. And how the cardinal could preside over it."

Walsh put her legislation where her mouth was. She filed a bill that would make it a crime to move a known sexual abuser from one job to another. Having been the cardinal's leading legislative ally for years,

Walsh was now leading the charge to create a law that, had it been enacted a decade before, might have landed him in jail.

In April, after the Father Shanley documents were made public, Walsh became the first state lawmaker to openly call for the cardinal's resignation. And when Law blamed poor record keeping for his failure to appreciate Shanley's perversions, politicians of all stripes let him have it. The Republican minority leaders in the House and Senate called Law's statement deeply troubling and said he should resign. Several Democratic gubernatorial candidates said the cardinal should go, either unconvinced or unconcerned that what previously would have been seen as a cheap shot would cost them votes. There had been a discernible change in the political culture of Massachusetts: the cardinal was fair game. And increasingly so were cardinals and bishops in other places where, as in Boston, the Church had enjoyed a long tradition of polite courtesy from secular authorities.

New York was one of those places. Church officials there had been even less forthcoming than their Boston counterparts, Cardinal Edward M. Egan less contrite than Cardinal Law. And while Reilly and the five district attorneys whose jurisdictions cover the Archdiocese of Boston had aggressively forced the Church to cooperate with their investigations, some of their New York counterparts were initially more deferential to Church leaders.

Enter Jeanine Pirro, the district attorney of Westchester County. Now in her third term, the fifty-year-old Pirro had initially established her reputation as a prosecutor by going after those who sexually abuse children. Her office became the first in the nation to proactively pursue pedophiles with Internet stings, in which police officers pose as children and arrange to meet with child molesters who seek them out in chat rooms. When the clergy sexual abuse scandal erupted, Pirro took it as a personal failing that she hadn't seen it coming. "I mean, this is what I pride myself most on, protecting children from sexual abuse. I can't think of a more important thing we can do in law enforcement. But I had no idea. No one called us. No victims, none of their lawyers. And the Church did an incredible job in covering this up," she said.

But if Pirro missed anything in the past, she was determined to make up for it now, and she didn't care whose toes she stepped on in the process. In April 2002 she assembled a group of seven other district attorneys whose jurisdictions cover the New York archdiocese, and she summoned five lawyers who represent the archdiocese to her fifth-floor office in White Plains, New York. Pirro opened the meeting by saying she was a devout Catholic, but she quickly cut to the chase: the archdiocese had information that she and the other prosecutors needed to see in order to determine whether the Church was shielding sexual predators. Egan's announcement that the archdiocese would turn over evidence to prosecutors only if Church officials concluded there was probable cause didn't cut it. She wouldn't lecture the Church on theology, and she didn't expect the Church to tell prosecutors how to do their jobs. They could do it the easy way, she said, or they could do it the hard way. If the Church didn't want to turn over the records, she said, there was always the grand jury route. Then she stared at the Church lawyers as if to say, "What's it going to be, boys, yes or no?"

The Church lawyers exchanged glances. One of them, a friend of Pirro's, looked at her with something approaching disbelief. And then the lawyers blinked. They agreed to turn over the information and to waive the confidentiality agreements that had bound victims to silence.

The archdiocese isn't happy with her, but Pirro said she could not care less. "I was raised in the Church. It was a big part of my family's life, and it continues to be," she said. "I'm still deferential to a point, but I draw the line when they harbor criminals. With all due respect, the Church and its leaders don't have the world experience that I and other prosecutors have. Maybe to them, the victims are nameless and faceless. The victims are real to me."

Years ago, when she was a young prosecutor, when cases involving sexually abused children were farmed out to women because most men didn't want to handle them, Jeanine Pirro opened a file about a brother and sister. He was five, she was six. The children's baby-sitter and the baby-sitter's boyfriend had repeatedly raped and sodomized them. The baby-sitter and her boyfriend put knives in the girl's vagina and in the boy's rectum.

"I worked with those kids for a year, building the case," she recalled. "This was before there was a lot known about this kind of sexual abuse, and how to prosecute it. The kids didn't have the vocabulary to say what had been done to them. I got some guys I know in the [carpenter's] union to build me an anatomically correct doll, and the kids were able to tell the jury what had happened." The baby-sitter testified against her boyfriend, pleaded guilty, and was sentenced to probation and psychiatric treatment. Appalled by the evidence, the judge sentenced the boyfriend to seventy-five years in prison, only to realize later that thirty years was the maximum allowed under the law.

Ten years later, after Pirro had been made a judge, she was presiding over a family court session when a "child in need of services" case came before her. A teenage girl had tried to kill herself, and the state was trying to figure out what to do with the troubled girl. Pirro looked up at the teenager before her. It was the little girl she thought she had saved a decade earlier.

"As soon as I looked into her eyes, I knew it was her, even before I saw her name. She still had that sweet face, and the blond hair. And the eyes. She still had the eyes," Pirro said. Disturbed, Pirro decided to find out what had happened to the girl's brother. He was on the streets, selling his body as a prostitute.

"Now remember," said Pirro, "these were two children who were taken under the wing of the state, who were believed, who were comforted, who were able to see that a jury had vindicated them, and know that the people who did this horrible stuff to them had been sent to prison for a long, long time. And still, look what became of them. It made me realize the enormous impact of sexual abuse on children, the lingering effects, the long-term ramifications. And it made me think — what about all the children who aren't believed, who aren't comforted, who don't see those who harm them held accountable?

"This is where the Church leaders were blind. They didn't make that human connection. They just wanted to protect the Church's reputation at the expense of children."

Pirro said the stories that continue to emerge about the extent to which Church leaders covered up the sexual abuse of children disturb her greatly, but she has not lost her faith. "I've raised my kids in the Catholic faith, and I will continue to raise them in the Catholic faith. There are many good things that the Church has done, and continues to do, for poor people. I'm just determined to make sure the Church learns from what they didn't do to protect the children. I will hold them accountable."

Pirro was dismissive of the archdiocese's idea of a commission to review cases of priests accused of sexual abuse. So were the other prosecutors who met with archdiocese officials at her office. After a Church lawyer sang the praises of potential commission members, including former judges and prosecutors, one prosecutor interrupted and said, "With all due respect, I don't care if Jesus Christ is on the commission."

"It was a great line," said Pirro. "I wish I'd said it."

Kevin Burke, the Essex County D.A., believes the sudden decline of the deference shown the Church by so many in society could lead to a "mini Reformation." "There's no Martin Luther here," he said, "and whether the Vatican pays attention, who knows?" It wouldn't be easy. "We're dealing with a medieval organization, an organization that represented authority to my grandparents and other immigrants. It was an organization that was respected because it educated them, it gave them a place in the New World, it gave them an identity. But with assimilation, with the educational and financial success of successive generations, the average Catholic's need of the Church is not social or political, it's moral and spiritual. And this behavior of the Church is so at odds with being moral and spiritual. The Church's leaders should be worried about a lot of things, but they should be most afraid of the lack of deference now shown them. They should not think that once this scandal fades, people will come running back to them. I know I won't."

7

His Eminence

In 1984, when he took over as archbishop of what was then the third-largest diocese in the United States, Bernard Law said, "After Boston, there's only heaven."

He could not have imagined that what were supposed to be his golden years in Boston would become something of a living hell.

Law's ambitious ascent in the Church was a fast and steady climb, from parish priest in the Deep South, to bishop in the Ozarks, where Catholics are few and far between, to Boston, which with New York, Chicago, Baltimore, and Philadelphia is one of the original great sees of the Catholic Church in America.

He rose from the buckle of the Bible Belt to preside over one of the Church's crown jewels. When his peer Cardinal John O'Connor of New York died in 2000, Law became indisputably the most influential American Catholic prelate and, more important, was seen as such in the Vatican. He was kingmaker of other bishops and cardinals. At the White House, presidents took his calls and valued his opinion. But Law's handling of the sexual abuse scandal that exploded on his watch ended all of that. Now the buzz about Cardinal Law revolved around how long he could weather the demands for his resignation.

Situated in the Brighton section of Boston, the chancery is the headquarters of the archdiocese. For eighteen years, the chancery and the cardinal's adjacent residence had been the places where Law presided over a $50-million-a-year operation, with hundreds of millions more in real estate, seeing to every detail, working the phones, sometimes two at a time, and cajoling rich Catholics to pony up to pay for the Church's schools, hospitals, and outreach programs. By January 2002, in the middle of what would be his winter of discontent, Law's compound had become his sanctuary — in effect a bunker. Within a few months of the story breaking, Law was a virtual prisoner, working all day and seldom venturing outside the splendor of his Italian Renaissance residence at night.

On the *Tonight Show*, Jay Leno used the scandal as fodder for his monologues, referring to the archbishop of his family's old parish, St. Augustine's in Andover, north of Boston, as "Cardinal Above the Law." Just outside his windows, Law could see protesters holding signs, demanding his resignation or indictment. Radio shock jocks, desperate for an audience, began doing live remotes outside the chancery.

Honk if you want the cardinal to resign.

It wasn't supposed to end this way.

Bernard Francis Law was born in 1931, in Torreón, Mexico, a place that, like others, was not home but was a way station in a childhood where moving was common. His father was a military and sometime commercial pilot, a job that caused the family to move six times while Law was young. His father was Catholic. His mother, Helen, to whom Law was devoted, was a Presbyterian who converted to Catholicism. Law went to high school in St. Thomas, in the U.S. Virgin Islands. If some children find frequent moves unsettling, Law said he recalled those nomadic years as exciting and enlightening. His parents, he said, enthusiastically embraced different cultures and settings. Law too was adaptable. One of the few whites at Charlotte Amalie High School in St. Thomas, he was elected senior class president by his mostly black classmates.

A good student, Law earned his way to Harvard, rooming with two Jews and a Southern Baptist. By his senior year, he had decided he wanted to become a priest. His four undergraduate years at Harvard would look easy in hindsight. Eight more years of study — two at a

Benedictine monastery in Louisiana, six at a pontifical college in Ohio — would follow. Only twelve of twenty seminarians in his class made it.

After his ordination, Law's first parish assignment brought him to Vicksburg, Mississippi, in 1961, as the civil rights movement gained momentum and John F. Kennedy, the first Catholic president, vowed to stand up to racists. Law took over as editor of the diocesan newspaper, using its columns to champion racial justice. Some local bigots didn't take kindly to the uppity priest, and it wasn't long before Law got death threats. But he did not back down.

In his twenty-fifth anniversary report to Harvard, Law looked back on those days in Mississippi as being not in the eye of a gathering storm but in the crucible of history. "To have been part of that significant moment of our history is in itself a grace, a gift," he wrote.

Law was an ambitious priest. He confided to friends in Mississippi that one of his goals was to become the first American pope. As someone who was always around and comfortable with black people, Law's position on civil rights was natural. But he also longed to get involved in the Church's nascent efforts to foster ecumenism. In 1968 he was made executive director of the National Conference of Catholic Bishops' Committee on Ecumenical and Interreligious Affairs, spending a few years in Washington, D.C.

In 1973 he was made a bishop and assigned to the Springfield diocese in the Missouri Ozarks. "He's a strategic leader, more an Eisenhower than a Patton," said Terry Meek, a prominent Catholic businessman in Springfield. But Law remained idealistic. "He's a dreamer, a visionary, and at times not that practical," said Rev. Philip Bucher, who served under Law in the Missouri diocese. "It's all overwhelming unless he has a good core of people around him who take suggestions for what they're worth."

After ten years in Missouri, where he was the leader of 47,000 Catholics, 90 priests, and 63 parishes, Law was sent to Boston to preside over 2 million Catholics, 1,100 priests, and 408 parishes. It was like going from running a car dealership to running General Motors. The death of Cardinal Medeiros in Boston and the confidence of Pope John Paul II in Rome gave Law not only the opportunity to become archbishop of one of the largest dioceses in the United States but a real shot at even greater advancement. Law's three previous predecessors — William O'Connell, Richard Cushing, and Medeiros — had been elevated to cardinal. So when he arrived in Boston in March 1984, Law had to know that becoming a prince of the Church was only a matter of time.

He was given a warm welcome, and a wide berth. His three predecessors were considerably different characters. O'Connell was an eccentric, vainglorious man, fond of the high life, driving around town in the middle of the depression in a limousine, accompanied by his poodles. He was also part of the bricks-and-mortar brigade, as the Catholic Church in America built the churches, schools, convents, and rectories needed to house a growing congregation. Cushing, a plain-speaking populist, continued the tradition in which the archbishop of Boston acted as much like the CEO of a construction company as he did the spiritual leader of 2 million Catholics.

In his book *Bare Ruined Choirs*, Garry Wills noted that the Church's obsession with creating enough parochial schools to make the Catholic community independent of secular public education also created a career ladder for priests, monsignors, and bishops who were promoted "by virtue of business skill." Wills contended it was this system that created a church hierarchy in America whose goal was not to help the faithful achieve eternal salvation but to achieve a healthy bottom line. "The priest had little time for theology, or for study of any sort. He adopted the businessman's no-nonsense ways and practicality," Wills observed. "The pastor was obnoxious, not for his theology or his transitional ties but for his lack of theology and parochialism."

By the time Cardinal Cushing died in 1970, the long growth period of the Catholic Church in America was coming to an end. Up to that point, the American Catholic Church had been dominated by the Irish. And for more than two centuries, ever since the Pilgrims landed at Plymouth Rock and quickly moved up to Boston, the capital of New England was a Protestant city for a Protestant people. But that changed in the mid-nineteenth century, when Ireland's potato blight and Britain's refusal to bail out its colony sent more than 1 million Irish to the emigrant ships. Almost overnight, Boston's religious demographic changed, and by the end of the century, Boston had elected its first Irish-born mayor. The Irish used political power to take control of a city where they were initially reviled and greeted with those "No Irish Need Apply" signs.

When Italians and then Poles and other Eastern Europeans followed the Irish, they became part of an American Catholic Church that was, in essence, an Irish church. As *Boston Globe* reporter Maureen Dezell noted in her book *Irish America: Coming into Clover,* 90 percent of men enrolled in American seminaries in the latter half of the nineteenth century had Irish names, while by 1900 three quarters of the American Catholic hierarchy was Irish. (Even by the 1990s, when Hispanics emerged as the biggest ethnic group in the American Catholic Church, and the Irish made up only 15 percent of the laity, a third of the priests and half of the American bishops were of Irish descent.)

Cushing's replacement, Medeiros, the son of a vegetable farmer from the Azores, could not have been more different from the two Irish priests-cum-pols O'Connell and Cushing. O'Connell and Cushing were larger than life, characters who could have been plucked out of Edwin O'Connor's novel *The Last Hurrah,* as comfortable in back rooms twisting arms as they were in confessionals handing out penance. Medeiros, by contrast, was shy, retiring, and pious, the antithesis of the bishop-as-businessman.

Within a few years of his arrival, Medeiros managed to alienate the heart of the archdiocese, the mostly Irish and Italian working class of Boston, by ordering that any student suspected of being part of the "white flight" to avoid court-ordered desegregation of the city's public schools was not to be allowed into Catholic schools. Medeiros's directive was largely ignored. The archdiocese's schools swelled in numbers, and many Boston Catholics swelled in resentment, seeing Medeiros as unfairly judging them as racist when many simply wanted to avoid the chaos of busing that no one in the wealthy suburbs had to endure.

Thomas H. O'Connor, a professor of history at Boston College and author of *Boston Catholics,* said Medeiros was never fully accepted in Boston. Medeiros was an outsider. He was visibly an outsider. People said, "He's not one of us." And he knew it. He made smiling references to the fact that Cardinal Cushing was a hard act to follow and that he wouldn't try to follow him. Even Medeiros's mannerisms — the folding of his hands, the upward thrust of his eyes, the exaggerated piety — had he been in a Latino country, it would have been no big deal. But they were out of character in Boston. So there was never a good fit here.

Although he was of Irish descent, Law was not a throwback to O'Connell and Cushing so much as a change from Medeiros. He had O'Connell's administrative skills and the political savvy of Cushing, who often boasted that he and old Joe Kennedy mapped out JFK's campaign for the White House inside the chancery. He had the intellectual gravitas that his predecessors lacked. Cushing came home from the Vatican II council early, complaining he couldn't understand the Latin. And while O'Connell seemed to regard the religious component of his job as a nuisance, Law seemed almost as pious as Medeiros, but considerably more approachable and down-to-earth.

"Much of the initial reaction to Law was, 'We got one of our own back.' A white, blue-eyed Harvard grad. He wasn't born here, like Cushing and O'Connell, but he looked Irish. The reaction in Boston was, 'Finally, Rome has come to its senses and sent us one of ours.' But I think that early assessment was wrong. The longer Law stayed here, the fewer people seemed to think he was one of us," said O'Connor. "He had a public persona and a private persona. Publicly, he's like O'Connell, very pompous in the pulpit, elongating his vowels while speaking, the gravitas, the weight of the words. But in social circles, in small groups, he would be charming and gracious and sophisticated and humorous. He was always conscious of his rank and position. He can laugh at himself, but no one else can."

Unlike Cushing, Law was no backslapping populist. He insisted on formality. He expected his staff to call him "Your Eminence" in conversation, and they did. They also insisted that others do likewise. Law's former spokesman once chastised a reporter who referred to the cardinal as simply "Law" during a telephone conversation.

While interviewing priests for his book, O'Connor asked them to give him one word or phrase to describe Boston's cardinals. For O'Connell, it was *pompous*. For Cushing, it was *gravel-voiced*. For Medeiros, it was *pious*. But Law stumped them.

"Finally, one priest who knows Law quite well told me: *rootless*. I looked at him in surprise and asked, 'Ruthless?' And he said, 'No, rootless.' And I understood what he meant. Law doesn't call any place home. He was an army brat. He really doesn't have any roots. In that respect, he's probably the first American cardinal and archbishop we had in Boston. He was an American, not a Bostonian."

Perhaps because he was not a native Bostonian, and not beholden to the city's ancient preoccupations and grudges, Law seemed to have a special affinity for immigrants — the Central and South Americans, the Haitians, the Vietnamese — who were the new faces of a changing Church in Boston. His history of advocating for racial and social justice, and his tireless campaigning for affordable housing for low-income families, made him a hero among immigrants. Hispanics loved a cardinal who could speak to them in fluent Spanish. When things turned sour for the cardinal, it was the immigrant groups that were his staunchest supporters.

And as the years passed, it was the old guard, not the newcomers, who came to question Law's stewardship. Critics saw him as patronizing, self-righteous, and increasingly isolated. Instead of his influence growing with his longevity, it waned.

The first priest to greet Law when he arrived in Boston, Rev. Bernard McLaughlin, then the chaplain at Logan Airport, said there was great hope when Law became archbishop, but that Law didn't fulfill his promise because he was too isolated, shut off from the flock, living in a palatial mansion, surrounded by advisers who gave him bad advice. "Boston is a village," Rev. McLaughlin said. "I don't think the cardinal ever learned that."

O'Connor came to share that view and said Law never appreciated the need to be out and about more, to be seen, to be a bigger part of the community, whether it was going to a Red Sox game or going to a restaurant. O'Connor remembered Law casually telling him that he had given back a lifelong ticket to the Boston Athenæum, one of the oldest and most prestigious private libraries in the United States. "My eyebrows went up. Every archbishop has had one. They are priceless. Bishop

Cheverus, Boston's first bishop, had helped found the Athenæum and had given it his personal library. When I asked Law why he gave the ticket back, he said, 'I never get down that way.' He figured he didn't need it. Maybe that's a small thing to some people, but you put it all together and you see he didn't understand Boston. He just didn't get it."

Instead of mixing with the masses, Law spent an inordinate amount of time in the office, his nerve center. It was there that O'Connor saw the Bernard Law who is a workaholic, and who is very much in charge.

"He's a compulsive micromanager," said O'Connor. "When notes come to him, he corrects the grammar. He's very much at home in the electronic age. He's got computers and faxes. I've been talking to him, and at the same time he's on the phone, calling someone else. The people he talks to, he gives them orders. 'Get him at his job. Get him on the golf course.' The furious energy of the man is fascinating. And watching him in action reminded me of something a priest once told me [about Law]. He said, 'You've got to remember that Bernie was an only child. All the toys are his. He never had to share.'"

The racial climate in Boston had cooled considerably by the time Law arrived. The passion Law once brought to the civil rights movement as a young priest, he devoted to the pro-life movement once he became part of the hierarchy. In his first speech as archbishop in Boston in March 1984, Law described abortion as a "national disgrace" and the "primordial evil of our time." Law and Cardinal O'Connor of New York, appointed as cardinals together in 1985, became the American tag team preaching Pope John Paul II's orthodoxy, lecturing the laity that abortion, contraception, homosexuality, and divorce were sins, even though polls showed a majority of Catholics considered those issues matters of personal conscience. The two cardinals became popularly known as "Law and Order," laying down the Pope's law and ordering the laity to not even discuss the idea of women becoming priests or priests getting married or ending priestly celibacy.

Law's aggressive stance on abortion alienated many liberal Boston Catholics. Boston's archbishop traditionally addresses the graduating class at Boston College every year, and O'Connor said Law's first address at the 1984 commencement set the tone for what would be a strained relationship between Law and the preeminent Catholic university in New England. Two years later, he told another Boston College graduating class that the Jesuit school was losing its Catholic identity. "I was there, in the audience, and I remember people just gasping, listening to their archbishop say that BC had moved away from the Catholic tradition, that it was no longer a Catholic college, that changes had to be made. He alienated a lot of BC graduates, and yet it was a core of BC graduates who were his biggest financial backers," O'Connor said.

Shortly after, he told a group of Catholic businessmen that they had "an obligation" to do more than just say they opposed abortion. A month later, Law made a dramatic and unprecedented appearance at a State House pro-life rally just as the Massachusetts legislature was about to consider an amendment that would restrict or prohibit abortion. Some suggested he was meddling with the constitutional separation of church and state. "If a preacher isn't meddling, he isn't really preaching," said Law, sounding like one of the Pentecostal preachers he counted as friends in the Deep South.

Thomas P. O'Neill III, the son of the late U.S. Speaker of the House Thomas P. "Tip" O'Neill Jr., remembered that Law's intolerance of the liberal views held by many Boston Catholics irked not only his generation but his father's. "It's interesting to look at the two of them in comparison," said O'Neill, a former lieutenant governor of Massachusetts who went on to found a successful public relations company. "The archbishop who came to Boston had a certain gravitas, especially on civil rights. But I've watched a lot of people come to power and have seen how power corrupts them and isolates them, cuts them off. My dad became big and powerful, but he never lost the common touch. He was never isolated from ordinary people, and he always knew what they thought. The cardinal came in and never understood the city, and that failure to understand the city eventually isolated him. It's a city that takes its tribalism seriously, and its Catholicism seriously. But it opens its arms to the disadvantaged and the dispossessed. And to be told, in this city, that you were somehow less a Catholic because you didn't agree with the Church's position on abortion or contraception was offensive.

"Cardinal Law came in here and judged people and politicians on one issue: abortion. It was almost as if the cardinal came in and said, 'Boston, you've had it your way, but there's a new Pope, there's a new cardinal, there's a new conservatism, and we're here. You're too progressive, you're too liberal. And it's going to change.'"

On December 30, 1994, a Catholic zealot named John Salvi walked into an abortion clinic in the Boston suburb of Brookline, the town where John F. Kennedy was born, and shot a receptionist dead. He went to a second clinic and killed another receptionist. Shortly after Salvi opened fire, Law answered the phone in the chancery. Barbara Thorp, director of the archdiocese's Pro-Life Office, was on the other end, crying. When Thorp finished explaining what had happened, the cardinal put down the phone and headed straight into his private chapel to pray and to write down his response to the murders. Law called for a moratorium on protests outside abortion clinics. Antiabortion activists were furious, saying Law gave ammunition to those who claimed Operation Rescue and other antiabortion demonstrators who took their protests and heated rhetoric to clinics were responsible for the murderous exploits of those like Salvi. Law's prohibition on protests was short-lived — he lifted it five months later — but it showed how profoundly the murders had shaken him.

Even abortion rights activists gave Law credit for changing his rhetoric over the years. "If I had to produce lists of inflammatory language, my O'Connor list would be ten times longer than my Law list," said Frances Kissling, president of Catholics for a Free Choice, a Washington lobbying group.

When he was a priest in the Deep South and later a bishop in Missouri, Law's commitment to ecumenism was as much an act of pragmatism as a theological imperative. In both places, Catholics were heavily outnumbered by Protestants, some of them hostile. These were places where the Ku Klux Klan once hated Catholics almost as much as they hated blacks. In Jackson, his first diocese, Catholics made up less than 3 percent of the population. In Missouri, they amounted to less than 5 percent. But in Boston, the Catholics were in the majority. Rather than the put-upon minority they were in other parts of the country, Catholics had power in Boston and sometimes used it to oppress others.

As he did in the Bible Belt, Law reached out to Protestants in Boston. But he especially reached out to Jews. This was, after all, a town where Nat Hentoff recalled in his memoir, *Boston Boy,* that Irish and Italian kids were taught in Catholic schools that the Jews killed Jesus Christ. Such teachings encouraged anti-Semitism. Gangs of Catholic boys would seek revenge on Jewish kids. Like many of his peers, Hentoff got beat up by the gangs. If a Boston cop intervened, he would be more likely to chastise the Jewish kid for being stupid enough to let himself get ambushed than he would be to hold the attackers accountable.

It was against that historical backdrop that Law sought to engage the Jews of Boston. They responded to him enthusiastically. "He really cares, and he really gets it," said Leonard Zakim, the longtime head of the Anti-Defamation League of New England. "Cardinal Law understands anti-Semitism and the importance of the Church to confront it."

When Zakim died of cancer at forty-six, Law leaned on an initially reluctant governor Paul Cellucci to name a new bridge spanning the Charles River after Zakim. Cellucci acquiesced this time. A year before, in 1999, Cellucci refused to bow to the cardinal's demands when Law urged the governor to reconsider the nomination of two judges. The cardinal implied that the women, Margaret Marshall and Judith Cowin, were anti-Catholic and had an "attitude and mentality which I find troubling."

Law especially wanted to derail Marshall's elevation to chief justice of the state's highest court. Marshall, like Law, had a long commitment to racial justice. She came to prominence in her native South Africa while leading college students opposed to apartheid and was banned from her own country for her trouble. But she ran afoul of the cardinal in her job before she became a judge, when she rebuked one of the cardinal's closest advisers. That adviser, Harvard Law School professor Mary Ann Glendon, was ordered by Marshall, then Harvard's chief legal counsel, to stop using Harvard stationery in her antiabortion efforts.

*   *   *

In the wake of the Father Porter scandal, Cardinal Law announced that he had appointed a nine-member board, including laypeople, that would recommend to him action to be taken against priests accused of what he called "the sin of sexual abuse." Still, the cardinal was determined to keep the Church's dirty laundry indoors. He ignored pleas that he institute a policy that would compel the archdiocese to turn allegations against priests over to civil authorities, and he envisioned returning offenders, once they had been treated, to parishes.

In May 1993, as the archdiocese tried to get a better handle on its abusive priests, the cardinal summoned to his residence a group of eminent experts in the field of child sexual abuse, a pair of husband-and-wife teams who were nationally known for their work.

It was a working lunch. Carolyn Newberger, a child psychologist, and her husband, Eli, a pediatrician, sat at the end of a large table with Ted and Carol Nadelson, a pair of well-regarded psychiatrists. At the other end of the table, the cardinal sat with the two priests, William F. Murphy and John B. McCormack, who were his point men in trying to get on top of the problem of priests abusing minors. "The scene struck me as something out of the Middle Ages," Carolyn Newberger recalled. "You had all these priests in clerical garb on one side, all these secular Jewish experts on the other, and all these nuns serving us."

The Jewish doctors respected the cardinal, in part because of his well-documented outreach to the Jewish community. They were flattered when Law explained that he had sought them out because they were nationally recognized experts in the field of pedophilia and the sexual abuse of minors. Carol Nadelson was the first female president of the American Psychiatric Association. But they realized early on, before the appetizers were cleared away, that the cardinal wasn't especially receptive to what they were telling him.

"The four of us were on the same page," said Carolyn Newberger. "We told them that the way they had handled these cases was wrong and was endangering children. We stressed the importance of reporting these cases to the civil authorities. And we told them that, no matter what they thought about priests having been cured or having put these problems behind them, there was a strong likelihood of a repeat of this behavior."

To illustrate their point, Newberger spoke at length about a case in Arizona. A boy who had been abused at a very young age was adopted by a family and was doing well until a priest molested the child again. Another priest had walked in while the abuse was occurring, but walked out without intervening.

"The boy went on to molest his own siblings," said Newberger. "I used the case to emphasize the insidiousness of this abuse, how devastating it is not just to the individual child, but to the extended family. I tried not only to emphasize the facts of the case but to engage the cardinal and the other priests there to empathize with the victim."

But neither Newberger nor her colleagues sensed they were getting through on the human level. While the experts talked about the real world, the priests seemed preoccupied with a higher realm.

"The cardinal said canon law had to be considered. We just looked at one another. Whatever we had just told him didn't seem to be registering," Newberger said. "Canon law was irrelevant to us. Children were being abused. Sexual predators were being protected. Canon law should have nothing to do with it. But they were determined to keep this problem, and their response to it, within their culture."

At the end of lunch, Newberger and the other experts offered to help the cardinal shape a new approach to aggressively rooting out the sexual abuse of minors by priests. Newberger said the cardinal smiled at them and looked deeply into their eyes as he shook their hands, thanking them. But he never contacted any of them again.

"I'm not Catholic, but I feel betrayed," Carolyn Newberger said. "I look to spiritual leaders of all faiths to be moral. And the Church's response to this problem has not been moral. I'm angry in that the cardinal asked for our advice and then ignored it."

In an ironic twist, Newberger was sought out by someone else: David Deakin, the prosecutor in charge of the sexual abuse unit in the Suffolk County District Attorney's Office in Boston. Now Newberger is a consultant for Boston prosecutors. The archdiocese's loss, it seems, was the prosecution's gain.

*   *   *

The next time the cardinal summoned a group to his residence to discuss his handling of sexually abusive priests, he expected a more sympathetic audience. In fact, many of the people called in on the morning of February 19, 2002, had been with Law in Rome when he was elevated to cardinal seventeen years earlier. They were among those who stood patiently in line for up to two hours, on a warm spring night, to shake hands with their new cardinal.

Now, as they once again greeted Law, they pondered the scandal that threatened his future and their Church. The meeting had been put together by Dr. Michael Collins, who heads the archdiocese's hospital system, and Jack Connors Jr., the founder of the biggest advertising agency Boston had ever produced and a longtime mover and shaker in Catholic philanthropic circles. Connors had been a confidant of the cardinal's since Law arrived in Boston, and as the storm clouds swirled around Law in the wake of the Geoghan disclosures, Connors remained protective and supportive of the cardinal.

Collins and Connors had assembled a group of savvy, successful spin doctors, lawyers, and businesspeople to advise the cardinal on how to steer his way through the burgeoning crisis. It was a Who's Who of the Boston Catholic elite: Tom O'Neill; James Brett, a former state representative who heads a business group called the New England Council; R. Robert Popeo, a lawyer and one of the city's top litigators and power brokers; William Bulger, president of the University of Massachusetts; John L. Harrington, former CEO of the Red Sox; John Hamill, the CEO of Sovereign Bank in New England; Rev. William Leahy, president of Boston College; Paul La Camera, president and general manager of WCVB-TV, the ABC affiliate in Boston; Jack Shaughnessy Sr., whose success in the construction equipment business made him among the archdiocese's most generous patrons; John Drew, the head of the World Trade Center in Boston. The only woman at the table, Donna Latson Gittens, head of one of the region's few black-run marketing firms, was also the only person who wasn't white. The only non-Catholic at the table was Jeffrey Rudman, a Jewish lawyer with the white-shoe law firm of Hale and Dorr, who had offered his services pro bono in appreciation of Law's "resolute opposition to anti-Semitism." Many of those called to the meeting were wealthy, people who gave and raised millions for the Church.

If the cardinal thought this was going to be a pep rally, however, he would soon be disappointed. There were, for sure, a few people who were with him all the way, come what may. Brett would not abandon Law, especially in light of the kindness the cardinal had shown his family, such as when his wife's parents were dying. Shaughnessy was fiercely loyal to the cardinal. Gittens too said she would not abandon him. But among the fourteen people invited that day, Law's unconditional supporters were clearly in the minority.

Connors tried to break the ice, and the tension, by drawing on an old gag from the *I Love Lucy* TV show.

"Well, Your Eminence," Connors began, "as Ricky used to say to Lucy, you sure got some 'splainin' to do."

Judging by the grins around the table, everyone thought it was funny. Everyone, that is, except the cardinal. He showed a poker face. That face quickly changed, however, as most of those assembled explained to him how grave they believed the situation was.

O'Neill said he noticed the cardinal's body language change as what Law assumed was a friendly group offered a less-than-sympathetic critique of his handling of the crisis. "I think he thought we were going to say, 'Hey, we're with you all the way, Your Eminence.' It wasn't that way at all."

Law spoke first, for about twenty minutes. He was very defensive, O'Neill recalled.

When the cardinal acknowledged that his handling of the crisis had been "flawed," Bulger uncharacteristically interrupted him, taking exception to what he considered a massive understatement of the problem. To Bulger, an erudite man with a formidable vocabulary who had been the president of the Massachusetts senate for seventeen years before moving into academia, *flawed* was not the word. "It's been disastrous," said Bulger, as heads nodded around the table.

Bulger's open contradiction of Law was a rebuke of enormous symbolic significance, suggesting that the deference Boston's archbishops had enjoyed for more than a century was under attack not just from the outside, as the laity rebelled and prosecutors convened grand juries, but from the inside, by the Church insiders convened around a huge table in the cardinal's residence.

Connors voiced the concerns of many when he said the crisis threatened all the Church's good works — the social service agencies funded by Catholic Charities, the hospitals that served the dispossessed, the schools that increasingly took in new immigrants. La Camera gingerly raised the prospect of resignation, saying, "If you're thinking about resigning . . ." But the cardinal would have none of it. Law said the Pope might not accept his resignation even if it was offered. "We said resignation needed to remain on the table, but he outright dismissed it," La Camera said.

Hamill said whatever reform was needed, women had to play a bigger role in the solution. The Church, he said, needed to be more inclusive. O'Neill picked up on that theme, telling Law, "You've got to get women to the table." O'Neill, the PR executive, said the cardinal could not treat the crisis as a PR campaign. It had to be about real reform; there was a dysfunctional priesthood that had to be fixed. He suggested Law could be like "Nixon in China": if Nixon could put aside his anticommunism and make peace with Chinese Communists, O'Neill reasoned, surely the most conservative American cardinal could get the Pope to buy into comprehensive reform of the Church.

But Gittens chastised O'Neill, saying it was presumptuous of him to speak for women. Dr. Collins said more women had been invited but couldn't make it.

The meeting broke up inconclusively, with the cardinal promising to consider what he had been told. As weeks and then months passed, people such as O'Neill and Connors began to conclude that while the cardinal may seek the counsel of others, the only counsel he kept was his own.

One by one, the influential Catholics who warned the cardinal that he wasn't responding to the crisis with enough fervor walked away from him. It began March 3, when La Camera went on his TV station with an editorial saying Law had lost his moral authority to lobby for good causes and should consider resigning. Two weeks later, *Boston Herald* publisher Patrick J. Purcell, once the cardinal's most influential friend in the Boston media, personally authorized an editorial calling on him to step down.

The *Herald* had been a steadfast supporter of Law since his installation in 1984, but Purcell was stunned by what he saw as Law's betrayal of children, and of Purcell's own family. Their parish was St. Julia's in Weston, where John Geoghan had officiated at the wedding of Purcell's daughter. Purcell's wife, Maureen, taught religious education at the parish, which Geoghan supervised. When Purcell and his wife lobbied on behalf of Geoghan's bid to become pastor of St. Julia's, the cardinal did not inform his friend that he was going to bat for a pedophile.

In March, a month after the big meeting at the chancery, Jack Connors told the *Globe* he was no longer advising the cardinal. For his candor, Connors was summoned to the chancery and given a dressing-down by Law. It was like a naughty altar boy being reprimanded by the pastor for laughing during Mass. As Connors later told O'Neill, only half jokingly, "I think I was just excommunicated."

Some of the richest, most influential Catholics did not abandon Law. But most did. Catholic Charities, the biggest private social services provider in Massachusetts, raised more than $1.4 million at its annual Garden Party at the cardinal's residence in 2001. But for the first time since it was established twenty-six years earlier, the Garden Party was canceled because wealthy donors said they would not give money if the cardinal was involved. Many of those who had been with Law in Rome the day he got the red hat and had waited hours to shake his hand were no longer willing to go through the routine of standing in line for a photo with him before dropping off a check.

Catholic colleges that a year before would have coveted Law as a commencement speaker let it be known his presence would detract from the joyous event. At Boston College, where Law had given the opening benediction at graduation almost every year, he was no longer welcome.

Law's days were long, his nights often lonely. The boredom was broken when his old friend Leonard Florence dropped by for their regular Saturday-night Ping-Pong game. Florence, seventy, the son of Russian Jews, made millions in the silverware business. He admired the cardinal's embrace of Jews and gave money to Catholic causes. The Saturday night before the Shanley papers were released, Florence showed up for their weekly game and noticed the cardinal was especially anxious.

"We had a good match that night," said Florence. "He beat me, and I think it helped."

On April 8, the day the Shanley documents hit the papers, Law drove north, to Maine, to preside over the funeral of a bishop. Copies of the *Globe* and *Herald* were on the car seat next to him, but he didn't read them. Returning to Boston the next night, Law learned about the outrage the Shanley documents had caused. According to one of his principal advisers, Law initially wanted to release a statement criticizing the press coverage of the Shanley story. But after a conference call with advisers outside the Church, Law decided to say nothing. Before hanging up, the cardinal asked them to report back to him the next day with their recommendations on whether he should resign.

The next day, the advisers told Law that he needed to step down, that he had lost his ability to lead the archdiocese. One tried to let him down gently, saying it was unfortunate and perhaps even unfair, but that his resignation was now the best way to begin restoring confidence in the Church.

But Law wanted a second opinion. He said he would decide on his future the next day, after conferring with his "college of consultors," composed of his six bishops and a handful of trusted priests. The members of the college serve at the pleasure of the cardinal, and they were, in effect, being asked to decide not just his fate, but most likely their own. Not surprisingly, they told him to stay on and tough it out. Law called his secular advisers and told them he was going to consult with the papal nuncio, the Pope's ambassador in Washington. The *Globe* reported that Law informed the papal nuncio that he thought he should resign, but that the cardinal was asked not to submit his resignation until the Pope and his top aides could deliberate on how to proceed.

The next day, April 12, Cardinal Law left Boston for Rome. That was not unusual. The cardinal sat on any number of important Vatican committees and traveled to Rome almost monthly. But Law's route was unusual. Instead of going to Logan Airport, just ten miles and a half hour from the chancery, Law drove more than two hundred miles and five hours to Newark International Airport. He did not want to be seen. There had been an outcry after the Shanley documents were unsealed. Public anger was growing. The cardinal's movements were becoming increasingly furtive. He was avoiding the press, he was avoiding the demonstrators who now dogged him regularly, he was avoiding just about everyone.

In a statement, the cardinal later acknowledged that he had gone to see the Pope and other Vatican officials, adding, "The focus of my meetings was the impact of the Shanley and other sexual abuse cases upon public opinion in general, and specifically upon the members of the archdiocese. The fact that my resignation has been proposed as necessary was part of my presentation."

Law was vague on whether he had offered to resign, or whether the Pope refused to accept his resignation. Vatican scholars believe the Pope was wary of letting Law step down, fearing it would establish a precedent that would apply to other cardinals and bishops who were complicit in keeping predatory priests within reach of their victims. The fear of a domino effect, some argued, was keeping Law from falling.

But there were indications that Law's peers, the other twelve American cardinals, were getting antsy. Publicly, some offered words of support. Privately, however, some seemed to think that Law's resignation might reduce the heat the entire Church was feeling. On April 15, with Law still secretly ensconced in the Vatican, the Pope called the American cardinals to Rome for a two-day meeting about the sexual abuse of minors by priests.

Law slipped back into Boston unnoticed to prepare for the meeting. When he returned to Rome several days later to join the other cardinals, his peers traveled in first class, but Cardinal Law settled for coach. While the other cardinals traveled with entourages, he traveled with only an aide, Monsignor Paul McInerny, the director of Boston Catholic Television. As he wheeled his bag through the airport in Rome, Bernard Law looked more like a confounded tourist than a prince of the Church. He couldn't find an exit. It was a task made all the more difficult by the media horde that surrounded him. Law seemed startled by the number of reporters and by the fact that they were waiting for him at seven o'clock in the morning. At one point, the cardinal stumbled as the reporters closed in on him. He seemed rattled and exhausted. "My God," he said. "My God, you are all up awfully early." Law could not find his way out of the terminal, backtracking, looking for an exit, shadowed by the pack. A reporter helped direct Law to the exit, and once the exit was in sight, Law seemed to relax a bit.

"How'd the Red Sox do last night?" the cardinal asked. It was a moment that hearkened back to the old days, when Law would banter genially with the press. Someone told him the score. But there was no warmth in the exchange, and there was no hiding the tension.

The relationship between Cardinal Law and the other American cardinals had also changed. On the eve of the Rome meeting, the *Los Angeles Times* reported that one of the American cardinals had told the newspaper that some cardinals planned to ask Vatican officials to urge the Pope to ask for Law's resignation. The newspaper said a bishop had confirmed the account and added that a majority of U.S. bishops thought Law should resign quickly. Many suspected Cardinal Roger Mahony of Los Angeles was the source of the report. Weeks before, Mahony had spurned an opportunity to express support for Law, and he implicitly criticized Law, saying he would find it difficult to walk down the aisle of his church if he had been guilty of negligence. After the *Times* story appeared, the newspaper later quoted three other cardinals by name as saying Law should not resign, but Mahony was not quoted in his hometown paper about what he thought.

In Rome, Mahony was sensitive about suggestions he had stabbed a fellow cardinal in the back. When *Globe* reporter Charles Sennott jumped into an elevator with Mahony in Rome, Mahony denied he was the source of the damning report.

When asked if he thought Law should step down, Cardinal Mahony offered less than a ringing endorsement. "That," Mahony said, "is up to Cardinal Law and the Holy Father."

Most of the American cardinals stayed in the North American College compound and were pestered constantly by reporters. Law stayed in a place that was off-limits to the press: the Domus Sanctae Marthae, a comfortable hotel for visiting clergy in Vatican City, behind gates patrolled by the Swiss Guards. Ever defiant, Cardinal Egan, second only to Law in being embattled, stayed in a five-star hotel near the Pantheon. While the other cardinals were driven together in a minibus to the Apostolic Palace for the meetings, Law was shuttled to the sessions by himself.

Inside the Apostolic Palace, surrounded by the Pope and his peers, Law was humble and contrite. He also seemed very much alone. "In a sense, if I had not made the terrible mistakes that I made, we would not be here. I apologize for that," Law said, according to several who were in attendance.

When the two-day meeting broke up, the waiting reporters were told that all of the cardinals would appear before them to take questions. But only Cardinal Theodore McCarrick of Washington and Cardinal Francis George of Chicago showed up. The reporters wanted to question Law, but he had slipped away again.

The thought of his peers possibly abandoning him must have been crushing to Law, according to O'Connor, the Boston College historian. "The one thing that all the priests I interviewed agreed on was that Law was very compassionate and very sensitive when it came to visiting the sick and dying clergy in the hospital. And that compassion extended to their families. At a banquet once, somebody mentioned that a priest's mother had had a stroke, and Law turned to Monsignor McInerny and told him to drive him to the hospital. It was a genuine warmth and concern. He was the priest's priest. It is so ironic that Cardinal Law was unable or unwilling to express that same sense of compassion to the victims of sexual abuse, and that that failure was the reason that so many priests turned on him, that that blind spot was his downfall. I find his lack of compassion for the victims inexplicable because I don't see him as a man lacking compassion. It's just a blind spot of his. I don't know. He leaves me confused because he's capable of so much. How can a man with so much talent, so sophisticated in so many other areas, be so blind?"

* * *

Back from Rome, again in the sanctuary of his compound, Cardinal Law got back to business. His humility, so in evidence in Rome among his peers, was nowhere on display as he engaged an angry and increasingly empowered laity. He had his top aide send out a letter to priests, cracking down on a proposed association of parish councils. In Law's view, the idea of a coalition of laypeople working together on common problems facing the Church was "superfluous and potentially divisive." Laypeople should express their desires to change the Church "within the hierarchical structure of the Church." In other words, sit down and shut up.

"It's astounding to me that this Church seems to be so afraid of dialogue with its own members, people who love it and who would give almost anything to see the Church get back on track," said David Zizik, a parish council leader whose idea it was to bring other councils together in a coalition.

If it was any consolation to laypeople like Zizik, Law wasn't being any easier on priests who were trying to band together to fill the vacuum created by the sexual abuse crisis, which had virtually silenced Law in speaking out on issues of social justice and morality. Law's auxiliary bishops began summoning the leaders of a nascent priests' alliance in an apparent effort to exert some control over the group. The message was clear: dissent will not be tolerated.

According to canon law specialists, the cardinal was fully within his rights to crush potential dissent. But his timing, so soon after his humiliation in Rome, did little to suggest that a man whose arrogance was cited by critics as a leading cause of the predicament he now found himself in had truly changed.

And for all the apologies, for all the expressions of deep regret to the victims of sexual abuse, Law seemed as though he still didn't get it when it came to taking their feelings into account. In his first legal response to charges that Shanley had molested a six-year-old boy, Law's defense included the assertion that the boy and his parents contributed to the abuse by being negligent.

Carmen Durso, a Boston lawyer who represents victims of priests, said that using such insensitive language, however much it was legalese, betrayed arrogance, ignorance, or both. "From the start, the archdiocese has been incredibly stupid in the way they have handled this crisis," said Durso. "And as hard as it was to do, they have managed to make things worse."

Rodney Ford, whose son was six when Shanley allegedly raped him for the first time, was almost speechless in his rage. Two weeks later, the archdiocese reneged on its earlier agreement to pay eighty-six of Geoghan's victims. The victims' lawyer, Mitchell Garabedian, called the cardinal "a despicable human being."

Judge Constance Sweeney ordered Law's immediate deposition, saying the Vatican might transfer him to Rome so he could avoid questions from the lawyers representing Geoghan's victims. On May 8, Law became the first cardinal questioned under oath for actions taken as a prince of the Church. It was as humiliating a moment as any he had endured. Law was smuggled into the underground garage of the Suffolk County Courthouse in a car with darkly tinted windows and used a back elevator to avoid the myriad cameras in the lobby. But some photographers captured Law moving quickly from the elevator to the closed courtroom where he was questioned. It was for all intents and purposes a perp walk. During the first day of questioning, Law said he could not recall any of the critical events surrounding his 1984 decision to send Geoghan to St. Julia's after abruptly removing him from St. Brendan's for molesting children. He said he had expected his top aides to handle the particulars involving a troublesome priest like Geoghan.

So as the victims seethed, and the demonstrators gathered outside his residence, Law soldiered on, rarely leaving his compound. When he did, to say Mass at the cathedral, the demonstrators followed him.

On TV, local-boy-made-good Jay Leno kept the jokes coming on the *Tonight Show*. "Tomorrow night, a very, very special edition of *E.R.*," Leno intoned. "Doctors in Boston desperately try to remove Cardinal Law's foot from his mouth."

If he was watching, His Eminence probably wasn't laughing.

8

Sex and the Church

From the time Peter Isely was seven years old, he knew he was to be his family's contribution to the Roman Catholic priesthood. One of six boys in a devoutly Catholic family in rural Fond du Lac County, Wisconsin, he saw his future on an isolated rise in nearby Mount Calvary, at a small seminary that had been founded by a pair of Capuchin friars in 1857.

His early model for life in the priesthood was his local parish's monsignor, an intimidating figure who would announce from his pulpit the names of parishioners whose weekly collection contributions he deemed insufficient. "I remember being out in the parking lot of the parish," Isely said. "He takes my hand in his gnarled hand — like a stone figure — and he looks straight at me. This is like God looking at me. And he said, 'Peter, you will be a priest.'"

Isely's mother liked the idea; it was understood that young Peter would be the Isely family's seminarian. And for a time, he was.

At the age of thirteen, Isely headed up that hill to St. Lawrence Seminary, which prepared adolescent boys for the rigors of college-level seminary study. Isely can still remember his boyhood bravado about the school's patron saint. "Saint Lawrence's claim to fame was that as he was being martyred — roasted alive — they asked him if he had any last words and he said: 'Turn me over on the other side.'" True or not, it was the kind of story that schoolboys liked. Rev. Gale Leifeld was gregarious, jolly — the sort of "neato" priest that could talk to a young kid without condescension. He taught modern history, and the pupils were drawn to him. And Leifeld took a special liking to young Peter Isely — too special, as it turned out. One day, Leifeld called Isely into his office. The class was preparing for its first oral exam, and the priest said he wanted to make sure his favorite student was ready. Leifeld leaned back in the chair behind his table, puffed away on his pipe, and asked Isely to give him the definition of *nationalism,* a concept the teacher had asked the students to memorize. "I gave it to him word-for-word and he leaned forward and said, 'No,'" Isely recounted in an interview years later. "I was so naive and so trusting I became completely confused and disoriented. I froze. He came up from his chair and came around and began massaging my shoulder. I had not a clue. What it felt like was that my head was being pumped with gas and my body was being pumped with gas. It was like anesthesia. He moved down my body, into my pants, and began fondling me. Then he stopped, like nothing happened." Leifeld fondled Isely several more times, Isely said, before the student learned to stay away from the popular teacher. Isely suffered a dramatic weight loss, a sleep disorder, and a sharp decline in his grades. Leifeld, who was eventually sent for extensive treatment to the Servants of the Paraclete center in New Mexico, never admitted his abuse of Isely, but in a 1994 deposition, he acknowledged abusing others. Isely blamed himself for the abuse. "I thought there was something in me that was so evil and I didn't know what it was that was making him do this," he said.

Why did Leifeld abuse seminarians? Was there an aspect of his character that made him desire adolescent boys? Was there something in the clerical culture that enabled or even encouraged such behavior? Leifeld has taken his own theories to his grave. And Isely, a psychotherapist who ran a Wisconsin treatment program for victims of clergy sexual abuse in the 1990s, isn't sure. "What he was doing, in his mind, I think, was some kind of initiation into a special experience of love," Isely said. "I was a boy who needed love and this was what love was to him. But it was really all coercion, force, and terror for me."

Long after the lawsuits are settled, the new policies are enacted, and names like *Geoghan* and *Shanley* have faded into the recesses of memory, scholars of the Church and human psychology will still be debating what happened in the second half of the twentieth century, when, it now seems clear, more than fifteen hundred priests sexually abused many thousands of minors who had been entrusted to their care. The debate is freighted with ideology — progressives are quick to blame celibacy and clericalism, while traditionalists are eager to fault homosexuality and sexual permissiveness. And, as is often true, an argument can be made that each of those factors played a role in some cases, with each abuser having his own story, and with no easy explanation in sight. "It's a great question, why do priests act out sexually against minors, and the answer is far more complex than saying it's just a reflection of society in general," said A. W. Richard Sipe, the monk-turned-psychotherapist. "People don't like to deal with multifactored realities, but this is a multifactored reality. It's not just one thing. You have to understand that the priesthood is a powerful, enduring, beautiful, productive culture that has a very, very dark side."

Social science has had little to say about the abuse of minors by priests — neither the Church itself nor academics who study mental health have undertaken a rigorous quantitative study that would shed some light on the frequency or nature of this startling phenomenon. But in the wake of relentless revelations about sexually abusive priests, even the most conservative defenders of the Church have abandoned the argument that the priesthood is no worse than any other profession in which adults work with children. "At the end of the day, this problem is more than a few rotten apples," said William Donohue, the Catholic League for Religious and Civil Rights president. "This is very big. I don't think this is a time for Catholics to become defensive. You can love the institution, and at the same time understand the need to get this out." Even in the absence of hard data, it seemed increasingly clear that, although clergy from every religious denomination have sexually violated children, no major denomination has had a problem of the scale that has plagued the Catholic Church. "There are absolutely no Protestant equivalents," said Anson D. Shupe, a professor of sociology at Indiana University–Purdue University in Fort Wayne who researches clergy misconduct. "If I could find some spectacular cases, that would help my career, but I can't. You don't have rapacious serial predators, and the Protestant establishment doesn't tolerate it the way the Catholic establishment has."

Catholic Church officials are also now acknowledging a characteristic of sexual abuse by priests that differentiates it from other kinds of child sexual abuse: the majority of victims are teenage, post-pubescent, and male. Some researchers were using a new term, *ephebophilia,* to differentiate this phenomenon from pedophilia, the attraction to pre-pubescent children. "Almost all the cases involved adolescents and therefore were not cases of true pedophilia," the American cardinals declared in a joint communiqué issued after their April 2002 meeting at the Vatican.

Part of the explanation for the high incidence of sexual abuse by priests seems to lie in the culture of the priesthood itself, a lonely profession that confers upon its members prestige and — at least in the years before the current crisis exploded — plenty of access to young children, especially young boys. "It has always been welcome to parents when they see a priest taking a boy to a ball game, or hunting or fishing or camping — the priest acts as a chaperone as well as companion — and conventionally, people have not raised an eyebrow," said Rev. James J. Gill, a Jesuit priest and physician who directs the Christian Institute for the Study of Human Sexuality at the Catholic Theological Union in Chicago. "If a priest is taking a girl off for walks or swimming or any of these social or athletic events, there is some question. I think parents are a little more skeptical about turning girls unreservedly over to the priest for companionship." And Sipe called the priesthood a "homosocial culture. All the values within the culture are male, and the reason there has been such a tolerance across the board of sexual activity by priests or bishops is that there is a boys-will-be-boys atmosphere. It's kind of a spiritual fraternity — like a college fraternity, but with a spiritual aura around it." Like many who have spent time in the clerical culture, a former Boston seminarian, Edward Cardoza, points to the twin factors of power and access. "The priesthood is a profession where you can find yourself around an incredible number of children, very quickly, and it is a profession that immediately grants you a certain amount of respect and standing in the community. If you have access to a vulnerable group like children, and you are able to come in as a person with power, you can really cause harm. It is a dangerous formula for havoc."

Church insiders, who as recently as 2001 would routinely shrug off clergy sexual abuse as no different from sexual abuse by a Boy Scout leader or a teacher, are increasingly adopting a more shaded view that acknowledges some unusual aspects of the Catholic clergy. "I think there were a lot of factors," said Rev. Christopher J. Coyne, an instructor at St. John's Seminary in Boston. "The most simplistic answer is that it happened because some men didn't embrace the life of the priest to which they were called. But why did that happen? If you look back at the fifties, for example, the number of men accepted into seminaries, without rigorous screening, was very high, and as you move all these men along in large classes, some are going to fall through the cracks. And then there was a second aspect: there was not recognition of the need to deal with issues of intimacy and sexuality. There were all kinds of euphemisms. And if you entered seminary as an adolescent, and had never had an opportunity to acknowledge who you were sexually, never got into a position of healthy relationships with others, then when you leave, to whom do you relate? Adolescents. And that caused all kinds of wreckage."

The most obvious distinction between priests and other men is the vow of celibacy, and many critics are quick to charge that celibacy, as well as the Catholic Church's general discomfort with talking about sex, contributes to a clerical culture in which some men choose children as an outlet for their sexual desire. But Church officials point out that most child sexual abuse occurs at the hands of married men, and there are no studies suggesting that celibacy actually causes sexual abuse.

In the spring of 2002, another factor came to dominate the debate over what causes clergy sexual abuse: homosexuality. The debate generally produced more heat than light — although it seems clear that there are a disproportionately high number of gay men in the priesthood, and a disproportionately high number of adolescent boys among victims, no one can be sure whether there is any causal link between those two factors. Most gay priests, like most straight priests, don't abuse children; some straight priests, like some gay priests, get sexually involved with adolescent boys. Scholars say there is no evidence about how — or whether — the misconduct of gay priests with adolescent boys differs from that of the gay male population in general. Nor, they said, do gay and straight adults appear to have different patterns of involvement with adolescents or younger children. "There is no evidence that an adult gay male is any more likely to seek out a boy for sexual activities than that an adult heterosexual man would seek out a little girl for sexual activities," said Dr. Fred S. Berlin, founder of the National Institute for the Study, Prevention and Treatment of Sexual Trauma in Baltimore. Asked why the vast majority of the victims are boys, Berlin echoed Gill's observation: "People have probably had the sense that if you have an adult male in the presence of teenage girls, there is probably a need for a chaperone and that presumably decreases the risk of something going on. Perhaps there is an assumption that an adolescent male in the presence of a priest doesn't need to be chaperoned. But we don't have statistics about any of these disorders. . . . We don't have anything to turn to."

Despite the lack of data, Church officials seemed increasingly concerned about the role of homosexuality in the priesthood. As the crisis in the Church tore through dioceses around the nation, the Pope was initially silent. But by early March, as the unrelenting scandal grew, the pontiff's spokesman could no longer avoid directly addressing the issue. And when he did, his remarks would jangle this rawest nerve in the clergy sexual abuse crisis. "People with these inclinations just cannot be ordained," the spokesman, a Spanish psychiatrist named Dr. Joaquin Navarro-Valls, declared to the *New York Times,* referring to gay priests. "That does not imply a final judgment on people with homosexuality. But you cannot be in this field."

Navarro-Valls's comments were swiftly and predictably condemned by many scholars and gay rights groups, which accused the Vatican of trying to shift blame. "The Christian response would be to make meaningful restitution to the victims, cooperate with law enforcement to bring perpetrators to justice, and learn how to prevent future abuse," said Mary Louise Cervone, president of Dignity/USA, the nation's oldest and largest group of gay Catholics. "Instead, they are trying to make gay priests the scapegoats for decades of criminal abuse." Some raised a more practical concern, arguing that if Rome really wanted to empty seminaries of gay men — a proposal under consideration at the Vatican — it would face more empty rectories and more barren altars. Some Church experts estimate that from 30 percent to fully one half of the forty-five thousand U.S. priests are gay. "If they were to eliminate all those who were homosexually oriented, the number would be so staggering that it would be like an atomic bomb. It would do the same damage to the Church's operation," Sipe said. "And it's very much against the tradition of the Church. Many saints had a gay orientation. And many popes had gay orientations. Discriminating against orientation is not going to solve the problem."

But the issue was now on the table. At the Vatican meeting, Bishop Wilton D. Gregory of Belleville, Illinois, president of the U.S. Conference of Catholic Bishops, told reporters that he was concerned about the increasing number of gays in the priesthood. "One of the difficulties we do face in seminary life or recruitment is when there does exist a homosexual atmosphere or dynamic that makes heterosexual men think twice" about joining the priesthood for fear that they'll be harassed. "It is an ongoing struggle. It is most importantly a struggle to make sure that the Catholic priesthood is not dominated by homosexual men [and] that the candidates that we receive are healthy in every possible way — psychologically, emotionally, spiritually, intellectually." And Cardinal Adam J. Maida of Detroit argued that clergy sexual abuse is "not truly a pedophilia-type problem but a homosexual-type problem. . . . We have to look at this homosexual element as it exists, to what extent it is operative in our seminaries and our priesthood and how to address it." Bishops need to "cope with and address" the extent of a homosexual presence in Catholic seminaries, he said. Cardinal Anthony J. Bevilacqua of Philadelphia said he wouldn't let gay men become priests.

"We feel that a person who is homosexually oriented is not a suitable candidate for the priesthood even if he has never committed any homosexual act," he said.

For several decades, the Catholic Church's main approach to priests who were sexually abusive to children was to send them off for treatment at one of a handful of psychiatric centers with close ties to the Church.

Rev. Jay M. Mullin was one of those priests. Ordained in 1969, Mullin had been in ministry for twenty-three years when Rev. John B. McCormack, then Cardinal Law's chief lieutenant for clergy personnel matters and now the bishop of Manchester, New Hampshire, summoned the priest to the chancery. Mullin was anxious on the drive into Boston, and with good reason. A man had accused Mullin of molesting him twenty years earlier, when the accuser was a teenager and Mullin was a new priest in Allston, a working-class neighborhood of Boston. Even though Mullin denied the allegation, he agreed to contribute $10,000 to an archdiocesan out-of-court settlement with his accuser, and the archdiocese removed him from his parish and told him he could not return until he spent time in one of the psychiatric hospitals at which the Catholic Church had spent millions to quietly treat accused sexual predators.

So in late 1992, Mullin's ticket to treatment brought him to the St. Luke Institute, a Catholic psychiatric hospital in suburban Maryland. Named for the patron saint of physicians, it was founded by Rev. Michael Peterson, a Washington doctor who was gay and who died of AIDS in 1987. For several days there, Mullin observed some of the Church's attempts to treat sexually abusive priests with one-on-one therapy, sex addiction support groups, and a device with a mercury ring, jokingly called a "peter meter," that measured a man's level of sexual arousal based on the circumference of his penis. "You go into this room with the doctor, who is from Johns Hopkins, and you get into a blue johnny. And he wants you to masturbate so that they can get a penis size," Mullin recalled. "And then, for the next hour or so, they show you pornographic images. They show male and female. They showed female with a female. A male with a male. In various age levels from people in their twenties and thirties. I'm alone in the room. They're observing me. They're videotaping it. And they have the instrumentation. They finish up with kiddie porn — my first introduction to the whole pornographic industry. It was not a joy."

For several decades before priests like Geoghan propelled clergy sexual abuse into a crisis, the Catholic Church saw places like St. Luke as one of their best defenses against recidivist rapists. The Maryland center, and counterparts like the Servants of the Paraclete centers, run by a religious order in Jemez Springs and St. Louis; the secular Institute of Living in Hartford; and the Catholic-run Southdown Institute in Ontario, took out ads in the remote advertising space of religious journals. The bishops shipped them their most troubled priests. Psychiatrists evaluated the priests, sent reports estimating the risk of relapse to supervising bishops, and then frequently returned them to their ministry. That process was costly — Sipe has estimated the Church spent $50 million on treatment over twenty-five years. And there was a human cost, too — some priests, like Geoghan, reoffended even after multiple visits to multiple centers. Critics charge that the Church tried to use psychology as a cover: priests got short-term treatment and were returned to parishes, in some cases despite psychological recommendations that they have no further contact with children. Victims, especially those who were molested by priests who had been in treatment, wonder bitterly now why the Church used its own treatment centers.

"No institution can police itself," said David Clohessy, national director of the Survivors Network of those Abused by Priests. "If the Church wants to restore trust, leaders should be more open about these treatment facilities. If chemical companies said, 'Just trust us — send us your dioxins; we'll clean them up,' the public would be wary."

The treatment centers had been born in a rush of Christian compassion. On a blustery night during the depths of the depression, Rev. Gerald Fitzgerald heard a knock on the back door of his rectory in the Brighton section of Boston. He gave food and a coat to a beggar who, as he walked into the dark, turned around and said that he, too, was once a priest. That was the genesis of the Servants of the Paraclete, a religious order whose mission was to care for troubled priests. In 1947, Fitzgerald opened the Jemez Springs retreat for troubled or alcohol-abusing priests; sexual misconduct was not part of the mission then. When Fitzgerald was asked about treating child molesters, his idea was to buy a small Caribbean island and isolate them there, according to Rev. Peter Lechner, servant general of the Servants of the Paraclete. By the mid-1960s, though, the Paraclete retreat began welcoming an increasing number of pedophiles and, more commonly, ephebophiles.

Throughout the 1960s, sexual disorders were treated with psycho-analysis in secular institutions — an approach now discredited — and the Paracletes lagged behind even in that. It wasn't until the 1970s that Jemez Springs began to "approach modern standards," Lechner said. It adopted regular therapy and employed an in-house psychiatrist. In 1976, the Paracletes opened the first treatment center in the world for psychosexual disorders. By 1995, psychiatrist Jay Feierman had consulted with a thousand priests about sexual disorders. "They knew more than anybody in the world," said Sylvia M. Demarest, the Dallas attorney who later represented victims of Jemez Springs patients. A *Rocky Mountain News* reporter who spent a week at the center in 1987 described an atmosphere that encouraged emotional exploration. Priests there had psychodrama therapy and role-playing. They wept together. Therapists encouraged them not to repress sexual impulses. Dr. Feierman, the program's chief psychiatrist, complained about the Church's message that a priest is "not allowed to be affectionate, he's not allowed to be in love, he's not allowed to be a sexual being." Officials at the Paraclete Center made the final decision about whether a priest was ready to return to ministry — but later some of those decisions would look like terrible mistakes. Of the two thousand priests who were treated at Jemez Springs from 1947 to 1968, Lechner said ten committed criminal acts after leaving. Among the "graduates" from the 1960s and 1970s were men accused of long lists of molestations, like James R. Porter, Jason Sigler, Rudy Kos, and David Holley — some of whom molested children when the Paracletes sent them out on weekends to officiate in local parishes. In 1993, the Paraclete center was forced to pay

$525,000 and set aside $7.6 million more from insurers to settle lawsuits with twenty-five plaintiffs who said they were attacked by Porter. They also settled with seventeen plaintiffs suing Holley, who is serving a 275-year sentence for molesting children. Bruce Pasternack, a lawyer who defended alleged victims in the Porter case, said the treatment center made New Mexico the world's "dumping ground for ecclesiastical waste." Demarest, who represented Kos's victims, still speaks with contempt of the treatment Kos received. "I can tell you what the atmosphere was. They flew in fresh fish and special food items and they went on hikes in the mountains and they were released over the weekend into local parishes, where they continued to abuse children," said Demarest. "There is not one single shred of evidence that anyone gave one whit about the victims." The Paraclete fathers shut down the sexual disorders treatment center in New Mexico in 1994. They would not rebuild it.

In 1981, a new kind of priest set about building a new kind of treatment center on the East Coast. Michael Peterson was a psychiatrist before he converted to Catholicism and entered the priesthood. An experienced substance abuse counselor, he founded the St. Luke Institute with alcohol treatment in mind. But by the mid-1980s, patients were joined by an increasing number of priests who had been accused of sexual misconduct. As patients like Geoghan, Kos, Gilbert Gauthé, and Monsignor Michael Harris moved in next door, the neighbors were told that they were "in training," said Nannie Presley, who lived across the street for fourteen years.

The relationship between the Church and its doctors was shaken by the priest abuse scandals in the mid-1990s. Minneapolis psychologist Gary R. Schoener remembered receiving a telephone call from a rattled John R. Roach, then Archbishop of St. Paul–Minneapolis. Roach wanted Schoener to review records the archdiocese had received from the centers that had been treating priests: the St. Luke Institute, the now-defunct House of Affirmation, and the Servants of the Paraclete in New Mexico. "The archbishop said, 'For God's sake, are we getting bad advice?'" Schoener recalled. "Are they using the wrong tests? Are they misinterpreting them? Is one of the centers better than the others?" Schoener reported back a few weeks later. He had been impressed by the psychiatric reports, and he said they would pass muster in secular hospitals. But he faulted the centers for accepting the Church's investigations at face value. They failed to contact victims. They left responsibility for follow-up to the priest's diocese. In short, the psychiatrists saw the Church as their boss. And, Schoener concluded, they wanted the boss to like them. "The mindset of these folks was to get him back there, that somehow the guy was fixable," said Schoener. "They are a key part of the mistake. It's not that I don't blame the Church. I blame them both."

Attorney Demarest said Church officials misused the treatment centers. "I don't think it's fair to blame the therapeutic community for problems," she said. "The issue was not what they were doing but whether the bishops were listening. That's what the problem is. The bishops were the ones putting these men back in circulation." And in March 2002, psychiatrists at the Institute of Living in Hartford charged that Church leaders intentionally disregarded their clinical advice — with sometimes-disastrous results. The institute, a secular psychiatric hospital situated on a leafy thirty-five-acre campus, had developed a specialized program for treating clergy and had been seeing a handful of priests every year. Cardinal Edward M. Egan had pointed to the institute's psychiatric reports as the justification to return priests to the ministry; some of them swiftly reoffended. Top psychiatrists at the institute quickly fired back at Egan. They told the *Hartford Courant* that Church leaders had used psychiatrists' advice as cover to rush potentially dangerous priests back into ministry. "I found that they rarely followed our recommendations," said Leslie M. Lothstein, director of psychology at the institute. "They would put [priests] back into work where they still had access to vulnerable populations." Lothstein's comments marked a new chapter — and a clear break — in the relationship between the Church and psychiatrists.

In Mullin's case, psychologists were unable to determine the validity of the accusation against him. In their confidential report, written in November 1992, the psychologists said that Mullin acknowledged loaning his car to his accuser, "rubbing his back while tutoring him, twisting his nipples while horsing around, going on an overnight trip to the

Berkshires, telling him he loved him, and making him the beneficiary of his life insurance policy for a period of time." Mullin said his behavior may have been immature, but not sexual. "Father Mullin has consistently denied both sexual activity with and sexual interest in boys," read the report, which Mullin willingly shared with a *Globe* reporter a decade after the traumatic treatment. "However, we believe that the behaviors he does acknowledge, such as twisting the boy's nipples, are cause for significant concern. We believe that most people would describe such behavior between an adult and a boy [as] at least inappropriate and probably sexual in nature." After his treatment, Mullin was in limbo for some time, but six years later he won assignment to a church in Wayland, Massachusetts.

On a frosty Cape Cod evening in 2002, Mullin sat in the front room of his small, quiet home wearing a cardigan sweater pulled tight against the raw chill of late winter. His large frame filled an easy chair bathed in low-watt lamplight as he calmly discussed the details of how his clerical career unraveled. He viewed the existence of St. Luke as evidence of the Church's concern, saying, "I wasn't aware there was anyplace like that. Seeing all of it, I thought, the bishops know where they're sending all of us. They know the magnitude of the problem." But he never saw his own behavior as part of that problem. "It was just one of those game-type things that adolescent, immature people sometimes do. . . . It was not a sexual-interest type of a thing."

For years — presumably for centuries — the Church simply did not talk about sex with future priests. Seminarians were on their own to figure out what it meant to lead a life of permanent chastity, and many struggled. "There was nothing," recalled Rev. Robert W. Bullock, who finished his training at St. John's Seminary in Boston in 1956. "We didn't talk at all. And then we emerged from this highly male, controlled situation into a very different kind of world, and that transition, for a lot of people, was harrowing. Looking back, I would have wished we were better prepared."

Some seminaries offered experiences that seem to reinforce the notion of a Church deeply uneasy with sex. Writer Paul Hendrickson attended a seminary in Alabama, where for five years, from the time he was fifteen until he was twenty, he would routinely visit his spiritual director for what was supposed to be instruction in managing sexual desire. "I did so, more or less willingly, in the name of conquering impure temptation," Hendrickson, the author of *Seminary: A Search,* wrote. "It was his idea, his proscription, his scenario. Sometimes it happened weekly. Sometimes it happened in the middle of the night. Sometimes it happened just before study period, or after evening colloquy, or when I had just come up from the gym. I'd go in, sit in a green chair beside his desk, unzipper my pants, take up a crucifix (it was called the Missionary Cross, and it had a tarnished green skull and bones at the base of the nailed savior's feet), begin to think deliciously about impure things, and then, at the point of full erection, begin to recite all of the reasons that I wished to conquer my baser self and longings. 'Father, I'm ready now,' I'd say. Having taken myself at his prompting to a ledge of mortal sin, I was now literally and furiously talking myself down, with the power of the crucified Jesus in my left hand. My director was always there, guiding me, urging me, praying with me."

But in 1992, there were two events, one official and one unofficial, that dramatically transformed the way the Catholic Church thought about the training of future priests. The first was an order from the Pope to overhaul seminary education to include franker discussion of sexuality and celibacy. The second was the case of Father Porter, in which the intense media coverage of the serial pedophile from the Diocese of Fall River, Massachusetts, became a major topic of discussion among priests.

In March of that year, Pope John Paul II issued an apostolic exhortation, *Pastores Dabo Vobis,* instructing the bishops of the world to overhaul their seminary programs in light of "the circumstances of the present day." Those circumstances included a persistent lack of candidates for the priesthood and the concomitant rise in clergy burnout. "Priests who have been actively involved in the ministry for a more or less lengthy period of time seem to be suffering today from an excessive loss of energy in their ever increasing pastoral activities," the Pope wrote. "Likewise, faced with the difficulties of contemporary culture and society, they feel compelled to re-examine their way of life and their pastoral priorities, and they are more and more aware of their need for ongoing formation."

"Formation" is Church-speak for education, training, and character development, and the Pope insisted that seminaries be restructured to focus on four areas of formation for new priests: human, intellectual, pastoral, and spiritual. The Pope placed a special emphasis on human formation, which he called "the basis of all priestly formation." And a key component of that formation of a priest as a person was clearly understanding his own sexuality. "Of special importance is the capacity to relate to others," the Pope wrote. "In this context affective maturity, which is the result of an education in true and responsible love, is a significant and decisive factor in the formation of candidates for the priesthood." And the Pope declared that in an era when sexuality "is reduced to nothing more than a consumer good," seminaries must be particularly attentive. "An education for sexuality becomes more difficult but also more urgent," the Pope said. "It should be truly and fully personal and therefore should present chastity in a manner that shows appreciation and love for it."

Even as seminaries were putting the Pope's orders into action, the Porter case began to focus broad attention on the issue of clergy sexual abuse, especially in Massachusetts. Seminaries began tightening their admissions requirements and watching seminarians more closely.

"In ninety-two, when the Porter case hit the seminary, the seminary didn't know how to proceed, but they knew whatever they were going to do, they had to address these issues," recalled Edward Cardoza, the former seminarian at St. John's in Boston throughout much of the 1990s, who decided not to pursue ordination. "I remember one conference where the spiritual director got up and actually said, 'As terrible as this is for the Church, it may well prove to be a sanctifying moment.'" Seminarians attended monthly conferences to discuss human formation, talked about their personal lives with spiritual directors, and took a course on human sexuality taught by a nun. "You were taught that even when the charism of celibacy and chastity is present and embraced, the attractions, the impulses, the desires will still be present. So the first thing you need to do is be aware that you are a human being, and no matter how saintly or holy you are, you will never remove yourself from those passions. But the idea was making prudent choices. You just walk away. Celibacy is a radical call, and you've made a decision not to act on your desire."

Today, seminaries say they screen applicants rigorously. In Boston, for example, a young man must begin conversations with the vocations director a year before applying for admissions, and then the application process takes at least four months. Most seminaries require that applicants be celibate for as long as five years before starting the program, just to test out the practice, and students are expected to remain celibate throughout seminary as they continue to discern whether they are cut out to lead the sexless life of an ordained priest. Some seminaries screen out applicants who say they are sexually attracted to other men, but most do not, arguing that there is no evidence linking sexual orientation to one's ability to lead a celibate life. The seminaries attempt to weed out potential child abusers, running federal and local criminal background checks, but there is currently no psychological test that can accurately predict whether a man who has never sexually abused a child is likely to do so in the future. So seminary officials say that in the screening process, and throughout seminary training, they are alert to any sign that a man is not forming normal relationships with adults, or seems abnormally interested in children. Many potential applicants are turned away from seminaries, and every year some students are forced out. "Just because there's a shortage doesn't mean we should lessen our standards," said Rev. Edward J. Burns, executive director of the Secretariat for Vocations and Priestly Formation at the U.S. Conference of Catholic Bishops. "A man is dissected in many ways when he comes forward to apply to a seminary. There are psychological tests to assess the psychosexual maturity of the man, because it's important they have a real grasp of their own identity. Tests are given to show any type of psychosis or mental imbalance. We do bloodwork. And it's not just tests —

in seminary we live with them, and you get a clear indication of how a man lives out life. You can be sure that we're alert to any red flags."

Many current seminary officials acknowledge what now seems obvious: screening standards in the past were inadequate. "Everyone hearkens back to the glory days when the seminaries were packed, but I wonder how many of them were people who never should have been priests," said Rev. James King, director of vocations for the Indiana province of the Congregation of Holy Cross, the religious order that founded the University of Notre Dame. "It was the popular thing to do, or a desirable thing to do, satisfying one's family. We're talking about people who were there when there was no awareness about the need to do any screening. You had people who were psychologically immature in an era when seminaries didn't have an idea about psychological screening." Today, as he sits across the desk from an aspiring priest, King said he looks not so much for the candidate with the highest test scores or most remarkable résumé or biggest collection of awards and achievements. He is looking for honesty. Someone who is genuine and straightforward. And he makes it a point to be clear that the priestly requirement for celibacy — a life without sexual activity of any kind, including masturbation — is not an ancillary part of the job. "The message pretty much is that celibacy is an absolute requirement," said King. "Everyone has urges. Married people have the same struggles fundamentally. They get to have sex, but they don't get to have sex with everybody else and still be faithful to their commitment. There isn't a person alive who isn't a sexual human being. But we have to manage it in healthy ways. In many ways, married people struggle with this as much as we do. Celibacy is a gift, but it's not something that most people are cut out for."

There is no magic trick to living a celibate life. Seminary instructors acknowledge that priests will have sexual feelings, but they encourage them not to put themselves in situations that heighten those feelings. They advise priests to pray for strength. And they frequently fall back on comparisons to married people, who the Church expects not to have sex with people other than their spouse, and single people, who, the Church teaches, should not have sex at all.

"I'll never forget when I was a vocation director, and a college student asked me, 'What do you do when you get an urge?' as if no one else would control it but a priest," Burns said. "Everyone is called to holiness, particularly in their sexual life. How do we manage our sexual desires? By being people of integrity, with respect for other people's sexuality, and for our own sexuality. Celibacy is a gift we give, in order to live out a service of life for others. It is a call from God. We are meant to be celibate men, working to build a Kingdom, here and now."

Today's seminarians are generally older than they once were, and seminary directors hope they are more mature. There are only nine high-school seminaries left in the country, and many men enter seminary only after they have completed college. Many have dated; some have been married. And dioceses now offer ongoing formation, a kind of continuing education for priests, to help newly ordained priests adjust to the challenges of living in a parish.

Of course, compliance is not universal. Some seminarians, and many priests, do violate their vows of celibacy, just as many married people violate their vows of monogamy.

Rev. Len Plazewski, director of vocations for the Diocese of St. Petersburg, Florida, has a recipe for a disciplined, healthy priesthood that he shares with the seminarians he supervises. It is a deceptively simple one. Have friends inside and outside of the priesthood, pals who don't feel the need to always address you as "Father." Take time to relax. God is important, but so are sports and the arts and a trip to the beach. Have hobbies or other distractions that don't make a celibate lifestyle more difficult to pursue. "Obviously, if my hobbies consisted of going to strip clubs and searching the Internet for pornography, those things are not going to help me live a celibate life. But there is no magic pill. . . . In a certain sense, I came to realize that the love of a single woman was not enough for me; that my call to love wasn't focused on a single person or a single family. Yes, I'm celibate. No, I'm not having sex. But I am loving. Love is an important part of my life."

Church officials repeatedly point to the fact that relatively few cases have emerged involving priests ordained during the 1990s as evidence that their new screening and training procedures are succeeding. But critics are skeptical, arguing that abusive priests will simply be more careful in the future not to attract attention. "I don't see this leadership having the ability from a moral or a human standpoint to be able to address this crisis," Demarest said. And there have been some recent cases: in January 2002, police in Haverhill, Massachusetts, arrested thirty-three-year-old Rev. Kelvin E. Iguabita, who had been ordained in 1999, and charged him with twice raping a fifteen-year-old girl in his parish rectory. Nonetheless, Plazewski is one of the optimists, those who believe the Church is now paying a price for past mistakes, but that things have improved. "The good news is that these [abuse] cases that we're dealing with now come from a time when the seminary system was not where it is now," he said. "A lot of effort has been made and that effort will bear fruit."

9

The Struggle for Change

The twelve U.S. cardinals who gathered in the Vatican's ornate Sala Bologna in the spring of 2002 were an unusual mix by most measures — a group of celibate men, with an average age of seventy-two, two of whom were themselves under fire for their failure to oust priests accused of sexually abusing minors. But they were the princes of the Church, men whose loyalty to the institution and its faith had earned them the red hats that symbolized their stature and influence, men who were now charged with correcting the course of a religion racked by scandal so great that even Cardinal Bernard Law, the man at the eye of the storm, had told worshipers it was "undermining the mission of the Catholic Church."

On the same late April day that the cardinals arrived in Vatican City for a presummit dinner, another gathering was taking place four thousand miles away, in the prosperous Boston suburb of Wellesley. There too a group of Catholics whose lives had been shaken by the sexual abuse crisis were gathering to talk about what they could do to help fix the problem. But instead of meeting in the tapestried halls of the Vatican's Palazzo Apostolico, these Catholics were assembling in the basement of a church school where each Monday night for three months they had been moving aside cafeteria tables to make room for a fast-growing group of heartbroken laypeople. These churchgoing suburbanites, many of them graduates of Catholic schools and colleges, had stuck with Catholicism all their lives despite disagreements over a variety of teachings, putting their money into the collection baskets and giving their time to the parish committees and enrolling their children in the parish schools. But now they were sitting in folding chairs on the linoleum floor at St. John the Evangelist School, beside a concrete-block wall decorated with paper letters spelling out their motto. On one side of a large cross, the letters spelled out the words KEEP THE FAITH. On the other side, the letters said CHANGE THE CHURCH.

Not since the heady days of the early 1960s, after Pope John XXIII summoned the world's bishops to Rome for the Second Vatican Council, has the future of Catholicism been more uncertain.

The crisis that began with the story of a pedophile priest opened a Pandora's box of grievances nursed by Catholics for decades: Homosexuality. The role of women. The nature of authority. Debates that had long taken place only at the margins of Church life suddenly seized center stage. Should married men, or women, be ordained as priests? Should laypeople play a greater role in governing the Church, including the selection of bishops and the assignment of priests? American Catholics struggled to understand what it was about their Church that had enabled more than fifteen hundred priests to molest minors and had caused numerous bishops to shuffle problem priests from parish to parish rather than fire them or turn them over to prosecutors.

Some Catholics began to predict a wave of change akin to that set off by the Protestant Reformation of the sixteenth century, when the Church's inability to rein in clerical corruption created an opening for Martin Luther to launch a broad theological critique that wound up splitting Western Christianity into Catholicism and Protestantism. Others speculated about some kind of geographic schism, in which U.S. Catholics would break from Rome. Neither scenario was given much credence by theologians, but even Pope John Paul II acknowledged that Catholicism might be forever changed by the events of 2002. "We must be confident that this time of trial will bring a purification of the entire Catholic community," he told the visiting U.S. cardinals in his sumptuous private library, "a purification that is urgently needed if the Church is to preach more effectively the Gospel of Jesus Christ in all its liberating force."

The first major call to arms was sounded by Mary Jo Bane, a professor of public policy at Harvard University's John F. Kennedy School of Government and a member of the parish council at her local church, St. William's, in the Dorchester section of Boston. Bane was no stranger to speaking out — she had drawn national attention by quitting her job as a high-ranking official in the Clinton administration to protest the president's support of a welfare reform measure that she saw as unfair to poor people. But previously she had relied on her Catholic social teaching to impel her lengthy career as a human services advocate and administrator; now she was relying on lessons learned in the secular arena to empower her to challenge her own Church. "I will give no money to the archdiocese until steps are taken to remedy structural and cultural flaws that created the current crisis," Bane declared in an op-ed piece. "I urge my fellow Catholics to do the same. Perhaps then the cardinal will pay attention to those of us who love the Church, who grieve for what has happened to it, but who hope for what it can become."

For many Catholics, the apparent coddling of priests who had molested minors stood in sharp contrast with the way they themselves had been treated as kids, threatened with eternal damnation for minor sins. "I remember back in the 1950s if you ate meat on Friday, did not wear a hat or veil to church, or ate breakfast before Communion, you could burn in hell for these sins," said one Catholic layman, Victor Conlogue. "How come there is no mention of Geoghan going to hell?"

Even worse, many saw evidence of astonishing hypocrisy. A Church that kept paychecks flowing to priests who raped children but cut off benefits to priests who married adult women. A Church that in many cases failed to oust priests who touched the genitals of little boys, violating their bodies and their souls, but that in 2000 fired and evicted the seventy-two-year-old baptizing nun, Jeannette Normandin, for touching water to the forehead of a baby. "I cannot imagine what is going through the mind of a cardinal who lets priests who change wine and bread into the Eucharist use those same hands to molest children," said a sixty-seven-year-old laywoman, Mary Leveck of San Antonio. "It is sinful of the cardinals and bishops who tried to cover this up."

For many, the clergy sexual abuse scandal was the final straw in their relationship with the Church hierarchy, a relationship that had been fraying for several generations as U.S. Catholics struggled to balance their American values of democracy and egalitarianism with their Catholic understanding of authority and clericalism. Thousands had simply left the Church — in some cases for other denominations; and in many cases for a life in spiritual exile, still culturally Catholic, but unwilling or unable to participate in the life of a Church whose politics they abhorred. Those who formed organizations to push for change were defined by Church leaders as marginal, fringe, even non-Catholic. In Boston, for example, Law barred Massachusetts Women-Church, a group advocating the ordination of women, from meeting on Church property — despite the fact that polls consistently showed that a sizable majority of U.S. Catholics support the ordination of women and the end of mandatory celibacy for priests.

Many scholars have argued that the Church's moral authority began seriously to erode in 1968, when Pope Paul VI, in the encyclical *Humanae Vitae*, reasserted the Church's opposition to the use of artificial birth control. That teaching has been widely ignored, and some argue that it opened the door for Catholics to reject other Church teachings, particularly on sexual matters, without abandoning their faith. The erosion of Catholic authority was aided by sociological factors as well; many Americans, regardless of faith, were according less deference to societal institutions and were increasingly determined to define their own sexual mores. In poll after poll, most Catholics acknowledged that they simply don't agree with Church teachings on birth control, divorce, premarital sex, and homosexuality, and many said they don't agree on abortion, either. Those disagreements led to a kind of religious cognitive dissonance, in which Catholics rejected and ignored the Church's teachings on matters of sexual ethics while embracing the Church's basic articulation of Catholic Christian faith and its rich liturgical practices.

American Catholics, of course, are also part of a larger American society that thrives on dissent, in which critics of corporations demand change through shareholder and public pressure and critics of government force change through the ballot box. In this context, the metaphor of bishops as shepherds and laypeople as sheep increasingly rang hollow. And the timing couldn't have been better for a lay-led transformation. Catholics, once a largely immigrant group in the United States, were now more highly educated and affluent than ever; as a result, they were increasingly confident in their ability to demand the same responsible roles in their Church as they held in other civic institutions. Vatican II, a gathering of the world's bishops from 1962 to 1965, had launched an era of reform in the Church most famously symbolized by the decisions to allow worship in vernacular languages, rather than in Latin, and to allow priests to face worshipers during prayer, rather than an altar along the rear wall of the sanctuary. Over the ensuing several decades, as the number of priests and nuns plummeted, laypeople took on increasingly important roles in the Church, often overseeing and administering parish churches, running Catholic schools and social service programs, and joining faculties of theology. One sign of the increasing importance of laypeople in the Church came in 2001, when Georgetown University, the oldest Catholic university in the United States, chose as its forty-eighth president John J. DeGioia, the first layman to head the venerable school founded in 1789 by a Catholic archbishop, John Carroll.

Not only has Catholic educational achievement been rising, but a growing minority of lay Catholics are also increasingly knowledgeable about the fundamentals of their own faith. In Boston, St. John's Seminary uses classrooms once intended for priests to train laypeople in theology and ministry. Many saw hope in Vatican II's promise that the *sensus fidelium,* the sense of the faithful, must be heard. "The holy people of God shares also in Christ's prophetic office," declares *Lumen Gentium,* the dogmatic constitution of the Church. "... The entire body of the faithful, anointed as they are by the Holy One, cannot err in matters of belief." That seemed clear to Catholics in the pews, if not to the cardinals who gathered at the Vatican.

Any doubt that the cries for reform had penetrated deep within the laity was erased March 9, 2002, the day of Law's annual convocation, a gathering of several thousand lay leaders from around the archdiocese, at the World Trade Center along Boston Harbor.

Many Catholics had been skeptical of the gathering, which was held under tight security, because the participants had been handpicked by parish priests. "Is Cardinal Law's March 9 convocation going to be a listening session, as touted, or a pep rally for Cardinal Law?" wondered one laywoman, Helene O'Brien of Acton, a suburb of Boston. But in a display of how the sexual abuse of minors by priests had galvanized local Catholics, many of the Church's top lay leaders told Law, to his face, that they wanted sweeping reforms of the Church's structure. The archdiocese refused to let reporters attend the six "listening" sessions, but those who were there said that Law appeared stunned by the anger directed at him — in remarks afterward, he acknowledged for the first time that many Catholics felt he had betrayed them. Some laypeople wore lavender ribbons to show their sorrow over the pain experienced by victims of abuse by priests. Others wore white buttons reading, "In Solidarity with Our Priest," in an effort to demonstrate the widespread concern parishioners were expressing about the psychological impact of the sexual abuse scandal on priests who were not abusers. A group of women from Wellesley wore red, which they said represented their penitence over their Church's conduct. "You've got a pretty outraged flock here," Paul A. Baier of Wellesley said that day. "And this is the core of the Church. These are three thousand hard-core believers willing to give up a Saturday, and if they're fifty to eighty percent pissed-off, you've got a problem."

Suddenly parish council members and religious education teachers were giving voice to concerns previously associated only with activist groups such as Call to Action, FutureChurch, and the Association for the Rights of Catholics in the Church. "We need to change the whole power structure of the Church," said Bonnie Ciambotti, a eucharistic minister and religious education teacher from Newton, an upscale suburb west of Boston. "We need more women. The power, and the male dominance, and the secrecy are how this whole thing started."

"In a strange way, this whole situation has really empowered Catholic people and priests at the parish level," said Patricia Casey, a member of the parish council at her church, St. Ignatius Loyola, in Newton. "I think we've kind of crossed a line, and I don't think we're going to go back. People will be asking, when we get together next year, 'What has changed in the Church because of this?' That's the question of the day." Another participant, Jane Audrey-Neuhauser, said, "What is significant about this call for renewal and reform is that it does not come from a splinter group outside of Catholic worship but from the leaders, workers, and priests within the parishes of the archdiocese."

Among the more radical proposals floated at the sessions were calls for a Third Vatican Council, and a suggestion that a coadjutor bishop be appointed in Boston to administer the archdiocese while Law would be required to focus full-time on protecting children. One speaker said the Church needed to make major changes to head off another Reformation. "What came across is that this is a very articulate, well educated, and deeply affected group of people who are going to say the truth," said Rev. Robert J. Bowers, pastor of St. Catherine of Siena's in the Charlestown section of Boston. "You're seeing loyalty at its very best. These people are going to love the Church into something else, into a new birth."

Law said he got the message. "I have heard you passionately and prayerfully plead for greater openness in the Church . . . [and] I have heard calls for greater and more meaningful involvement of the laity in the life of the Church, and specifically of women in the life of the Church," he said. "I don't have the answers today for all the things that I have heard. . . . I have heard a great deal. And I need and I want . . . to really take in what you have offered." But a month later, as he outlined his goals for the meeting in Rome, Law didn't mention the word *women,* and as soon as the meeting ended, he ordered a crackdown on the most mainstream lay organization to spring up from the crisis, a proposed association of parish councils that Law warned might be divisive.

Dr. James E. Muller could still recall the Gregorian chants echoing from behind the black curtains of the Carmelite monastery of his Indiana childhood, when he served as an altar boy while his uncle said Mass. In his mind's eye, he could see his uncle Paul, the pastor of a large Indianapolis parish, and his aunt Lea, a Sister of Charity who served as vice president of Mount Saint Joseph College in Ohio. He could hear his Catholic teachers, at Joan of Arc grade school and Cathedral High School in Indianapolis; at the University of Notre Dame, where he and his brothers and his father and his uncles went, and where he later sent his son; and at Georgetown University, where he did graduate work. He could cite *Pacem in Terris,* Pope John XXIII's 1963 encyclical on peace, and the writings of Thomas Merton, which together inspired Muller to cofound Physicians for the Prevention of Nuclear War in 1980, work for which he shared a Nobel Peace Prize in 1985. And he could remember the shame he suddenly felt about his faith in January 2002; how he wanted to smash the glass plaque he had won for celebrating Catholic values; how for the first time in memory he and his wife deliberately skipped Mass and wondered if they could ever go back. He contemplated flight from the Church. But he decided instead to stay and fight from within.

Now, from that basement in the parish school at St. John the Evangelist, the fifty-nine-year-old Muller, a renowned cardiologist on the faculty of Harvard Medical School and on the clinical staff of Massachusetts General Hospital, was leading a movement that seemed to be spreading like wildfire. Voice of the Faithful's meetings were packed with hundreds of mainstream Catholics, and its website was hosting raging debates on electronic bulletin boards and recording hits from all over the planet, including Vatican City. In just three months of existence, the group attracted 6,800 supporters from all over the Archdiocese of Boston and twenty-two countries around the world.

At his grandest moments, Muller dreamed of unprecedented change. "We are witnessing a conflagration of the hierarchical Catholic Church on a worldwide basis," he said. "A dense and aged forest with dark shadows and many dying trees is in the final stages of the burn. From the ashes, within months, new life will emerge, green and fragile against the gray. Somewhat later a full, warm, and living landscape will appear — a Catholic Church enriched by the Voice of the Faithful, a pilgrim Church again on its way forward, after centuries of darkness." His dream seemed unimaginably ambitious: he wanted to enlist half of the world's Catholics, 500 million people, in an international congress of laypeople, with chapters in every parish, that would debate policies and then represent the positions of the faithful in shaping the future of their Church. Muller sought solace from the existence of similar institutions, although much smaller, in Protestant and Jewish denominations, and he insisted there were parallels in the peace movement. "In 1980 the governments were talking about winning a nuclear war, and the people had no voice, so we tried to find the voice of the people against nuclear weapons, and I think it changed the climate for confrontation," he said. "Now, here we have a billion Catholic laypeople that have no voice against this hierarchy, so we're trying to create a structure in which one fifth of humanity can have a voice."

Progress was painstaking. The group spent three weeks just trying to hammer out a mission statement. They tried to find consensus on a statement calling for Law to quit, but gave up when nine people objected. At every meeting, a handful of people objected to every action. And each time someone would propose a secular action, such as urging some kind of financial boycott of Church coffers, someone else would get up to propose people pray the Rosary or stage a day of fasting. Muller was hopeful but also realistic. "My nightmare scenario is that the Church successfully papers over the clergy sexual abuse problem and leaves intact an abusive power structure," he said. "That's why we're moving so fast, why we're meeting four times a week now. Because we know we have to seize the moment."

* * *

Even as the laity was awakening from a long, uneasy slumber, so too were priests. At first, many were shell-shocked, ashamed, scared, and angry. Rev. Robert J. Carr, parochial vicar of the Cathedral of the Holy Cross in Boston, where Law says Mass whenever he is in town, reported getting catcalls from construction workers as he walked back to his rectory after celebrating Mass for prisoners at the Nashua Street Jail. Rev. Robert Bowers, the Charlestown pastor, recalled a Halloween party at which someone came dressed as a pedophile priest. "Now, when you look out at an audience, it crosses your mind, 'What do they think of me?'" said Monsignor Peter V. Conley, pastor of St. Jude's Church in Norfolk, a suburb southwest of Boston. "I know a priest who stood outside of his rectory and a car slowed down and a guy yelled out, 'Hey, pedophile!' He was in a funk for days."

But very quickly, some priests also began to realize a new sense of power. As Cardinal Law lost influence, they gained it. Polls taken in February and April showed that even as Law's popularity plummeted, that of parish priests was sky-high — and many priests responded in kind, demonstrating far more sympathy to their parishioners than to their bishop. A number of priests sensed that Law, who had been known for summarily yanking priests out of parishes for even the slightest perceived mistake, could no longer afford to be so authoritarian. The cardinal himself began making noises about attempting to improve relations with his "brother priests."

Priests began to organize. A few of them had already started a small support group to talk about burnout and loneliness, and that group would be the seed for a much larger organization, ultimately called the Priests' Forum, which promised to provide a voice for priests who feel alienated by their leaders. They brought in the leading thinkers about the state of the priesthood, including Rev. Richard P. McBrien, a Notre Dame theologian, and Rev. Donald B. Cozzens, the author of *The Changing Face of the Priesthood*. They anticipated discussing tough issues: perhaps suggesting that Law rein in his extensive travel to focus on the needs of Boston, or encouraging him to stop the practice of reassigning priests whose preaching or style of worship has offended Church conservatives. Some wanted to go even further and talk about celibacy. "We need to bring that up for conversation, and discuss the theological ramifications," said Rev. Paul E. Kilroy, pastor of St. Bernard's Church in Newton. "We are not trying to create a bandwagon for every issue, but we need to find a way to create a ministry so that burnout does not become the soup of the day."

But as in the lay organizations, achieving consensus on anything proved difficult. Some priests wanted their group to call for Law's resignation, but others argued against it, citing priests' obligation to be loyal to their bishop. "We want to get the forum off to a positive start with as many priests as we can," explained one of the forum's leaders, Rev. Walter H. Cuenin of Our Lady Help of Christians in Newton. Nonetheless, chancery officials were clearly getting nervous. In mid-April Law's auxiliary bishops began summoning the eight leaders of the Priests' Forum for chats that some described as reprimands. Some priests expected Law eventually to try to ban the group; some priests even began to speak of unionizing. "Nothing's going to be the same again," said Rev. Robert W. Bullock, the seventy-two-year-old pastor of Our Lady of Sorrows Church, as he sat in the front room of the rectory across from his white clapboard church in suburban Sharon, Massachusetts, south of Boston. "We're going through a sea change."

One change seemed certain as a result of the clergy sexual abuse crisis: never again would the Catholic Church in the United States knowingly allow a sexually abusive priest to have access to children. All over the country, bishops broomed out of churches those priests who had once been accused of misconduct. Numerous bishops, including Cardinal Law, began voluntarily turning over to prosecutors the names of dozens of priests accused of abuse. In many states, such a step was already mandatory; others, including Massachusetts and Colorado, were poised to make it so. The U.S. Conference of Catholic Bishops agreed to devote its June 2002 meeting, in Dallas, to the issue of clergy sexual abuse and was ready for the first time to approve mandatory rules for all 194 dioceses in the United States, a step the bishops' conference had resisted for nearly two decades. The new requirements would likely insist that all priests who sexually abuse minors be removed from ministry and be reported to prosecutors, that dioceses reach out to victims, and that Church workers be trained to recognize and report indications that a child might have been harmed.

But reformers wanted much more. Many argued that the hierarchy's handling of abusive priests revealed systemic problems with their Church. "It isn't just the cardinal; it's the way we operate," Bullock said. "There are structural issues. What is it that has made us priests be so supine, and unwilling to stand up and take risks? To speak out when something awful is happening, and not to cover up? To name things for what they are? The leadership has not protected children, and we have not protected children."

For some, the answer seemed obvious: the all-male, celibate priesthood attracted, created, or facilitated men who were uncomfortable with their own sexuality, and some fraction of those men acted out their sexual maldevelopment in inappropriate ways. Many began to ask, if women were priests, or had any role in the Church power structure, wouldn't they have acted more quickly to protect children? Such questions had been percolating beneath the surface for years, but now laypeople felt free to join the debate. Many pointed out that celibacy, although valued from the earliest days of Christianity and first mandated in the fourth century, was widely enforced only starting in the twelfth century. Defenders of celibacy have described it as a gift, a charism, a witness to sanctity. But critics have noted that celibacy was legislated to avoid the problem of Church property being passed along from a priest to his children. They have also pointed out that today married men can be ordained as Eastern Catholic priests and that there are even a handful of married men serving as Roman Catholic priests — those who were ordained as priests by the Anglican Church but then chose to enter the Catholic Church.

"The issue at the core of this is the reforming of the priesthood," said Tom O'Neill. "If the cardinal is looking for a role in the future, he should go to His Holiness and provide leadership in the reform of the priesthood. If he's not going to provide the type of leadership needed, he will never win back the backing of the faithful nor be exonerated for his management."

Numerous scholars have argued that celibacy was the main reason for the plunge in the number of priests in the United States, although there clearly were also sociological factors. In the decades after Vatican II, thousands of men left the priesthood, most often to marry women. The number of priests in the United States dropped by 23 percent, from 58,632 in 1965 to 45,191 in 2001, according to Georgetown University's Center for Applied Research in the Apostolate. And the research center found other signs of trouble: the number of parishes without a priest skyrocketed, from 549 to 3,151, over those same years, and the average age of priests was rising, so that by 1999 the average diocesan priest was fifty-nine, and 24 percent of all diocesan priests were over age seventy. Catholic University of America sociologist Dean Hoge, who has studied the priesthood extensively, found that dissatisfaction with celibacy was the primary reason priests quit during their first five years, and he predicted that the number of seminarians would quadruple if celibacy were made optional.

Some Church leaders openly began to question mandatory celibacy. Although the Church insists that the ordination of women is theologically off-limits, because Jesus did not call any women as disciples, the proscription against married Roman Catholic priests is not doctrinal and could be changed if a pope were so inclined. "I have no problems with celibacy withering away," said Archbishop Keith O'Brien, president of the Scottish Bishops' Conference. "There is no theological problem with it ending. The loss of celibacy would give liberty to priests to exercise their God-given gift of love and sex rather than feeling they must be celibate all their lives." When asked at a news conference about discussion of priestly celibacy, Cardinal Roger M. Mahony of Los Angeles said, "I think all these questions are open." And Bishop William S. Skylstad of Spokane, the vice president of the U.S. Conference of Catholic Bishops, said that celibacy "is not a doctrinal matter. It's a discipline. I feel it has great merit, but it's not a closed issue."

But after Cardinal J. Francis Stafford, president of the Vatican's Pontifical Council for the Laity, told the *New York Times* that he expected celibacy to be discussed at the gathering of U.S. cardinals in Rome, the Pope quickly shot down that possibility. "The value of celibacy as a complete gift of self to the Lord and his Church must be carefully safe-guarded," the Pope told a group of visiting Nigerian bishops.

Pope John Paul II himself had been an outspoken proponent of the important role of laypeople in changing the Church. "The renewal of the Church in America will not be possible without the active presence of the laity," he said in the 1999 apostolic exhortation *Ecclesia in America*. "Therefore, they are largely responsible for the future of the Church." Nonetheless, the obstacles to change in the Catholic Church are immense.

As fast as progressives and centrists demand sweeping change, traditionalists rise up to demand a return to orthodoxy. Where progressives call for reform — the ordination of women and married men, an increased role for laypeople in decisions such as the selection of bishops — conservatives call for restoration: a renewed emphasis on celibacy, the barring of gay men as seminarians, and more traditional teaching standards in the formation of priests. "People on the far left and the far right greet bad news for the Church as good news for them, because the left can smile and say, 'We told you so — you didn't make enough reforms,' and the right can say, 'We had too many reforms, and let's go back to pre–Vatican II,'" said William Donohue of the Catholic League for Religious and Civil Rights. "People on the left have been itching for reform regarding the totality of the Church's teachings on sexual ethics, and they're going to seize this moment. And on the right, a lot of people have been arguing for a long time that the Church has gone soft and doesn't have the courage of its convictions."

Some Catholics sought to discredit voices of dissent. They complained when progressive priests, such as Rev. Richard McBrien, were quoted on television or in the newspapers; they objected to poll results that included the views of people who go to Mass less than once a week, though the Church itself counts such people as Catholics. Some orthodox Catholics queried leaders of Voice of the Faithful about their stance on issues such as birth control, saying that only if the leaders agreed with all Church teachings could they really be Catholics; others posted notes on electronic message boards suggesting that unhappy Catholics should just become Protestants. Catholic commentators such as William J. Bennett, William F. Buckley Jr., and Patrick J. Buchanan articulated the conservatives' concerns in newspaper columns. "What the Church needs, to restore its moral authority, is to stand up to the moral confusion of modernity, not embrace it," Buchanan wrote. "That way lies total ruin." The famously conservative editorial board of the *Wall Street Journal* warned that "we aren't about to join those whose real agenda is to leave the Church crushed and humiliated." And Ronald P. McArthur, the president emeritus of Thomas Aquinas College, a conservative Catholic institution in California, argued that "there has been an attempt by so-called theologians and liturgists and leaders within the Church to literally midwife another religion, and that has had repercussions in the seminaries and in the wider life of the Church. What is happening now, if not predictable, is at least compatible with the flight from orthodoxy."

Then, of course, there was the danger of apathy. Even as the clergy sex abuse scandal triggered a flurry of angry e-mail and a surge of participation in Voice of the Faithful, street protests and petition drives around Boston drew a few hundred participants at most, a tiny number in an archdiocese of more than 2 million Catholics. Numerous scholars and activists suggested that perhaps the only way for laypeople to wield power was by withholding contributions, but a consensus on some kind of financial boycott seemed elusive because many were concerned about hurting the poor who benefit from Church ministries. "Americans have a short memory — they get all angry about something or other, but then as soon as the wave has crested, they move on," said Lisa Sowle Cahill, a Boston College theologian. "Can the lower structures in the Church really keep up the momentum, even with a new archbishop or cardinal? That's the real question."

Despite all kinds of societal and Church change over the past several decades, the Catholic Church remains the most hierarchical of the world's major religious traditions, and John Paul II, over his twenty-four-year tenure, has appointed hundreds of bishops and cardinals who share his traditionalist — sometimes called restorationist — views. Not surprisingly, the Vatican expressed no interest in sweeping reform in response to the clergy sexual abuse crisis. "Rome can't be open to changing the faith," Cardinal Stafford told the *New York Times*. "That's the gift of God, and Rome has no power to make any changes there. The power of the pope or bishops is very restricted. One has to be humble enough to admit that."

The Vatican was also keenly aware that the American energy for change was not universal. The 60 million–plus Catholics in the United States made up a vibrant, and affluent, segment of the Church but were only 6 percent of Catholics worldwide, and many officials of the Curia believed that the desire for change was more reflective of Americanism than Catholicism. Although incidents of clergy sexual abuse were reported worldwide, the scandal was clearly most intense in the United States; in the developing world, where the Church sees its future, many Catholics were more concerned with issues of day-to-day survival. At the Vatican's first news conference on clergy sexual abuse, a curial cardinal, Darío Castrillón Hoyos of Colombia, made note of the fact that most of the questions were posed in English, calling that fact "an X ray of the problem."

Even in the United States, some bishops, while declaring an interest in openness, reverted to type. In Dallas, where the diocese had been hailed as a model of how to protect children, Bishop Charles V. Grahmann barred priests from speaking to the news media without his permission. In Boston, Cardinal Law declared that "we now realize both within the Church and in society at large that secrecy often inhibits healing and places others at risk," but his spokeswoman, Donna M. Morrissey, largely stopped returning reporters' phone calls and was content to let most news stories appear without comment from the archdiocese. Law also repeatedly asserted his concern for victims, but then allowed his lawyers to file a legal document asserting that negligence by a six-year-old boy and his parents contributed to the boy's abuse by Rev. Paul R. Shanley.

And in a step that infuriated many in Boston, the night that the cardinals' meeting ended in Rome, Law phoned his vicar general, Bishop Walter J. Edyvean, and ordered him to fax a letter to all priests barring them from assisting a proposed association of parish pastoral councils, declaring to the pastors, "You are not to join, foster or promote this endeavor."

"While all the Christian faithful possess 'a true equality regarding dignity and action . . . according to each one's own condition and function,'" Edyvean wrote, quoting from canon law, "this equality is lived out within the hierarchical structure of the Church. Within this structure bishops, priests and deacons fulfill a special role in the functions of teaching, sanctifying and governing."

By the time the clergy sexual abuse crisis forced Pope John Paul II to summon all the American cardinals to his side in April, the once vigorous pontiff was a frail man, nearing his eighty-second birthday. He had survived an assassination attempt in 1981, and chronic joint problems after a hip replacement in 1994, but was now physically hobbled, with slurred speech, apparently as a result of Parkinson's disease.

This Pope, the sixth-longest-serving in history, was beloved as a spiritual leader and a symbol of holiness, and renowned for his staunch anticommunism and his unprecedented efforts at interfaith and ecumenical relations. But his record on internal Church issues was much more controversial, because he was perceived as closed to debate over many aspects of Church life. In 1986 his administration engineered the resignation of Archbishop Raymond G. Hunthausen of Seattle, who was perceived as too liberal, and the ouster of Rev. Charles Curran from the faculty of Catholic University of America, for teachings deemed out of step with Catholic theology. In 1999 the Vatican ordered a nun, Sister Jeannine Gramick, and a priest, Rev. Robert Nugent, to stop their ministry to gays and lesbians because they refused to condemn homosexual activity. And in 2001, amid what appeared to be a crackdown on progressive theologians, and as the Church was putting into place a requirement that American Catholic theologians seek approval from their local bishops to teach at Catholic colleges and universities, the Vatican barred a Massachusetts theologian, Rev. Roger Haight of the Weston Jesuit School of Theology in Cambridge, from teaching while the Vatican investigated whether a book he wrote on salvation might have contradicted the magisterium. "For the world he's been a marvelous pope, but for the Church his legacy is going to be more problematic, because there's a good deal of division now within the Catholic community," said Thomas H. Groome, a Boston College theologian. The communiqué issued by the cardinals who gathered with the Pope in Rome to discuss the issue of clergy sexual abuse reinforced the sense that the hierarchy had little interest in a no-holds-barred debate. "The Pastors of the Church need clearly to promote the correct moral teaching of the Church and publicly to reprimand individuals who spread dissent," the communiqué said.

As long as John Paul II was in charge, the Church's fundamental organization would not change, and the restriction of the priesthood to celibate men would not be lifted. The Pope, like other members of the Vatican leadership, saw clergy sexual abuse as part of a broad societal problem, not as a reflection of structural problems within the Church. "The abuse of the young is a grave symptom of a crisis affecting not only the Church but society as a whole," he told the U.S. cardinals. "It is a deep-seated crisis of sexual morality, even of human relationships, and its prime victims are the family and the young. In addressing the problem of abuse with clarity and determination, the Church will help society to understand and deal with the crisis in its midst."

But many theologians had already begun to think about the Church post–John Paul II. Although few people talked openly about the pontiff's passing, it was widely understood that the Pope was ailing — twice during Holy Week 2002 he was unable to finish Mass — and speculation had begun about who would be next to sit in the throne of Saint Peter. The conventional wisdom held that the next pope would be someone equally conservative, because over the course of his lengthy papacy John Paul II had appointed the vast majority of the College of Cardinals. But the conventional wisdom is often wrong. "Media commentators routinely use phrases such as 'stacking the deck' to express the idea that John Paul II has influenced the outcome of the next papal election by creating cardinals in his own image and likeness," wrote John L. Allen Jr., Vatican correspondent for the *National Catholic*

Reporter. "History, however, suggests a different view. Conclaves full of cardinals appointed by the deceased pope do not elect photocopies of the man who named them. More often, the opposite holds true: they elect popes who pursue different policies."

Few people expected the cardinals to choose a man who would support a Third Vatican Council, at which issues of reform would be fully ventilated. But some looked to a new Holy Father with a more sympathetic ear to laypeople with proposals for change. And the *Vaticanistas,* the corps of journalists and others who make a living observing the Holy See, saw some likelihood that the next papacy would be a short one — that the cardinals would choose one of their older colleagues as the next pope to increase the odds that he wouldn't live too long. That's because long papacies tend to concentrate power in Rome, and after the unusually long reign of John Paul II, many bishops were hoping to see some power devolve from the Curia to their own dioceses around the world.

In Wellesley the Voice of the Faithful crowds kept growing through the spring of 2002. Gatherings turned into revival-style meetings, with a charismatic emcee, Mary Scanlon Calcaterra, prone to shouting things like "praise the Lord" after a newcomer would get up to give personal testimony about why he or she joined the group.

"I am sixty-one years of age, benefited from seventeen years of Catholic education, have always been involved in ministry of some sort in the Church, did a year of missionary work in Alaska, worked in a chancery, taught CCD for years, have been on a pastoral council and a eucharistic minister and did a thirteen-part series for Boston Catholic television," said one participant, Mary Ann Keyes. "What I am mostly is someone who loves my Church, and my hope is that out of this enormous pain will emerge a new way for our Church to carry on." Another participant, Donna Salacuse, declared, "Voice of the Faithful has brought hope to me that the laity will assume the role given it by Vatican II and stand together with the clergy as Church. The laity represents a vast resource of talent and energy. We seek our rightful place in the

Church so that together we may deal with the challenges facing us. We must never again be the mute people in the pews."

Some of the laypeople were quite clear on what they had to offer, urged on by Dr. Muller, who was fond of reminding gatherings that it took laypeople, led by Galileo, to convince the hierarchy that the planetary system is sun-centered. "We're trying to save the hierarchy from itself, from its own insularity, its own tendency to secrecy, its own medievalism, by bringing in the laity, with our ideas," said Luise Cahill Dittrich, one of the group's leaders. "They need us. They don't know how to police themselves; they don't know anything about human sexuality, about the democratic process, or about the equality of women. And they're so busy defending themselves, they lack compassion and love, which is what Jesus was all about."

Thanks in part to the global nature of the Internet, supporters began enlisting from around the country and the world — in one weekend in April, twelve hundred people signed up as members of the group. They began planning a convention, raising money to hire staff, figuring out how to create an international organization, meeting with survivors, and setting up a fund for Catholics unwilling to route charitable contributions through the cardinal. "I consider myself a committed Christian and Catholic, and feel that the clergy, and most especially our bishops, must start listening to those of us they describe as laymen," said Richard W. Rohrbacher of San Joaquin, California.

Theologians saw something remarkable happening — the clergy sexual abuse crisis had energized Catholics who had long remained silent. "There have always been people on the activist agenda who have wanted to change the Church, either on the left or on the right, and who haven't had much impact, but this crisis has moved the broad middle of the Church, people who have been pretty content and have been complacent," said Boston College Theology Department chairman Stephen J. Pope. "There are a lot of mainstream, middle-of-the-road Catholics who are feeling called to be active in the Church in a new way, and that's one of the significant elements of this crisis."

But none of them seemed sure exactly where they were heading. "I don't know what's going to happen in the end, but this is a very important time," said Gisela Morales-Barreto, a psychologist with the Boston Public Health Commission and a parishioner at Our Lady Help of Christians in Newton. "These sexual abuse victims endured horrific pain and trauma, and the good that is coming out of it is people coming together to support them, and looking for change in the Church while keeping faith alive. As always happens, from evil comes good."

Afterword to the 2015 Edition

After a burst of apologizing in January and February 2002, Cardinal Law pondered how he could ride out the storm.

He convened a meeting of lay Catholic leaders, a who's who of Boston's top businessmen, politicians, doctors, and lawyers — like Jack Connors, one of the founders of the city's leading advertising agency, and William Bulger, then president of the University of Massachusetts, who was also a former president of the Massachusetts state senate. Those in the room had been longtime supporters of Law, but now they demanded that he account for himself.

"Well, Your Eminence," Connors told Law, "as Ricky used to say to Lucy, you sure got some 'splainin' to do."

When Law started to say that his handling of the crisis had been "flawed," Bulger bluntly cut him off. "It's been disastrous," he said.

Most of Boston's richest and most powerful Catholics began abandoning the cardinal. Catholic Charities, the biggest social service provider in Massachusetts, canceled its annual fundraising event at the cardinal's residence for the first time because donors said they wouldn't contribute if Law was involved.

In early April, after another spate of bad press caused by the release of damning documents concerning the rampage of one abusive priest, Father Paul Shanley, Law's inner circle of advisers told him he should resign. The cardinal asked for a second opinion from his "college of consultors," six bishops and a group of trusted priests. Not surprisingly, the group, which served at Law's pleasure, told him he should tough it out.

The cardinal then embarked on a secret trip to Rome — via Newark, so he'd avoid being seen at Boston's Logan Airport — to consult with the pope and other Vatican leaders on his handling of the abuse crisis. On April 15, with Law still in secret discussions at the Vatican, Pope John Paul II summoned the American cardinals to Rome for a two-day meeting to discuss the issue.

Meeting with the pope and his peers, Law was contrite. "If I had not made the terrible mistakes that I made, we would not be here," he said, according to several people who were in the room. "I apologize for that."

Returning to Boston after winning at least a temporary reprieve from the pope, Law lay low. He canceled his scheduled 2002 graduation speeches and turned down an honorary degree, knowing his presence at happy occasions would serve as a major distraction.

But then, after months in the bunker, he attempted to reintroduce himself to the public, a chastened man who now understood the incorrigibility of abusers and the importance of protecting children. At the U.S. bishops' spring meeting in Dallas in June, Law met for five minutes each with the individual newspaper and television reporters from Boston, testing the waters for reentry into the public eye. He settled eighty-four of the Geoghan lawsuits, for a relatively affordable $10 million—far less than initially anticipated. And in an effort to address the archdiocese's increasingly dire financial straits, Law won a loan of up to $38 million from the Knights of Columbus.

The cardinal's reemergence seemed to accelerate in early October, when he showed up at the dedication of the Leonard P. Zakim Bunker Hill Bridge spanning the Charles River in Boston, sitting patiently as Bruce Springsteen told a story about meeting the pope. Four days after the bridge dedication, Law held a special Mass at the Cathedral of the Holy Cross for striking Boston janitors. Such an event would not have been unusual a year earlier, but Law's once-loud voice on public policy had almost entirely disappeared. So for him to weigh in on a labor dispute took on new significance.

By the time of the November bishops' meeting in Washington, Law was almost ready to return to normal. He walked through the halls, shaking hands with his brother bishops, even receiving a round of applause for his three years of service as chairman of the bishops' international policy committee. Most remarkably, after months of being held up as an example of moral turpitude, he led the bishops in two days of debate over the pressing moral question of the day—whether the United States would be justified in invading Iraq—and then showed up at two press conferences to discuss the possibility of military action.

Law changed his approach toward priests and laypeople, meeting with large groups of archdiocesan clergy, as well as with the leadership of Voice of the Faithful, a Catholic lay group formed to press the Church to do more to address the sexual abuse crisis. The organization had attracted four thousand people to a midsummer meeting in Boston.

Most dramatically, Law changed his approach to the victims, and launched what amounted to an apology tour.

"Apology is a weak thing, but I don't know how else to begin," he told a group of seventy-five people gathered on a fall night in the small northeastern Massachusetts town of Dracut. All seventy-five had been sexually abused by one priest—the Rev. Joseph E. Birmingham. "I beg your forgiveness, and I understand that can be a very difficult thing to give, because the hurt is so deep, the memory so raw, and the wound so searing."

Then, at the request of the Dracut victims, Law issued a dramatic public apology at the cathedral in October, for the first time seeming to accept personal responsibility for mishandling child abusers.

"I did assign priests who had committed sexual abuse," he said, at times choking up. "The forgiving love of God gives me the courage to beg forgiveness of those who have suffered because of what I did. Once again, I want to acknowledge publicly my responsibility for decisions which I now see were clearly wrong."

But the words rang mostly hollow. It was too little, and too late. A year of revelations had taken an extraordinary toll on the reputation of the man who was once mentioned as a possible pope. The story that began with Father Geoghan had come to include so many characters that few people could keep track of them all. More than a hundred priests in Boston had been accused of sexual abuse by some five hundred people in lawsuits against the archdiocese that could carry a price tag of $100 million.

Under public pressure or because of litigation, the personnel files of accused priests were made public at several dioceses around the country, including Boston, Los Angeles, and Chicago. Lurid tales were revealed in the process, like that of the Rev. William J. Cloutier in Chicago, who allegedly raped a thirteen-year-old boy in his summer cottage, then pulled a gun and threatened to kill the boy if he ever told what happened.

In Boston, the steady drip of revelations in the personnel files was simply too much for local Catholics to stomach. By early December 2002, the documents had shown allegations that a priest had terrorized and beaten his housekeeper, another had traded cocaine for sex, and a third had enticed young girls by claiming to be "the second coming of Christ." The demands for Law's resignation had reached a tipping point throughout the archdiocese. But the loudest voices came from the most unexpected quarter: fifty-eight of his own priests signed a letter saying it was time for Law to quit.

As the furor intensified, Law traveled to Washington for a meeting with the pope's apostolic nuncio, Archbishop Gabriel Montalvo, who was the Vatican's top emissary to the United States. Law told Montalvo he had decided to step down.

From Washington, the cardinal flew to Rome, and on December 13, he met with Pope John Paul II and told him he was ready to resign. An eighteen-year career as archbishop of Boston then officially ended with a terse, legalistic statement from the Vatican that made no reference to priests, children, or the crisis in the Church. In a perfunctory list of the pope's activities that day, the Holy See announced that the pope "accepted the resignation from the pastoral care of the archdiocese of Boston, U.S.A., presented by Cardinal Bernard Francis Law, in accordance with Canon 401, para. 2, of the Code of Canon Law."

Church officials tried to cast the most positive light on the resignation, suggesting that, at last, the Church could move on.

Cardinal William H. Keeler of Baltimore declared, "I join Cardinal Law in praying that this will be an act of purification for our Church, allowing us to begin healing and reconciliation. Many people have suffered. Trust has been betrayed. Yet, now is not the time to turn away. It is time for us to come together to answer scandal with witness and service."

But victims were unsatisfied, saying they wanted to see other bishops ousted and even taken to court. Two days after Law resigned, protesters showed up at Boston's Cathedral of the Holy Cross. "Law's gone — the fight goes on," read one sign. "Let the dominos fall," read another. One quoted Winston Churchill: "This is not the end. It is not even the beginning of the end. But it is, perhaps, the end of the beginning."

A somber Cardinal Law made one final appearance in 2002, speaking for about three minutes to a group of reporters hastily summoned to a church library near his residence. As a roar of camera shutters tracked his every expression, Law said he could never have imagined a story that would end this way.

Eight months later, in a shocking coda to the saga of the priest whose abuse rampage Law had in part facilitated, John Geoghan was murdered in a Massachusetts prison, where he had been serving a nine-to-ten-year sentence for fondling a boy in a public swimming pool a decade ago. Geoghan, sixty-eight, was strangled by a convicted killer with a white supremacist past.

The following year, the disgraced Law was given a soft landing when Pope John Paul II announced that he was naming the cardinal archbishop of St. Mary Major Basilica, an elegant Vatican church in the heart of Rome. The tender sinecure outraged victims who said it rubbed salt in their wounds and was evidence of the Church's fundamental indifference to their plight. Law left the basilica job in 2011 and is now retired and living in Rome, eighty-three years old at this writing.

In Boston, a broad, far-ranging conversation continued about the future of the Church — including the roles of women and gays, priestly celibacy, the hierarchy's authority, and other questions the bishops largely wouldn't touch. Boston College, the preeminent Catholic university in the Archdiocese of Boston, kicked off a multiyear effort exploring issues challenging the Church and drew thousands to its inaugural event. Regis College, a Catholic women's college in Weston, Massachusetts, held a fiery two-day event to discuss the role of women in the Church. Even Tufts University, which is not Catholic, launched a new course entitled Catholicism in Crisis.

The abuse scandal unfolded in a Church already beset with problems. In the United States, only one in four of the nation's 67 million Catholics attend Mass weekly, according to Georgetown University's Center for Applied Research in the Apostolate. In 2015, the number of American priests, 38,275, is 64 percent of what it was at its peak in 1967. And ordinations of new priests, 545 in 2015, though somewhat improved over the previous year, were still only 60 percent of what they were fifty years ago.

In 2002, the bishops themselves had set in motion a lay effort of unpredictable results: they chose Oklahoma governor Frank Keating, a former FBI agent, local prosecutor, state lawmaker, U.S. attorney, and top official in the Reagan and Bush administrations, to head a national lay review board charged with producing a series of reports examining what went wrong in the Church.

The Church's deepest thinkers, its theologians, called for a broad conversation about the Church. The president of the Catholic Theological Society of America asked three top theologians to prepare a discussion paper, and their consensus was clear: "The scandals facing the Church today have led us to conclude that a thoroughgoing Church reform is both legitimate and necessary."

Over the course of a year that Law had described as a "nightmare," the crisis had reached down into the pews and up to the papacy, ultimately forcing the Church to rethink its whole approach to abusive priests in an effort to protect children and placate an angry public. The clergy and the laity struggled to deal with the fallout. As the intensity of the crisis waned, the Church woke up with a hangover: fewer people at Mass and less money in the collection basket.

The crisis seeped deep into American popular culture, transforming how Catholicism was viewed and treated. Catholic priest jokes became a staple of late-night television and were traded even at Catholic social gatherings. Abusive priest and abused altar boy costumes were featured at Halloween parties. At a fall 2002 football game between Columbia and Fordham, the Columbia announcer taunted his Jesuit-educated rivals with a crude joke about clergy sexual abuse. By November, a network television drama, *The Practice,* had featured a protagonist who leaves the Catholic Church over the crisis. The most popular movie in Mexico, *El Crimen del Padre Amaro,* was a tawdry melodrama about a handsome priest who has an affair with his house-keeper and her daughter. And despite objections from the Vatican, the top prize at the Venice Film Festival went to a Scottish film, *The Magdalene Sisters,* about abusive nuns in Ireland.

Although incidents of abuse by priests were reported throughout the Catholic world, the scandal resonated most deeply in English-speaking developed countries, such as the United States, Canada, Britain, Ireland, and Australia. In Ireland, one of the most Catholic countries in Europe, the Church's attempt to reform itself and min-imize the scandal with a handpicked blue-ribbon commission was overwhelmed by public outrage, especially after a documentary on the state-run broadcast service showed the extent of the problem and the Church's cover-up in Dublin. The Irish government, which had once afforded the Catholic Church a "special position" in the country's 1937 constitution, decided the Church was incapable of policing itself and set up its own inquiries.

In the spring of 2002, American bishops, meeting in Dallas, adopted a policy requiring that any allegation of sexual abuse against a priest toward a minor be turned over to police for investigation, and that any priest found to have sexually abused a child be defrocked. But the Vatican became concerned that in the zeal to weed out bad priests, the priests' rights were being trampled. So that fall, the U.S. bishops toned down the policy they'd adopted in the spring, no longer requiring that sexual abuse allegations against priests be referred to the police.

Pope John Paul II, though a beloved figure, was criticized for doing little to grapple with sexual abuse by priests, and much of the known misconduct took place during his twenty-seven-year tenure from 1978 until his death in 2005. In 2001, he apologized for the first time for abusive priests in an e-mail sent to Catholic churches worldwide. In

2002, the pope authorized the use of ecclesiastical courts to try abusive priests, but since the trials were secret, the Church left itself open to criticism that it was still concealing misconduct. And John Paul's long-time friendship with the Rev. Marcial Maciel Degollado — a serial sex abuser and the founder of the Legionaries of Christ, a powerful religious order — contributed to a perception that he was less than zealous in confronting the abuse problem.

John Paul chose Joseph Ratzinger, a German cardinal, to be in charge of adjudicating abuse cases for the Vatican in his office at the Congregation for the Doctrine of the Faith. While he was archbishop, Ratzinger had been touched by scandal for his handling of an abusive priest in his diocese, in a case akin to the way Cardinal Law dealt with Father Geoghan. After the German priest was accused of molesting boys, and given therapy, he was allowed to resume his duties despite warnings from his psychiatrist that he was unfit to work with children. The priest was later convicted in 1986 of molesting other boys. While a subordinate took responsibility for letting the priest resume his duties, Church officials acknowledged that Ratzinger knew of the priest's reassignment.

When John Paul died, it was Ratzinger who was elected to be his replacement. Ratzinger became Pope Benedict XVI, and was largely defensive in dealing with the abuse issue as he faced a constant barrage of news stories detailing new pedophilia scandals around the world. Though Benedict notably did remove Rev. Maciel, the compromised Legionaries of Christ cleric, from the ministry, he relied mainly on apologia in dealing with the abuse problem. "We, too, insistently beg forgiveness from God and from the persons involved, while promising to do everything possible to ensure that such abuse will never occur again," Benedict told priests in St. Peter's Square in 2010.

In 2011 the Vatican did issue guidelines instructing Church officials to report allegations of sexual abuse by priests to police where required by law to do so, but not all did. Bishops in Asia, Latin America, and Africa resisted, claiming they had little expertise or experience with the abuse problem.

But authorities in America grew more assertive on their own, and they began to devote attention to an area that the Church hierarchy had been roundly criticized for ignoring: its own culpability in failing to protect parishioners from the wayward priests it was supposed to be supervising.

In 2012 Monsignor William J. Lynn, secretary for clergy in the Philadelphia diocese, became the first cleric ever to face trial on charges that he covered up for abusive priests and thereby endangered the welfare of children. Lynn was convicted and sentenced to three to six years in prison. The same year, Bishop Robert W. Finn, head of the Kansas City–St. Joseph diocese in Missouri, became the first bishop criminally implicated for shielding an accused priest when he was convicted of failing to report the cleric, who had taken pornographic photos of girls. Finn resigned in 2015.

Two months after Finn's resignation, two bishops in the diocese of Minneapolis and St. Paul resigned in the wake of complaints about the way they handled abuse cases involving priests who served under them. Since 1978, seventeen American bishops have resigned under a cloud following allegations that they mishandled the abuse cases of subordinate priests, according to BishopAccountability.org, a research group based in Waltham, Massachusetts.

Pope Francis, who assumed the papacy in 2013 after Benedict resigned, has been more proactive than his predecessor. In his first year, Francis amended Vatican law to make sexual abuse of children a crime, and he appointed a commission to advise him on the issue.

In 2014 Francis met with six victims of sexual abuse from Ireland, Germany, and Britain and, in his strongest comments on the scandal to date, likened abusive priests to "a sacrilegious cult." In his homily to the six victims, Francis said, "Before God and His people, I express my sorrow for the sins and grave crimes of clerical sexual abuse committed against you. And I humbly ask forgiveness. I beg your forgiveness, too, for the sins of omission on the part of Church leaders who did not respond adequately to reports of abuse made by family members, as well as by abuse victims themselves."

A month before Francis's meeting with the six victims, the Vatican defrocked its former ambassador to the Dominican Republic,

Archbishop Józef Wesołowski, after he was accused of abusing boys while he was stationed in the country from 2008 to 2013. Vatican prosecutors later put him under house arrest in Rome. Wesołowski was found dead of natural causes in August of 2015 as he was awaiting trial. He could have faced a prison sentence of up to eight years, and would have been the first high-level prelate to stand before a Vatican tribunal.

Despite Francis's steps, the Vatican found itself under attack by the United Nations in 2014 for still lagging on the sexual abuse issue. That February, a UN committee report harshly criticized the Church for failing to abide by an international commitment to protect children, saying its policies had continued to allow wayward priests to prey upon young victims. The Vatican largely rejected the findings of the UN's Committee on the Rights of the Child, arguing that while it had ratified the Convention on the Rights of the Child it was responsible for enforcement only within Vatican City, not among its denominations globally. In May, another UN panel, the Committee against Torture, criticized the Vatican anew—for failing to report accused priests to police, and for not ensuring compensation for victims. The committee, monitoring Rome's compliance with an international treaty prohibiting torture, found that the sexual abuse of victims by priests itself amounted to torture. It praised the guidelines adopted by the Church in 2011 instructing its hierarchy to cooperate with civil authorities, but said it was concerned that the Vatican continued to "resist the principle of mandatory reporting."

In 2014 the Vatican said it had defrocked 848 priests worldwide for sexual abuse between 2004 and 2013, and that 2,572 clerics had been disciplined for abuse violations.

But in June 2015, Francis, perhaps swayed by the UN criticism, approved the creation of a Vatican tribunal to judge bishops accused of covering up or enabling sexual abuse by priests they supervise, a step long demanded by victims' rights advocates. While Rome had defrocked hundreds of priests accused of sexual abuse and penalized thousands more, little or no action had been taken against bishops, and this was the first time a mechanism was created for disciplining the so-called princes of the Church.

Today the scope of the crisis is difficult to define precisely. In the United States alone, 17,259 people have complained that they were abused by 6,427 priests from 1950 through 2013, according to data from the U.S. Conference of Catholic Bishops, the Church's official arm in America. But those figures are incomplete. They include only those complaints that the conference deemed "not implausible" or "credible," and none for 2003, the year after the scandal exploded in Boston and throughout the country. In Boston, during the same period, 249 priests were accused of sexual abuse by 1,476 people, according to BishopAccountability.org.

Financial settlements with victims of abuse have put an increasing strain on Church finances. Nationally, the Church paid more than $3 billion to settle abuse complaints between 1950 and 2015. In Boston, the archdiocese paid $154 million to settle with 1,230 victims from 2002 through June 30, 2014, the most recent figures available. Between 2004 and 2015, twelve dioceses nationwide filed for bankruptcy protection.

As the costs, financial and psychological, of the greatest crisis the Church has had in generations continue to reverberate, a silver lining has been the growing strength and empowerment of the victims who together have found a voice.

In 1988 Peter Pollard wrote Cardinal Law a letter telling him that he had been sexually abused by a priest when he was in his teens. He asked Law to get the priest into treatment, to make sure that he was never alone with a child again, and to begin an outreach program for other victims. But Pollard said one of Law's deputies told him that after a five-day evaluation the Church had concluded that the priest was not a danger to children. He suggested the sexual activity was a mere display of affection.

Now a father of one and a social worker who works with neglected and abused children, Pollard is encouraged by the recent empowerment of other victims, whom he calls survivors. While he endorses the Christian concept of bearing witness, he is less enamored with another principle in Church teaching.

"To those who ask that we forgive and forget, please understand,"

Pollard wrote in an opinion piece for the *Globe*. "The survivors, each of us in his own way, have spent our lives trying to move on, always weighing those two options. For some of us, suicide, substance abuse, or violence ended the struggle early.

"To varying degrees, those of us who have survived have begun to heal. We reclaimed dreams, earned degrees, formed families, went to work, even sought solace in spiritual practice. But we cannot escape the effects of the betrayals that were committed against us in God's name. They are inexorably woven into the texture of who we have become.

"That betrayal may not be a chargeable offense in a court of law. But there is no statute of limitations on its impact. And there should be no forgetting."

Ben Bradlee Jr. and Michael Paulson
September 8, 2015

Appendix:
The Documents

NOT ACKNOWLEDGED BY
CARDINAL'S...

CARDINAL'S RESIDENCE
RECEIVED
NOV 4 1980
OFFICE OF THE SECRETARY

)Humberto Cardinal Medeiros
2101 Commonwealth Avenue
Brighton, Massachusetts

Your Eminence,   file- John Geoghan
This is an acknowledgment of your kind
letter of October 28ᵗʰ. Thank you for
your prayers and offer of assistance.
I have been receiving excellent care or
direction from two wonderful Catholic
physicians; Dr. John Brennan and Dr.
Robert Mullins.
They assure me that within a
relatively short time I shall be able
to return for fruitful years of
... the Ministry. I am eager to

return and I thank God for His many
blessings.

Gratefully In Christ,
John J. Geoghan

37 Pelton St. /
W. Roxby, MA. 02132

November 2, 1980. Rev. John J. Geoghan, answering a note
from the late Cardinal Humberto S. Medeiros extending
his sick leave, says he is receiving excellent medical care
from two doctors and expects to return to service soon.

BOSTON CLINICAL ASSOCIATES, INC.
JOHN H. BRENNAN, M. D.
17 HENSHAW STREET
BRIGHTON, MASSACHUSETTS 02135
───
TELEPHONE: 787-3915

January 13, 1981

Most Reverend Bishop Thomas V. Daley
Archdiocese of Boston
One Lake Street
Brighton, Massachusetts 02135

Re: Reverend John J. Geoghan
    37 Pelton Street
    West Roxbury, Massachusetts 02032

Your Excellency:

I met with Father Geoghan in my office on the 12th
of January and it was mutually agreed that he was
now able to resume his priestly duties.

If you would like to have me talk with you or to write
to you about this matter, Father Geoghan has given
me permission to do so.

Respectfully,

John H. Brennan, M.D.

JHB:eg

January 13, 1981. Psychiatrist John H. Brennan tells Bishop Thomas V.
Daily that Geoghan is "now able to resume his priestly duties."

CHANCERY
ARCHDIOCESE OF BOSTON
2121 COMMONWEALTH AVENUE
BRIGHTON, MASSACHUSETTS 02135

OFFICE OF THE CHANCELLOR

January 26, 1981

John H. Brennan, M.D.
Boston Clinical Associates, Inc.
17 Henshaw Street
Brighton, MA   02135

Dear Doctor Brennan:

I write to thank you for your letter of January 13, 1981
regarding the Rev. John J. Geoghan of 37 Pelton Street, West
Roxbury, Masachusetts 02032 and am happy to note that in
your opinion Father Geoghan is able to resume his priestly
duties. Thank you so much for this recommendation and I
shall certainly make a note to His Eminence, the Cardinal
and look forward to the assignment of Father Geoghan very
soon.

With best personal regards, I am

Sincerely in Christ,

Most Rev. Thomas V. Daily
Auxiliary Bishop of Boston
Chancellor

TVD/mbg

January 26, 1981. Bishop Daily thanks Dr. Brennan for his opinion that Geoghan is fit to return to work.

"EXHIBIT E"
AUG 1 6 1982

OFFICE OF THE SECRETARY

RECEIVED
AUG 1 7 1982
OFFICE OF THE CHANCELLOR

Dear Emmanuel,

As you know, our family had a conference with Bishop Daly over two weeks ago.

Since that priest is still in his parish, it appears that no action has been taken. Am I to assume now that we were patronized?

Our family is deeply rooted in the Catholic Church, our Great-Grandparents and parents suffered hardships and persecution for love of the Church. Our desire is to protect the dignity of Holy Orders, even in the midst of our tears and agony over the 7 boys in our family who have been violated. We cannot undo that, but we are obligated to protect others from this abuse to the Mystical Body of Jesus Christ.

It was suggested that we keep silent to protect the boys — that is absurd since minors are protected under law, and I do not wish to hear that remark again, since it is insulting to our intelligence.

I have a tremendous love and respect for you Cardinal, and regret now for not writing to

August 1982. Margaret Gallant complains in a four-page handwritten letter to Cardinal Medeiros that her family's claims that Geoghan molested seven boys in her extended family have been ignored. She demands that Geoghan be removed and denounces a suggestion that she keep silent.

humility and holiness, but I am very angry with
you now, and do not understand this.

While it is true that a layman in the same
situation would only be confined for observation
for a limited time — he would also be exposed.
Parents would know then not to allow children
near this type person. In this case, not
only do they not know, but by virtue of his office,
he gains access quite easily, which compounds
our responsibility! His actions are not
only destructive to the emotional well being of
the children, but hits the very core of our
being in our love for the church — he would
not gain access to homes of fallen away Catholics.

Regardless of what he says, or the Dr. who
treated him, I do not believe he is cured, his
actions strongly suggest that he is not, and there
is no guarantee that persons with these obsessions
are ever cured.

Truly, my heart aches for him and I pray
for him, because I know this must tear him
apart too, but I cannot allow my compassion
for him cloud my judgment on acting for
the people of God, and the children in the
church.

My own children were not directly

sensitive to my nephews and grandnephews who were involved; I am far enough removed to be slightly more objective. I have not told my sister or my nieces that that priest is still functioning — I fear the consequences of telling them. I have told my brother, and he and I will take this case to the Holy Father if need be.

We did not question the Authority of the Church two years ago, but left it entirely in your hands — Now, we will not settle for this, but must insist on knowing what action is taken — where he is sent — etc — I will not allow this Temple of God to be overshadowed by a sin of ommission. We, our family and all of us who look to the Authority of the Church — are the Church — and have the right to expect service from the Ordained

My two sisters and my niece never as much as received an apology from the church, much less any offer for

counseling for the boys - It embarrasses me
that the Church is so negligent.

Father Damien the leper went after a child
molester once and beat him up. His cause
was held up because of it -- Now the cause
of Damien is in the Vatican. I am praying
to him now to bring this cause to Jesus
Christ. Father Damien would not sit
of his fanny - he would act.

My heart is broken over this whole
mess - and to address my Cardinal in
this manner has taken its toll on me
too. May Almighty God. Father,
Son and Holy Spirit have mercy on
all of us.

Margaret Gallant

Transcription of Margaret Gallant's letter
to Cardinal Medeiros:

August 16, 1982

Dear Eminence,
As you know, our family had a conference with Bishop Daly over two weeks ago. Since that priest is still in his parish, it appears that no action has been taken. Am I to assume now that we were patronized?

Our family is deeply rooted in the Catholic Church, our great-grandparents and parents suffered hardship and persecution for love of the Church. Our desire is to protect the dignity of the Holy Orders, even in the midst of our tears and agony over the seven boys in our family who have been violated. We cannot undo that, but we are obligated to protect others from this abuse to the Mystical Body of Jesus Christ.

It was suggested that we keep silent to protect the boys — that is absurd since minors are protected under law, and I do not wish to hear that remark again, since it is insulting to our intelligence.

I have a tremendous love and respect for you Cardinal, and regret now for not writing to . . . [at this point in letter, part of text is cut off] . . . humility and holiness, but I am very angry with you now, and do not understand this.

While it is true that a layman in the same situation would only be confined for observation for a limited time — he would also be exposed [word *exposed* is underlined twice]. Parents would know then not to allow children near this type person. In this case, not only do they not know, but by virtue of his office he gains access quite easily, which compounds our responsibility! His actions are not only destructive to the emotional well-being of the children, but hits the very core of our being in our love for the church — he would not gain access to homes of fallen away Catholics.

Regardless of what he says, or the doctor who treated him, I do not believe he is cured; his actions strongly suggest that he is not, and there is no guarantee that persons with these obsessions are ever cured.

Truly, my heart aches for him and I pray for him, because I know this must tear him apart too; but I cannot allow my compassion for him to cloud my judgment on acting for the people of God, and the children in the church.

My own children were not directly . . . [at this point in letter, part of text is cut off] . . . sensitive to my nephews and grandnephews who were involved; I am far enough removed to be slightly more objective. I have not told my sister or my niece that that priest is still functioning — I fear the consequences of telling them. I have told my brother, and he and I will take this case to the Holy Father if need be.

We did not question the Authority of the Church two years ago, but left it entirely in your hands. Now, we will not settle for this, but must insist on knowing what action is taken—where he is sent, etc. I will not allow this Temple of God to be overshadowed by a sin of omission. We, our family and all of us who look to the Authority of the Church — [word illegible] the Church — and have the right to expect service from the Ordained.

My two sisters and my niece never as much as received an apology from the church, much less any offer for counseling for the boys. It embarrasses me that the Church is so negligent.

Father Damien the leper went after a child molester once and beat him up. His cause was held up because of it. Now the curse of Damien is in the Vatican. I am praying to him now to bring this cause to Jesus Christ. Father Damien would not sit on his fanny — he would act.

My heart is broken over this whole mess — and to address my Cardinal in this manner has taken its toll on me too. May Almighty God, Father, Son and Holy Spirit have mercy on all of us.

Margaret Gallant

August 20, 1982

Mrs. Margaret Gallant
346 Walnut Street
Stoughton
Massachusetts 02072

Dear Mrs. Gallant:

Thank you for your letter of August 10, 1982 and your candid expression of opinion concerning the priest of the Archdiocese of Boston who has caused hardship to your family and most especially to several of the boys.

While I am and must be very sensitive to a very delicate situation and one that has caused great scandal, I must at the same time invoke the mercy of God and share in that mercy in the knowledge that God forgives sins and that sinners indeed can be forgiven. To be sure, we cannot accept sin, but we know well that we must love the sinner and pray for him. I take great comfort in noting these thoughts in your letter to me and at your compassion for Father. Please be assured that I am speaking to the priest in order to find the most Christian way to deal with the problem with him and at the same time remove any source of scandal for the sake of the faithful.

With every good wish, I am

Devotedly yours in Our Lord,

+ Humbert Cardinal Medeiros

Archbishop of Boston

August 20, 1982. Cardinal Medeiros responds to Margaret Gallant's letter by suggesting that "sinners indeed can be forgiven." He says he is speaking with Geoghan.

PERSONAL

CHANCERY
ARCHDIOCESE OF BOSTON
212 COMMONWEALTH AVENUE
BRIGHTON, MASSACHUSETTS 02135

Copy to: Fr. Oates/Fr. Mc
Personal/Confider

FOR THE LOCKED FILE

FICE OF THE ARCHBISHOP

September 21, 1984

Mrs. Marge Gallant
346 Walnut Street
Stoughton
MA 02072

Dear Mrs. Gallant:

Thank you for your letter of September 6, 1984 concerning the priest at St. Brendan's, Dorchester.

The matter of your concern is being investigated and appropriate pastoral decisions will be made both for the priest and God's people.

Thank you for your concern. Please pray for me.

With warm personal regards, I am

Sincerely yours in Christ,

[signature]

Archbishop of Boston

September 21, 1984. Bernard F. Law, then the archbishop of Boston, tells Margaret Gallant he is investigating her claim that Geoghan sexually molested seven boys in her extended family.

ROBERT W. MULLINS, M.D.
77 COREY STREET
WEST ROXBURY, MA. 02132
TELEPHONE 323-6110

Dear Rev. Oates,

Rev. John Geoghan, a long-time friend and patient of mine, has recently terminated his ministry at St. Brendan Parish, due to a rather unfortunate traumatic experience. Following a brief, but beneficial, respite from his duties, Father Geoghan has adjusted remarkedly well.

In my opinion, he is now able to resume full Pastoral activities, without any need for specific restrictions.

Respectfully yours,

Robert W. Mullins M.D.

RECEIVED

October 20, 1984. Dr. Robert W. Mullins, Geoghan's family doctor, writes that Geoghan, despite an "unfortunate traumatic experience" at another parish, is now ready to resume his ministry.

MOST REVEREND JOHN M. D'ARCY

AUXILIARY BISHOP OF BOSTON
OFFICE OF THE REGIONAL BISHOP

December 7, 1984

Most Reverend Bernard F. Law
Archbishop of Boston
Archbishop's Residence
2121 Commonwealth Avenue
Brighton, Massachusetts 02135

Dear Archbishop Law:

Just a word on the recent assignment in this region of Fr. John
Geoghan as an associate at St. Julia's in Weston. There are two
things that give me concern.

1) Fr. Geoghan has a history of homosexual involvement with
young boys. I understand his recent abrupt departure from St.
Brendan's, Dorchester may be related to this problem.

2) St. Julia's for some time has been a divided and troubled
parish. There is great animosity on the part of many parishioners
towards Monsiger Rossiter. It is difficult to deal with the
situation because Monsignor is a good priest - he is always there,
he is concerned, he does the traditional things very well, but
there are many complaints from good people and there have been
since I have come here to this region and, indeed, long before
that.

A large number of parishioners go elsewhere. Many attend Mass
at Pope John Seminary or they go to St. John's, Wellesley or
other parishes. At the same time, there is a core of parishioners,
mostly older, who are loyal to Monsignor Rossiter. The complaints
center around his style and manner that is perceived by many to
be overbearing and authoritarian. There is no question he, himself,
has experienced a great deal of pain in this situation. I believe
he might even be willing to be moved to another parish now and
perhaps this can be considered, although that might present other
problems. His Sunday collection, in this parish which is probably
the most affluent in the Archdiocese, is only $900.00. At the
request of about fifteen or twenty parishioners, we recently have
initiated the Spiritual Development Program and Monsignor has been
most cooperative, but we know there will be difficulties.

70 LAWRENCE STREET, LOWELL, MASSACHUSETTS 01852

December 7, 1984. Bishop John M. D'Arcy protests to Archbishop Bernard F. Law when Geoghan is transferred to St. Julia's Church, Weston, Massachusetts. Geoghan, writes D'Arcy, "has a history of homosexual involvement with young boys."

Archbishop Law
December 7, 1984
Page 2

I am afraid that this assignment has complicated a difficult situation. If something happens, the parishioners already angry and divided, will be convinced that the Archdiocese has no concern for their welfare and simply sends them priests with problems. On the other hand, if Fr. Geoghan is now removed, parishioners will quickly claim that once again Monsignor Rossiter cannot live with other priests.

I have had helpful and constructive conversations on this with both Fr. Banks and Fr. Oates. Both are keenly aware of the problem and, as you well know, they are hoping to set up some kind of structure so that we can handle this in a better way in the future. I am concerned about further scandal in this parish and further division and more misunderstanding by this assignment. I am anxious to help you in any way I can to relieve the difficult pastoral situation there and it is my obligation to keep you fully informed at this time so you would not be "blindsided" later on. While no parish can handle these shocking situations that we have witnessed recently, this parish is most vulnerable. I wonder if Fr. Geoghan should not be reduced to just weekend work while receiving some kind of therapy.

You know how grateful I am to you for your constant concern about this region and the constructive steps you have already taken in several parishes here. Many thanks.

Sincerely yours in Our Lord,

Most Reverend John M. D'Arcy

copies: Rev. Robert J. Banks
Rev. Thomas Oates

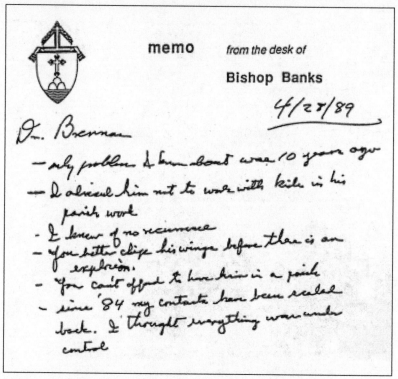

memo   *from the desk of*

Bishop Banks

4/28/89

Dr. Brennan
- only problem I knew about was 10 years ago
- I advised him not to work with kids in his parish work
- I knew of no recurrence
- You better clip his wings before there is an explosion.
- You can't afford to have him in a parish
- since '84 my contacts have been scaled back. I thought everything was under control

April 28, 1989. A note from Bishop Robert J. Banks, apparently made during a conversation with Dr. Brennan, who says of Geoghan, "You better clip his wings before there is an explosion."

ST. JULIA'S RECTORY
374 BOSTON POST ROAD
WESTON, MASSACHUSETTS
02193

June 29, 1990

His Eminence Bernard Cardinal Law
2101 Commonwealth Avenue
Brighton, Massachusetts 02135

Your Eminence:

Monsignor Rossiter has told me that he will be submitting his letter of resignation. I respectfully request that I be appointed his successor.

At the Emmaus Program it was stated that there would be a "stampede" for St. Julia Parish. I feel that I am qualified. I have been six years in Weston. I know the people, the parish and its problems. I am confident that I can build a vibrant Faith Community.

During my twenty-eight years in parish ministry, I have been the following:

* Deacon Supervisor, St. John's Seminary;
* Instructor in Catechetics, St. John's Seminary;
* President of an Ecumenical Association;
* Member of Board of Directors, Catholic Charities of Lynn.

I have been faithful to continuing education:

1. Master of Divinity, Master of Theology degrees, B.T.I. and Weston School of Theology;
2. Institute for C.T.E., the North American College, Rome;
3. Lectures and Workshops on Canon Law at the Gregorian University;
4. Lectures and Workshops on Liturgy at San. Anselmo University;
5. Biblical Institute and Pilgrimage, Jerusalem.

Assuring you of my filial obedience, Your Eminence,

Respectfully,

John Joseph Geoghan

Rev. John J. Geoghan
Parochial Vicar

June 29, 1990. Geoghan, in a letter to Cardinal Law, asks to be named pastor of St. Julia's, citing his long service to the parish.

The Most Reverend Robert J. Banks D.D.
2121 Commonwealth Avenue
Brighton, Massachusetts 02135

Re: Fr. John Geoghan

Dear Bishop Banks,

I haven known Father Geoghan since February 1980.

There is no psychiatric contraindication to
Fr. Geoghan's pastoral work at this time.

                              Very truly yours

                              John H. Brennan, M.D.

JHB/mk
cc: Fr. John Geoghan

December 7, 1990. Dr. Brennan notes that there is no "psychiatric contraindication" against the priest's returning to work.

File

CONFIDENTIAL

CARDINAL'S RESIDENCE
2101 COMMONWEALTH AVENUE
BRIGHTON, MASSACHUSETTS 02135-3192

December 30, 1994

Reverend John J. Geoghan
Associate Director - Office for Senior Priests
Regina Cleri
60 William Cardinal O'Connell Way
Boston, MA 02114

Dear Father Geoghan:

I was sorry to learn of the recent allegations made about you. In light of the steps being taken to address the allegations and in line with the agreement you reached with Reverend Brian M. Flatley, Assistant to the Secretary for Ministerial Personnel, I have assigned you to an Administrative Leave effective today, December 30, 1994.

During this period, you are free to celebrate Mass privately. Otherwise, I ask that you refrain from all pastoral activity and public ministry until a resolution has been arrived at regarding the allegations. During this period, your regular monthly remuneration will be provided through the Clergy Benefit Trust of the Archdiocese.

I realize this is a difficult time for you and for those close to you. If I can be of help to you in some way, please contact me. Be assured you are remembered in my prayers.

Please send written notification to Reverend Monsignor William F. Murphy, Vicar for Administration, and Reverend James J. McCarthy, Clergy Personnel Director, indicating that you have received this communication.

With warm personal regards, I am,

Sincerely yours in Christ,

Archbishop of Boston

December 30, 1994. Cardinal Law, saying he is "sorry to learn of recent allegations made about you," puts Geoghan on administrative leave.

ARCHDIOCESE OF BOSTON
OFFICE FOR SENIOR PRIESTS
60 WILLIAM CARDINAL O'CONNELL WAY
BOSTON, MASSACHUSETTS 02114
TEL. (617) 523-1861

REV. JOHN J. GEOGHAN

Nov. 17, 1995

Dear Monsignor Murphy,

I know it is not the end of the world but for me with the many burdens I am bearing, it feels like it !

I will be happy to meet with Cardinal Law any time he wishes to meet with me. At this time it would be inappropriate for me to resign from the position of associate director of this office. I believe it would be a terrible injustice to remove me from this office.

I have been falsely accused and feel alienated from my ministry and fellowship with my brother priests.

I cannot believe that one would be considered guilty on an accusation or based on speculation but I have experienced this. Where is there justice or due process?

It is not any consolation to be told I am in the company of many priests, bishops and cardinals. What hurts the most is being told by non-professionals "your in denial" therefore not credible.

I will do all within my power to maintain my innocence. Please have patience. I must.

Respectfully

John J. Geoghan

November 17, 1995. Geoghan, in a letter to Monsignor William F. Murphy, angrily denies abuse allegations and refuses to resign as associate director of the Office for Senior Priests, where he had been assigned after his administrative leave.

CARDINAL'S RESIDENCE
2101 COMMONWEALTH AVENUE
BRIGHTON, MASSACHUSETTS 02135-3192

August 4, 1996

Reverend John J. Geoghan
64 Oceanside Drive
Scituate, MA 02066

Dear Father Geoghan:

It is my understanding that after significant conversation with Reverend Brian M. Flatley, Assistant to the Secretary of Ministerial Personnel, you have accepted the recommendation recently made to you for professional assistance. I am encouraged by your positive response in that regard.

In that light, I am writing to advise you that I have granted you Sick Leave status. I have made the effective date retroactive to July 28, 1996.

Since December 30, 1994 you have been on Administrative Leave and I have indicated that you should refrain from all pastoral activity and public ministry. It is important that you understand that during your period of Sick Leave the same conditions would apply with regard to pastoral activity and public ministry.

Please send written notification to Most Reverend William F. Murphy, Moderator of the Curia, and Reverend James J. McCarthy, Clergy Personnel Director, indicating that you have received this communication.

I know that the time ahead has the potential to be an opportunity for much personal insight and growth and response to God's care and love in the various ways it may be made manifest to you. Be assured of frequent remembrance in my prayers.

With warmest personal regards and my appreciation for your cooperation and your efforts, I remain.

Sincerely yours in Christ,

Archbishop of Boston

August 4, 1996. Cardinal Law places Geoghan on sick leave, noting that "the time ahead has the potential . . . for much personal insight and growth."

REGINA CLERI, INC.
60 WILLIAM CARDINAL O'CONNELL WAY
BOSTON, MASSACHUSETTS 02114

October 19 1996

Dear Cardinal Law,

I request that I be granted Senior
Priest Retirement Status, for reasons
of health.

I feel privileged that I have shared in
the active ministry for these thirty
four years. God has been and
continues to be good to me.

Sincerely,
Rev. John J. Geoghan

October 19, 1996. Geoghan requests retirement.

CARDINAL S RESIDENCE
2101 COMMONWEALTH AVENUE
BRIGHTON MASSACHUSETTS 02135-3192

December 12, 1996

Reverend John J. Geoghan
Southdown
1335 Saint John's Sideroad East
R.R. #2
Aurora, Ontario L4G 3G8
CANADA

Dear Father Geoghan,

I am writing in response to your request, made October 19, 1996, for Senior Priest Retirement status. I am granting your request. I am also assigning you to full time residence at Regina Cleri in Boston. The effective dates of these actions is January 3, 1997.

As you know, it is unusual for a man of your age to be granted this status. However, your particular situation makes it advisable. In regards to your situation, I feel it prudent to remind you that your ministry within the Archdiocese is restricted to the celebration of private Mass. This allows for you to be the principal celebrant at the community Mass at Regina Cleri. Any other ministry must be specifically requested through the Office of Delegate of the Archbishop.

Please send written notification to Most Reverend William Murphy, Moderator of the Curia, and Reverend James J. McCarthy, Director of Clergy Personnel, indicating you have received this letter.

Yours has been an effective life of ministry, sadly impaired by illness. On behalf of those you have served well, and in my own name, I would like to thank you. I understand yours is a painful situation. The Passion we share can indeed seem unbearable and unrelenting. We are our best selves when we respond in honesty and trust. God bless you, Jack.

Please stay in close touch with Reverend William F. Murphy, Delegate of the Archbishop. I have asked him to be in contact with you on an informal but regular basis.

Asking God's blessings on you and those you love, I am,

Sincerely yours in Christ,

Archbishop of Boston

December 12, 1996. Cardinal Law grants Geoghan senior priest retirement status. Seventeen months later, Geoghan was defrocked.

ARCHDIOCESE OF BOSTON
2121 COMMONWEALTH AVENUE
BRIGHTON, MASSACHUSETTS 02135-3193
(617) 254 0100   FAX (617) 783-2947

VICAR GENERAL
MODERATOR OF THE CURIA

May 8, 1998

PERSONAL & CONFIDENTIAL

M E M O R A N D U M

TO: Reverend James McCarthy

FROM: Monsignor Richard Lennon *RGL*

RE: John J. Geoghan

For your records John J. Geoghan was dismissed from the Priesthood on February 17, 1998. He was informed of this action on April 27, 1998 (CDWDS 372/98).

RGL:dh

May 8, 1998. The notice that Geoghan was officially defrocked on February 17, 1998.

COMMONWEALTH OF MASSACHUSETTS

MIDDLESEX, SS.

SUPERIOR COURT DEPARTMENT
DOCKET NO.

COMMONWEALTH

V.

JOHN J. GEOGHAN

STATEMENT OF THE CASE

Now comes the Commonwealth and offers the following statement of the facts of this case. This statement does not constitute a bill of particulars nor does it recite all facts known to the Commonwealth.

During the late 1980's and early 1990's, John J. Geoghan was a priest at St. Julia's Parish in Weston, Massachusetts. Father Geoghan often would spend time at the Boy's & Girls Club at 20 Exchange Street in Waltham, Massachusetts. He spent most of his time in the pool and shower area.

Father Geoghan befriended many young boys who lived in the Prospect Hill area in Waltham, which is an area of low income housing. Father Geoghan encouraged these boys to attend the Boys & Girls Club and to become involved in activities there, telling the parents of these children that this was the best way to keep the children off the streets and not involved with "bad kids." Often Father Geoghan would attempt to recruit these young children to serve as altar boys with him at St. Julia's Church.

December 9, 1999. The Statement of the Case, *Commonwealth* v. *John J. Geoghan*, filed in Middlesex Superior Court.

When ███████████ was 11 years old, he was living in the Prospect Hill area in Waltham. He spent time at the Boys & Girls Club, having been encouraged to do so by his mother. One day, when ███ was at the pool with his mother and younger sister for a family swim, an incident occurred with Father Geoghan. ███ was in the deeper end of the pool, practicing his diving. Father Geoghan approached ███ and was assisting him in his efforts. At one point, Father Geoghan reached his hand inside ███ swim trunks and grabbed ███ buttocks. ███ cried out, squirmed out of Father Geoghan's reach, swam down to his mother and climbed out of the pool. He insisted that the family leave the Boys & Girls Club immediately. ███ pulled his pants on over his wet swim trunks and left the building. On the way home, ███ told his mother what had happened and told her he never wanted to return to the Boys & Girls Club.

Respectfully Submitted
For the Commonwealth,

MARTHA COAKLEY
DISTRICT ATTORNEY

By: _____

Lynn C. Rooney
Deputy First Assistant
40 Thorndike Street
Cambridge, MA 02141
617-494-4060
BBO No. 555399

Dated: November 22, 1999

Report of Rev. Paul Shanley's talk.   Oct. 4, 1977
  to Dignity—Integrity 9-23-77
  St. Luke's Episcopal Church, Rochester, N.y.

Dear Jean,
    In regard to Fr. Paul Shanley, the following are some of
his statements per your request.

Homosexual acts are not sinful, sick, a crime, nor are they
immoral.

What has been done to gays by the straight community calls
out for vengeance from heaven. Gay persons aren't angry
enough, they should become more angry at society.

He has been following Lewis Crew, who is an advocate for gay
teachers and gay curriculum in schools, and he (Fr. Shanley)
agrees with Crew, that gay children should have gay teachers
and gay curriculum.

Most first homosexual encounters are with straights. It is
straights who seduce youngsters.

Further, "straight people cannot tell the truth about sex".

Straights spend time worrying about the bedsores of gays in
regard to their sexual activity. (This brought a big laugh).

He doesn't advocate as some clergy do that gays form gay unions
(2 forming a pr.), because in his experience counseling those
in gay unions, he finds that gay unions invariably fall apart.
(He laughed) and said just as heterosexual unions are falling
apart, but in gay unions no children are involved.

He stated celibacy is impossible, therefore, the only alter-
native is for gays to have sex with different persons whenever
they want to.

He spoke of pedophilia (which is a non coerced sexual man-
ipulation of sex organs including oral-genital sex between an
adult and child). He stated that the adult is not the seducer--
the "kid" is the seducer and further the kid is not traumatized
by the act per se, the kid is traumatized when the police and
authorities "drag" the kid in for questioning.

He stated that he can think of no sexual act that causes psychic
damage--"not even incest or bestiality".

He stated that clergy donot work with gays because they are fear-
ful of losing their reputation--that they may be thought to be
gay. He said this is an indictment of the clergy. He said it
would be a good idea, if people thought the clergy was gay becau

October 4, 1977. A shocked woman writes about the topics of a recent
speech given by Rev. Paul R. Shanley that included subjects such as
"homosexual acts are not sinful" and "celibacy is impossible."

it would have a radicallizing effect. Fr. Shanley described himself as an ultra liberal.

To top off his speech he said, "Homosexuality is a gift from God and should be celebrated".

I have a clipping which states that Fr. Paul Shanley, of the Archdiocese of Boston represents "sexual minorities" on the Young Adult Ministry Board of USCC. Also a Fr. Patrick O'Neill OSA is the USCC's representative for young adult ministry.

Fr. Shanley said he was appointed to his position by a Cardinal Maderis (my spelling of the cardinal's name may be incorrect).

Fr. Shanley also stated that he had spoken to several clergy the afternoon of the evening meeting of Dignity/Integrit; Sept. 23, 1977, St. Luke's Episcopal Church. 8.P.M. Fr. Shanley was wearing full Roman garb.

Sorry I didn't get this off to you sooner, but have been very busy. Hope it helps.

Spiritually,

Francis Stevens

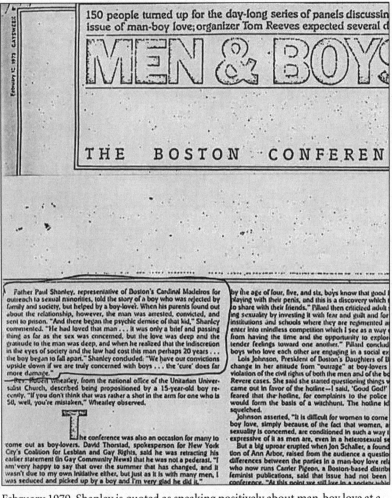

150 people turned up for the day-long series of panels discussin[g] issue of man-boy love; organizer Tom Reeves expected several d[...]

MEN & BOYS

THE BOSTON CONFEREN[CE]

Father Paul Shanley, representative of Boston's Cardinal Madeiros for outreach to sexual minorities, told the story of a boy who was rejected by family and society, but helped by a boy-lover. When his parents found out about the relationship, however, the man was arrested, convicted, and sent to prison. "And there began the psychic demise of that kid," Shanley commented. "He had loved that man . . . it was only a brief and passing thing as far as the sex was concerned, but the love was deep and the gratitude to the man was deep, and when he realized that the indiscretion in the eyes of society and the law had cost this man perhaps 20 years . . . the boy began to fall apart." Shanley concluded: "We have our convictions upside down if we are truly concerned with boys . . . the 'cure' does far more damage."

Rev. Robert Wheatley, from the national office of the Unitarian Universalist Church, described being propositioned by a 15-year-old boy recently. "If you don't think that was rather a shot in the arm for one who is 50, well, you're mistaken," Wheatley observed.

The conference was also an occasion for many to come out as boy-lovers. David Thorstad, spokesperson for New York City's Coalition for Lesbian and Gay Rights, said he was retracting his earlier statement (in Gay Community News) that he was not a pederast. "I am very happy to say that over the summer that has changed, and it wasn't due to my own initiative either, but just as it is with many men, I was seduced and picked up by a boy and I'm very glad he did it."

by the age of four, five, and six, boys know that good [...] playing with their penis, and this is a discovery which [...] to share with their friends." Pillard then criticized adult [...] ing sexuality by investing it with fear and guilt and for [...] institutions and schools where they are regimented a[nd] enter into mindless competition which I see as a way [of] from having the time and the opportunity to explor[e] tender feelings toward one another." Pillard conclud[ed] boys who love each other are engaging in a social ex[...]

Lois Johnson, President of Boston's Daughters of B[...] change in her attitude from "outrage" at boy-lovers violation of the civil rights of both the men and of the b[...] came out in favor of the hotline—I said, 'Good God!' feared that the hotline, for complaints to the police would form the basis of a witchhunt. The hotline ki[...] squelched.

Johnson asserted, "It is difficult for women to come boy love, simply because, of the fact that women, a[s] sexuality is concerned, are conditioned in such a way [...] expressive of it as men are, even in a heterosexual se[...]

But a big uproar erupted when Jon Schaller, a found[er] tion of Ann Arbor, raised from the audience a questio[n] differences between the parties in a man-boy love rela[...] who now runs Carrier Pigeon, a Boston-based distrib[...] feminist publications, said that issue had not been conference. "At this point we still live in a society whic[h]

February 1979. Shanley is quoted as speaking positively about man-boy love at a conference on the topic in Boston.

CARDINAL'S RESIDENCE
2101 COMMONWEALTH AVENUE
BRIGHTON, MASSACHUSETTS 02135

Protocol Number: 173/74

February 12, 1979

His Eminence
Franjo Cardinal Seper
Sacred Congregation for the Doctrine of the Faith
Il Piazza del S. Uffizio
Roma, 00193 (Vatican City)

Your Eminence:

I wish to acknowledge your letter of November 14, 1978 concerning the matter of Reverend Paul Shanley and his tapes in which he presents doctrine directly opposed to the teaching of the Church. Because this matter involves a serious pastoral problem which confronts the Church in the United States at this time, I have decided to reply at some length and after some serious reflection on my part and to present my reply in person at the Sacred Congregation.

I wish to place my answer to your questions in its fullest pastoral context and also to give to the Holy See the fullest awareness of how I, as a pastor, see this problem and how I have tried to face it. At the beginning of this letter, I will explain my general overall response to this serious problem and then I will answer your questions more directly.

I. General Context of Homosexuality as a Pastoral, Spiritual and Moral Problem in Large Urban Areas of the United States

The following points confront me as a pastor:

There is a widespread homosexual culture especially, although not exclusive among young people. But there is a relatively new element present. This new element is found in the fact that homosexuals band together to assert: (1) the open fact of their homosexuality, (2) the fact that this is of no consequence to anyone except themselves - thus to be a homosexual differs from having a heterosexual orientation as being right handed differs from being left handed, and (3) the strong efforts to secure their civil rights and human rights.

February 12, 1979. Cardinal Medeiros tells the Vatican that Shanley "is a troubled priest." Medeiros also lays out his views on homosexuality "as a pastoral, spiritual and moral problem."

Protocol Number: 173/74   - 2 -   February 12, 1979

From the Church, some of these are asking: (1) that they be ministered to as a group and (2) that they be admitted to seminaries and novitiates. It is often asserted that in the past the Church has condemned the condition of homosexuality as in itself sinful. Implicit and sometimes explicit is the assertion that homosexual acts and behaviour constitute a morally acceptable way of life. It is my belief that the very fact of banding together in such groups for social and religious purposes usually includes the recognition and even the fostering of homosexual activity. All of these elements which are widespread throughout the United States are intensified in the Archdioce of Boston because of two factors: (1) We are largely urbanized and (2) We have the largest concentration of young people in the world due to the great number of colleges and universities flourishing here.

There is one final, significant factor which though not widespread is especially ominous for the life of the Church. Affected by the above element a few priests are beginning to proclaim their own homosexuality and an eve larger number is beginning to foster the assertions and claims outlined abo In addition, some priests are said to assert that homosexual acts under certain conditions are not sinful.

II. General Response

I have felt an obligation to respond to the root of this problem without, how neglecting to respond to its symptoms as well. First, may I indicate my efforts to get at the root of the problem.

Priestly Formation

Since our seminaries reflect the local American culture, the problem of homosexuality has surfaced there in a manner which is widespread and qui deep. It has even been asserted by some seminary faculty members that the Church does not have the right to inquire into the lives of candidates fc the priesthood in a penetrating way. Such a philosophy, which is an illicit expansion of American political philosophy, would paralyze the Church in its mission of calling only true vocations to the priesthood. In response t this:

> (1) I have worked with seminary priests towards a complete transformation of our admission process to the college seminary and to the theologate.

(2) I have also worked to strengthen the evaluation process by which men are voted on towards the priesthood.

(3) I have encouraged the spiritual directors of our seminary to work in the internal forum - always respecting proper confidentiality - to exercise their influence to remove from the path to the priesthood young men who are homosexuals.

(4) I have also sent at regular intervals outstanding priests to be prepared for the delicate work of spiritual direction.

The danger in seminaries, Your Eminence, is obvious. Where large numbers of homosexuals are present in a seminary, other homosexuals are quickly attracted. Other healthier young men tend to be repelled. As a result of the efforts in our seminary, a large number of candidates have been dropped. Yet some of these, who are from other dioceses, have been transferred by their bishops to other seminaries despite complete disclosures from our seminary.

As a result of my actions and the cooperation of some of our faculty, the numbers to be ordained in our Archdiocese for the next several years will be small. Had we not taken these actions, a large number of active homosexual men would have been ordained. In this, as you know, I have only been following the requirements of the Holy See in its teaching on priestly formation. We have a seminary which has now - within a five-year period - become almost fully transformed into a community of healthy, well-balanced young men. Our numbers are much smaller but now we will attract more young men who will be the right kind of candidates.

Naturally, there has been criticism for our actions. But I am convinced that these actions were correct. I am also convinced that there are other seminaries where this problem has not begun to be faced. In order to attack this problem at its root, I am now working with some bishops in our Region to compose a letter to all seminaries in the United States and Europe where the bishops of New England send young men to prepare for the priesthood. While there are several foundational areas treated in this letter, the following are especially pertinent to your inquiry and to the issues as outlined above:

(1) The teaching of moral theology in the seminary especially as it relates to the Magisterium. We are trying to strengthen the place given to Magisterial teaching by theology professors, especially by teachers of moral theology.

(2) In this letter, we are trying to strengthen the admissions proceedures in several ways. We are saying quite explicitly that homosexuals should not be admitted to the seminary.

(3) We are trying to strengthen the core of trained spiritual directors as I have found this necessary for many reasons - but especially helpful in weeding out overt or latent homosexuals.

(4) We are strengthening the means and also the criteria through which seminarians are evaluated each year.

I believe this letter which is based on and draws heavily from the teaching of the Holy See can have an enormous effect over the next generation of priests formed in New England. We believe it will bring about more orthodox moral teaching, less priests who are inclined to foster and encourage the rising homosexual culture (at least where its demands contradict Church teaching) and that we can turn back the number of homosexuals who, for many reasons, are being drawn towards the sacred priesthood.

I hope that this document which is also addressed to vocation directors will also be helpful to our National Conference as it draws up new five-year guidelines for seminary formation within the next few years.

I also took one other significant step within the last year which I believe is related to this matter. I was approached by one of our priests who has been on a Leave of Absence for about seven years asking if he could return to active ministry. I made an investigation which indicated to me that this priest has been living in a homosexual relationship with another man for a large part of those years. He proclaimed that this was over and that, through a Charismatic Prayer Group, he had experienced a conversion. I felt that to receive him back could create scandal and would undermine the slow but steady reform I was trying to lead in the seminary. So, despite pressure, I refused to receive him back until he had sought spiritual direction and counselling over a five-year period under my direction. He refused to do this. He was refused permission by some other dioceses but - unfortunate I believe - was accepted by a neighboring diocese.

May I say that I always try to be compassionate and helpful to a priest who finds himself to be a homosexual but who wishes to live a life of chastity and who struggles to do good priestly work.

III. Efforts Made in the Archdiocese of Boston to Insure Proper Pastoral Action
on Questions of Sexual Ethics

(1) In 1975, the Bishops' Committee on Pastoral Research and Practices
released a paper entitled, Principles to Guide Confessors in Questions of
Homosexuality. I found this paper to be sound and helpful. I immediately
mailed it to all the priests of the Archdiocese of Boston. Working with two
theologians and a priest psychiatrist, I also prepared a letter to all our
priests in which I tried to set down some further principles on this urgent
question. I have enclosed a copy of my letter dated June 10, 1975 and also
a copy of the document from the National Conference of Catholic Bishops.

(2) In 1977, the Holy See issued "Humana Persona", a document which gave
the authentic Church teaching on a broad range of questions concerned with
sexual ethics. The document asked individual ordinaries to prepare further
teaching which would apply the principles in "Humana Persona" to their
local situation. In response to this request, I immediately set about to
write a Pastoral Letter entitled, Growing Together in Holiness. I consulted
several theologians during the writing of this letter as I always do on such
matters. A copy of my Pastoral Letter is enclosed.

(3) In general, my Pastoral Letter along with the Document from your
Congregation, was well received in this Archdiocese. I did, however, receiv
some'sharp criticism because I was not lenient enough. I have enclosed an
exchange of correspondence which I received from one Franciscan priest
which will point out to Your Eminence the unfortunate thinking which I find
among some priests and which indicates that they base their position more on
the currents of our culture than on revelation and Church teaching.

(4) I am sure that you are familiar with the recent study of the Catholic
Theological Society of America on sexual ethics. As you know, this study
treats questions of sexual ethics in a manner which is opposed to Catholic
teaching. In order to counteract its approach as quickly as possible, I took
the following two steps:

   a) I asked Bishop Thomas J. Riley (now deceased) to write a theological
critique for our Archdiocesan newspaper. Bishop Riley was a respected
moral theologian who taught in our seminary for many years and later served
as rector. A copy of this article from The Pilot, July 1, 1977, is enclosed.

   b) I, myself, wrote a Pastoral Letter concerning this study in which I
tried to attack its basic foundation. This letter also addressed another questi
which was receiving a great deal of publicity at that time. A copy is enclosed
It also appeared in the enclosed pamphlet entitled, Questions and Answers for
Our Times.

Protocol Number: 173/74   - 6 -   February 12, 1979

Having now given to your Sacred Congregation for the Doctrine of the
Faith my basic efforts on the broad and difficult question of homosexuality
as a pastoral, moral and spiritual problem, I am happy to respond to
your questions in a direct way.

IV. Efforts Made by me to Confront Directly the Work of Reverend Paul Shanley

When I assumed the office of Archbishop of Boston in 1970, Father Paul
Shanley came to see me. He had been working with young people who were
so-called "runaways" with the permission of the late Cardinal Cushing. I
did not remove him from this work. Neither did I at anytime assign him
in any direct way to work with homosexuals or with the so-called "homosexua
community". There are no letters in our files to this effect nor did I ever
write any such letter.

When reports reached me that he was teaching in ways that seemed contra-
dictory to the teaching of the Church, I immediately summoned him. I have
met with him privately at least five times. I have told him what the
allegations were and he has denied them. He has told me that he does not
teach against what the Church teaches. I have been very specific in my
questions and he has responded quite directly. On one occasion, I have calle
in to our meeting three other priests - one a moral theologian, one a spiritua
theologian who is a respected and very orthodox spiritual director at our
seminary, and one who is a widely-known and respected priest-psychiatrist.
All four of us, working as a panel, addressed Father Shanley with direct
questions. Many other questions were concerned with the morality of
homosexual acts. He assured us that he spoke only according to Church
teaching and that he did not violate it or encourage others to violate it.

V. What Will be Done in the Future Concerning Father Shanley

I trust that the above presentation answers the first part of your question -
namely, What has been done in the past to deal with Father Shanley as well
as positions which he allegedly espouses?

Now, however, I have been apprised by your letter that the Holy See has
found him to be still teaching in a way that is directly opposed to the Holy
See. So I feel obliged to answer your second question - namely, What do
I plan to do in the future on this matter?

It is my intention to send a letter to all our priests relative to this question.
I will re-state in a brief manner the teachings of the Church on matters of
homosexuality and refer the priests to recent documents of the Holy See, the
National Conference of Catholic Bishops, and my own office. More to the

point, I will indicate that no priest is assigned by me to work specifically or only with homosexuals. I will indicate that whatever confusion may have arisen on it in the past, no priest in the future will have the right to make that claim. I will urge all our priests to minister to any homosexual person with kindness but will teach again that the best way of affirming that person is to lead him or her to the following of Christ and the avoidance of homosexual acts or the so-called "homosexual culture".

Recently, an organization called "Dignity" mailed to all our priests a piece of literature which would be destructive if followed and which supports the activity of the gay liberation movement and tries to enlist priests in behalf of that movement - a movement which, as I indicated above, holds positions which could be destructive of Church life and which are held under a veneer of seeking full rights within the Church and also within civil society. A copy is enclosed entitled, An Introductory Letter to Religious and Clerics by Brother William Roberts. Also enclosed is a copy of an editorial which appeared on page 1 of Dignity's Cross Currents, Vol. 1, No. 2. This letter from the organization called "Dignity" will give me a good occasion to write a brief letter indicating my position and the position of the Church and mention the fact that no one priest is assigned to this apostolate.

Now, I wish to tell you about my recent meeting with Father Paul Shanley. I called Father Shanley to my office and met with him in early January of 1979. I told him that he was to take a regular parish assignment, that he was not to work with homosexuals, and that his teaching was confusing people and giving them ideas contrary to Church teaching. Father Shanley, as always, said that he was not teaching against what the Church teaches. However, what I want to indicate most of all is that shortly after our meeting, Father Shanley went to the press. He had an extended interview with the Boston Globe and I have enclosed a copy of that report. Father Shanley was also interviewed at length on a WEEI local radio station program. His loudest protest was that homosexuality as an orientation was not a sin and that he would continue to proclaim that to the rooftops. Of course, the Church has never said that it was sinful but that homosexual acts are sinful. It is on this subject of homosexual acts that Father Shanley presents confusing and distorted teaching.

I believe that Father Shanley is a troubled priest and I have tried to be understanding and patient with him while continuously affirming - both privately to him and publicly to my people - the Church teaching on sexual ethics. Finally, in an effort to cooperate with your findings, I have taken these difficult but necessary steps. I hope and pray that you will find them appropriate and wise.

Protocol Number: 173/74   - 8 -   February 12, 1979

I trust, Your Eminence, that I have given you a complete picture of this delicate matter. When I have completed my letter to priests in another month or two, I will forward a copy to you.

Please pray for Father Shanley and for all our young people whose souls are attacked constantly by voices which distort and scandalize. Also, I ask your prayers above all for our seminaries and for me. I shall, as always, be pleased to receive your response to this matter as well as your good counsel and advice.

With sentiments of esteem and my prayerful best wishes, I remain

Devotedly yours in Our Lord,

Humberto Cardinal Medeiros

Humberto Cardinal Medeiros
ARCHBISHOP OF BOSTON

Enclosures

April 12, 1979

Reverend Paul R. Shanley
49 Milton Street
Milton, Massachusetts 02186

Dear Father Shanley:

I am writing to inform you that I am ending your appointment to the Ministry to Alienated Youth and am appointing you as Associate Pastor at Saint John the Evangelist Parish in Newton. The effective date of these actions is April 15, 1979. The special ministry you had undertaken to homosexuals was ended when you last visited me.

It is understood that your ministry at Saint John Parish and elsewhere in this Archdiocese of Boston will be exercised in full conformity with the clear teachings of the Church as expressed in papal documents and other pronouncements of the Holy See especially those regarding sexual ethics. The pastoral ministry of priests can hardly be effective apart from the healing and saving truth of Christ proclaimed by His Church, even when "the saying may be hard."

I am confident that as an obedient priest you will render fine priestly service to the People of God at Saint John Parish.

Please notify Most Reverend Thomas V. Daily, Chancellor, and Reverend Joseph P. Smyth, Personnel Director, that you have received this letter.

I take this occasion, Father Paul, to ask for a remembrance in your Masses and prayers that I may be a worthy instrument of Our Lord as Archbishop of Boston.

Invoking the blessing of Christ, the Eternal High Priest, on our mutual priestly endeavors, I am

Devotedly yours in Our Lord,

Humberto Cardinal Medeiros
Archbishop of Boston

RCAB 00352

April 12, 1979. Cardinal Medeiros's letter ends Shanley's appointment to the Ministry to Alienated Youth and appoints him associate pastor at St. John the Evangelist parish. The letter also orders Shanley to fulfill his duties in "full conformity" with Church teachings.

January 16, 1990

The Very Reverend Philip A. Behan
Diocese of San Bernadino
1450 North D Street
San Bernadino, California 92405

Dear Father Behan:

Reverend Paul R. Shanley, a priest in good standing and of the Archdiocese of Boston, was recently granted a medical leave for one year by His Eminence, Cardinal Law. He plans to live in the area of Palm Springs, California, during this time and, if possible, in a religious house or parish rectory. Afterwards he plans to return to the Archdiocese for an assignment.

The purpose of my letter is to inform you of this and to express my hope that this would be agreeable to you. I expect that Father Shanley will make these arrangements on his own. However, he may call upon you for assistance. It is my understanding that he would be willing to provide a minimum of ministry such as a celebration of Mass in lieu of room and board. If his assistance is not needed, the Archdiocese would be pleased to reimburse the parish or institution for the room and board provided him.

His Eminence, Cardinal Law, will appreciate whatever assistance can be given to Father Shanley. If you have any questions about this matter, I will be happy to answer them. I can assure you that Father Shanley has no problem that would be a concern to your diocese. He has resigned from his parish on his own, and we shall place him in parish ministry when he returns.

With warm regards, I am

Sincerely yours in Christ,

Most Reverend Robert J. Banks
Vicar for Administration

RJB:mo'l
1297M

RCAB 00656

January 16, 1990. Rev. Robert J. Banks's letter to San Bernardino's Rev. Philip A. Behan recommends Church-provided room and board for Shanley while on sick leave from the Boston archdiocese. It refers to Shanley as "a priest in good standing."

MEMORANDUM

RECEIVED
DEC 9 1991
...AB FOR ADMINISTRATION

TO: Bishop Hughes

FROM: Father McCormack

DATE: December 9, 1991

RE: Reverend Paul Shanley

Attached to this memo are copies of letters I have received from:

     a.   Dr. James W. Shaner - the doctor for Paul Shanley in California

     b.   A letter I sent to Dr. Cassem regarding Dr. Shaner's letter.

     c.   Dr. Cassem's response to my letter.

It is clear to me that Paul Shanley is a sick person. I really question the advisability of asking Fr. Shanley to return to Boston for a psychiatric consultation with the view that he would be able to return to active ministry. I think Paul would be terribly threatened by this and would be uncooperative with the effort.

From what I can gather, Paul is free-lancing in California - that is, helping out in the parish where he lives once in a while or in other parishes but nothing more than that.

Based on Dr. Shaner's and Dr. Cassem's observations, my recommendation would be to place him on disability. What I am not sure about is whether it should be full or partial. If we keep him on partial disability, we maintain a regular contact with him which is something he would like to avoid. If we make it permanent, we have no contact with him or, at best, minimal contact. We would have no idea what he is doing.

I am going to talk to Dr. Cassem about this. Do you have any insights or observations before I approach him?

Many thanks.

F. McCormack   '12/10

Jack:
1) I would be inclined to favor
partial disability
2) I think that we need to keep contact
even if cloaked.

JBM:mo'l
3908M
Attachments

RCAB 00660

December 9, 1991. Rev. John B. McCormack, now a bishop in New Hampshire, tells Bishop Alfred C. Hughes that Shanley "is a sick person."

CARDINAL'S RESIDENCE
2101 COMMONWEALTH AVENUE
BRIGHTON, MASSACHUSETTS 02135-3193

February 29, 1996

Reverend Paul R. Shanley
The Leo House
332 W. 23rd Street
New York, New York 10011

Dear Father Shanley:

Let me extend my apologies for being a little bit tardy in my response to your letter under date of January 16, 1996 in which you indicate that after consultation with Father Brian Flatley and having reached the age of sixty-five on January 25, 1996 you are requesting Senior Priest/Retirement status.

I write now to advise you formally that in line with your request I am ending your Sick Leave status and I am granting you Senior Priest/Retirement status. The effective date of this action is March 1, 1996.

Please send written notification to Most Reverend William F. Murphy, Vicar for Administration, and Reverend James J. McCarthy, Director of Clergy Personnel, indicating that you have received this communication.

This letter provides me with an opportunity to thank you in my name and in the name of the people of the Archdiocese for the ministry which you offered both in parishes and in a specialized way over the years from your ordination in 1960 until your Sick Leave began in 1990. For thirty years in assigned ministry you brought God's Word and His Love to His people and I know that that continues to be your goal despite some difficult limitations. That is an impressive record and all of us are truly grateful for your priestly care and ministry to all whom you have served during those years. Without doubt over all of these years of generous and zealous care, the lives and hearts of many people have been touched by your sharing of the Lord's Spirit. You are truly appreciated for all that you have done.

I am aware that there are some specific considerations which call for attention at this time in order to be sure that we have a mutual understanding with regard to this new status. Thus I have asked Father Flatley to follow-up on this communication. I am certain that you will hear from him very shortly.

With grateful remembrance and with my blessing and promise of prayer, I remain,

Sincerely yours in Christ,

Archbishop of Boston

cc: Reverend Brian M. Flatley

RCAB 00737

February 29, 1996. Cardinal Law grants senior priest retirement status to Shanley.

CARDINAL'S RESIDENCE
2101 COMMONWEALTH AVENUE
BRIGHTON, MASSACHUSETTS 02135-3192

June 12, 1997

His Eminence John Cardinal O'Connor
1011 First Avenue
New York, NY 10022

Not Sent

Your Eminence:

I am writing regarding a proposed change in the staffing of Leo House, the Catholic Hotel for Travelers on W. 23rd Street. Reverend Paul R. Shanley, a retired priest of the Archdiocese of Boston, has been serving as Assistant Director of the facility since the Spring of 1995. On June 3, 1997, the Board of Directors asked Father Shanley to consider the position of Executive Director.

Father Shanley has done good work at Leo House and is well regarded by the staff, but, as you know, some controversy from his past has followed him to New York.

Two conflicting issues arise in considering Father Shanley for the post. The first is that he has done good work and is surrounded by a competent staff which is aware of his situation. Opposing this is the likelihood that the role of Executive Director will bring with it a greater notoriety. That could draw publicity to him, to Leo House and to the Church.

I am aware that you will be discussing this with Monsignor Edward O'Donnell. It is my understanding that he has the most complete information of anyone. If you do decide to allow Father Shanley to accept this position, I would not object.

I look forward to seeing you in the near future.

Asking God's blessings on you and those you serve so well, I am,

Sincerely yours in Christ

Archbishop of Boston

June 12, 1997. Cardinal Law, in a letter to New York Cardinal John O'Connor that apparently was not sent, writes that he would not object if Shanley were named executive director of the Leo House.

Confidential
Memorandum

To: Cardinal Law

From: Reverend William F. Murphy

Date: June 18, 1997

Re: Fr. Paul Shanley

I received a letter from Fr. Shanley in which he reports that Cardinal O'Connor has rejected the proposal that Paul become Executive Director of Leo House in New York. Because of this I have not sent the enclosed letter. Would you like any letter to go to Cardinal O'Connor?

I confirmed the decision with Msgr Edward O'Donnell, Priest Personnel Director of the Archdiocese of New York. Msgr. O'Donnell says that Cardinal O'Connor feels the situation in the Leo House neighborhood is too volatile to risk the publicity which might arise.

I spoke to Fr. Shanley, who is disappointed that he did not receive the appointment. He will have to leave his position, which was de facto Executive Director (but without the title). He does not know when he will have to vacate Leo House.

I assured him that he will not be stranded by the Archdiocese. He asked about Regina Cleri. I said I would investigate that. I will ask Bishop Murphy about the possibility of that arrangement.

June 18, 1997. Rev. William F. Murphy tells Cardinal Law that Shanley's application to run the Leo House in New York City was rejected because Cardinal O'Connor felt it was "too volatile to risk the publicity which might arise."

Shanley

COPY

ARCHDIOCESE OF BOSTON
2121 COMMONWEALTH AVENUE
BRIGHTON, MASSACHUSETTS 02135-3193
(617) 254-0100
September 6, 1997

SECRETAR Reverend Paul R. Shanley
332 West 23rd Street
New York, NY 10011

Dear Paul,

I have spent considerable time reviewing your file. Among the many letters you received from Brian Flatley and John McCormack I have been able to piece together the restrictions of not doing any ministry, living without a roommate and not living in a rectory. Together with the Cardinal's acceptance of the Review Board recommendations (of October, 1994), I can safely explain to you what your current restrictions must be.

GT
Redaction

All that is written in stone is that you are not allowed to engage in any parish ministry. The restrictions against living with a roommate and not living near children or known homosexuals were prudent while you were under such close scrutiny by ▮▮▮▮▮▮ but I feel comfortable in lifting those now. You may have a roommate and you may live wherever you choose.

If you are able to engage in any ministry outside of a parish or a setting which regularly involves children, you may do this. Before beginning such a ministry, I would ask you to carefully review it with me so that the Cardinal and I will be fully informed. If residence in a rectory or a religious house is an option made available to you, I would ask that you let me know the details so that we can discuss them before you accept.

I understand that you will be leaving New York within the next six weeks. Please inform me of the exact date you will be departing. I would like to restate my offer to have your air travel to the West coast paid by the Archdiocese. That is only fitting.

I have submitted your request to the Clergy Fund Advisory Board. The Board meets on Thursday, September 11. It is important to know that currently none of the 182 senior priests receives a housing allowance. I hope that your circumstances will make you the exception.

Have you contacted Monsignor Dillabough in San Diego yet? I hope you are well. I enjoyed meeting with you last month. I trust that you will continue to live your limited priesthood in the manner in which we met: with dignity and a genuine concern for those in need.

Sincerely,

Reverend William F. Murphy
Delegate of the Archbishop

September 6, 1997. Murphy tells Shanley that some restrictions on him have been lifted. "All that is written in stone is that you are not allowed to engage in any parish ministry."

Notes

This book is based primarily on original reporting by the staff of the *Boston Globe*, including hundreds of interviews with victims and perpetrators of clergy sexual abuse; numerous church officials, including bishops, priests, nuns, seminarians, lay leaders, and lay staff; government officials, including prosecutors and elected officials; academics, including sociologists and theologians; interest groups representing victims, priests, and Catholic laypeople; and attorneys. We also relied on a large number of Church documents filed in connection with criminal and civil court cases, on statements and other documents published by the Church and by advocacy groups, on the past and current coverage of the clergy sexual abuse crisis by the *Globe* and other news organizations, on the scholarly work of academic researchers and other authors, on opinion polling conducted by the *Globe* and other organizations, and on public statements by Church leaders at news conferences and from the pulpit. In these notes we acknowledge the people we interviewed and the publications we quoted in this book.

Chapter 1: Father Geoghan

Interview quoted: Frank Leary.

Sources quoted: A considerable amount of material for this chapter was drawn from ten thousand pages of court documents obtained by the *Globe* under a court order. The documents, from eighty-four civil lawsuits filed against former priest John J. Geoghan and seventeen Church officials, include depositions, correspondence, and psychiatric evaluations.

Cardinal Law's letter to Geoghan, concluding "God bless you, Jack," is dated December 12, 1996, and is part of Geoghan's court file.

The letter from Monsignor John J. Murray, rector of Cardinal O'Connell Seminary, to Rev. Thomas J. Riley, rector of St. John's Seminary, is dated July 31, 1954, and is part of the court file.

Geoghan's recollections about his father, his struggles with his father's death, and his thoughts about his early childhood are taken from a confidential 1989 report prepared by St. Luke Institute in Maryland. It is part of the court file.

Details of Geoghan's earliest days in the priesthood are taken from a series of letters between his uncle, Monsignor Mark H. Keohane, and Rev. Thomas J. Riley, rector of St. John's Seminary, dated July 1955.

Geoghan's remarks to therapists about his earliest sexual feelings are taken from the 1989 St. Luke report.

The acknowledgment of Geoghan's sexual arousal in the company of boys is noted on page 55 of the deposition of Dr. Edward Messner, a Massachusetts General Hospital psychiatrist, taken on December 27, 2001.

Geoghan's assertion that only on "rare occasions" did he touch a seven-year-old boy and was "careful never to touch" one family's only girl is noted on page 19 of Geoghan's sentencing report of February 15, 2002, prepared by the Commonwealth of Massachusetts.

Geoghan's quotation about his wish that he had sought advice about "how to deal with children from dysfunctional families" is from a critique prepared by Geoghan of a 1995 St. Luke Institute report. It is contained in the sentencing report, page 22.

The quotation from Geoghan observing that "the children were just so affectionate" is taken from a June 1996 evaluation of Geoghan conducted by Dr. Mark Blais of Massachusetts General Hospital. Blais's comments are noted on page 26 of the sentencing report.

Rev. Thomas W. Moriarty's assessment that "something is not right" with Geoghan is from Moriarty's deposition of February 23, 2001.

Joanne Mueller's account of Geoghan's assault on her son is taken from Mueller's deposition of August 17, 2000.

Maryetta Dussourd's description of Geoghan's abuse of one of her sons is from her August 24, 2001, deposition.

Rev. William C. Francis's statement that "there was talk that [Geoghan] had been fooling around with kids" is from Francis's deposition on March 30, 2001.

Leonard Muzzi's recollection about Geoghan at his home in Hingham, Massachusetts, is from a sworn statement contained in Geoghan's court file.

Geoghan's fondling of a young boy on the eve of the child's First Communion is described on page 6 of the Commonwealth's sentencing report.

The accusation that Geoghan fondled a young boy in the bleachers at Fenway Park is detailed on page 8 of the sentencing report.

The quotation from Geoghan that "youngsters I was involved with were from troubled homes" is taken from Geoghan's critique of the St. Luke report about him. It is excerpted on page 24 of the sentencing report.

Rev. Francis H. Delaney's comment about a housekeeper's contention that Geoghan had children upstairs at the rectory is from Delaney's deposition of April 27, 2001.

The quotation from Cardinal Medeiros that Geoghan "will receive a grant of $2,000 to help with your expenses" is from a letter from Medeiros to Geoghan dated August 26, 1982, and is contained in Geoghan's court files.

Catherine Geoghan's comments about her brother's feeling "upset" about the charges against him and Geoghan's victims showing up at his home in Scituate, Massachusetts, are taken from her deposition of September 8, 2000.

Rev. Brian M. Flatley's assessment of Geoghan as a "pedophile, a liar, and a manipulator" is noted on page 53 of Messner's deposition of December 28, 2001.

Geoghan's admission that he had "inappropriate sexual activity with prepubertal boys in the early 1960s" is contained on page 18 of the Commonwealth's sentencing report.

Catherine Geoghan's account of the decision to place the family real estate holdings in her name alone is from her September 8, 2000, deposition.

The description of Geoghan's emotions and actions in the mid-1990s is drawn chiefly from Messner's deposition.

Geoghan's resistance to attending meetings of Sex and Love Addicts Anonymous and his statements about being on "the verge of death row" are from Messner's deposition.

The decision to fund Geoghan's retirement from its clergy medical fund is discussed in a December 4, 1996, archdiocesan memo.

Chapter 2: Cover-Up

Interviews quoted: Rev. Thomas P. Doyle, Air Force chaplain; Mitchell Garabedian, attorney; Roderick MacLeish Jr., attorney; Raymond Sinibaldi, alleged clergy sexual victim.

Other interviews: Jeffrey R. Anderson, attorney; Robert Anderton, alleged victim; Jason Berry, author; Sylvia Demarest, attorney; Maryetta Dussourd, mother of alleged victims; David Finkelhor, director, Crimes Against Children Research Center, University of New Hampshire; William H. Gordon, attorney; Mark Keane, alleged victim; Donna M. Morrissey, spokeswoman for the Boston archdiocese; Matthew J. McNamara, attorney; Patrick McSorley, alleged victim; Dr. Robert W. Mullins, physician; Jeffrey A. Newman, attorney; Jean Palermo, alleged victim; Monsignor Thomas E. Reidy, vicar general, Springfield–Cape Girardeau diocese; Philip J. Saviano, New England director, Survivors Network of those Abused by Priests; A. W. Richard Sipe, author and psychotherapist.

Sources quoted: Much of the material used for this chapter is taken from the Geoghan court documents.

Margaret Gallant's letter to Cardinal Bernard F. Law is dated September 6, 1984; Law's reply is dated September 21, 1984.

Law acknowledged consulting with Bishop Thomas V. Daily and placing Geoghan in the category of "in between assignments" in a public court document filed on June 4, 2001.

Rev. James H. Lane's contact with Geoghan was described in confidential interviews.

Rev. Francis S. Rossiter's knowledge of the allegations against Geoghan are noted in a confidential Church chronology of Geoghan's career, dated August 22, 1994. Rossiter's denial that he was informed of Geoghan's troubled past is made on pages 75–81 of his deposition, taken on April 11, 2001.

Cardinal Bernard F. Law's 1984 arrival in Boston was covered by *Boston Globe* religion reporter James L. Franklin in several newspaper stories.

John Logue's comparison of Law and the late president John F. Kennedy was taken from a *Globe* story dated March 30, 1984.

Rev. Paul A. White's comparison of Law and the late Cardinal Richard Cushing was published in the *Globe* on March 30, 1984.

Bishop John M. D'Arcy's letter to Law is dated December 7, 1984.

Geoghan's activities at the Waltham Boys & Girls Club are detailed in Suffolk County civil lawsuits and a Middlesex County criminal complaint dated November 22, 1999. On January 18, 2002, Geoghan was sentenced to a 9-to-10-year prison term for indecently touching a ten-year-old boy in the club's swimming pool.

Geoghan's evaluation by the St. Luke Institute as a "homosexual pedophile, non-exclusive type" and the characterization that he was a "high risk" are dated April 26, 1989.

Bishop John J. Banks told Geoghan he would have to leave the ministry on April 28, 1989, according to a confidential chronology of Geoghan's career prepared by a Church official.

Law's statements about the Church's lack of knowledge of child sexual abuse was reported in the July 27, 2001, edition of *The Pilot*.

The estimate that Geoghan molested at least thirty children after Law reassigned him to St. Julia's Church, on November 13, 1984, was made by examining allegations in civil lawsuits and criminal complaints.

The 1981 removal of Rev. Leonard R. Chambers from a Missouri parish was confirmed in an interview with Monsignor Thomas E. Reidy, vicar general of the Springfield–Cape Girardeau diocese.

The story of Rev. Gilbert Gauthé is drawn from Jason Berry, *Lead Us Not into Temptation: Catholic Priests and the Sexual Abuse of Children* (Urbana and Chicago: University of Illinois Press, 2000), pages 7, 11, 18, 156, and from interviews with the author.

The account of the House of Affirmation and the Rev. Thomas Kane was drawn from a *Boston Globe* story dated April 24, 1993, and from a story in the *New York Times* dated April 19, 2002.

Law's support for the writing of the 1985 confidential report "The Problem of Sexual Molestation by Roman Catholic Clergy" was described in an interview with Rev. Thomas P. Doyle, one of the report's authors. All quotations from the report are taken from an original copy of the document.

Mark Chopko's comments on behalf of the National Conference of Catholic Bishops were made in 1992 to *Globe* religion reporter Franklin. Franklin also reported that Doyle lost his position at the Vatican embassy in Washington and was unable to renew his teaching contract.

Bishop James A. Quinn's statements are taken from a transcript of his speech to the Midwest Canon Law Society in April of 1990, a copy of a deposition taken from him on May 26, 1995, in a clergy sexual abuse lawsuit against the Cleveland diocese, and a story in the *New York Times* dated April 14, 2002.

The story of Gregory J. Riedle's lawsuit against Rev. Thomas Adamson and the Archdiocese of St. Paul and Minneapolis is drawn from an interview with attorney Jeffrey R. Anderson and a May 23, 1992, story in the *Minneapolis Star-Tribune*.

The account of the clergy sexual abuse scandal in New Mexico relies on numerous newspaper stories, including the *Santa Fe New Mexican,* March 8, 1998; the *Albuquerque Tribune,* March 20, 1998; *USA Today,* March 26, 2002; and the *Palm Beach Post,* June 26, 1998.

The lawsuit and criminal charges against Rev. Rudolph Kos of the Dallas diocese are drawn from an interview with attorney Sylvia Demarest and newspaper stories in the *Dallas Morning News* dated July 25, 1997; March 29, 1998; July 11, 1998; and September 30, 2000.

The case of Rev. James R. Porter was the subject of extensive reporting by the *Globe* in newspaper stories by Don Aucoin, Linda Matchan, and other reporters. The account of the Porter story also relies on interviews with attorneys Roderick MacLeish Jr. and Matthew J. McNamara, confidential sources, and Porter's alleged victims.

The story of the alleged abuse suffered by Raymond Sinibaldi and Robert Anderton is drawn from interviews with them and their attorneys.

Accounts of the Church's fight against state legislation that would have required clergy to report allegations of sexual abuse of children are drawn from stories in the *Boston Globe*.

Accounts of Law's 1993 policy on clergy sexual abuse come from reporting by the *Globe* and interviews with Law published in 1992 and 1993. Law's pledge to "report such incidents to civil authorities in accordance with the law" was taken from a *Globe* story dated January 15, 1993.

The characterization of an unholy alliance among the Church, victims, and their lawyers was drawn from numerous interviews with attorneys and victims.

The legal strategy employed by attorney Mitchell Garabedian was drawn from court documents and interviews with Garabedian and his associate, William H. Gordon.

Rev. David A. Holley's story is drawn from an August 31, 1997, article in the *Dallas Morning News,* and from an interview with one of Holley's victims, Philip J. Saviano.

Wilson D. Rogers's statement about medical evaluations of priests accused of sexual misconduct was published in the July 27, 2001, edition of *The Pilot*.

The story of Geoghan's doctors — John H. Brennan and Robert W. Mullins — and their spotty credentials is drawn from public court documents, state medical files, and interviews, as well as from correspondence and records of Geoghan's psychiatric treatment that were unsealed by the court.

Brennan's letter saying that he had met with Geoghan and that they had "mutually agreed" he could resume his ministerial duties is dated January 13, 1981.

The evaluation from Mullins describing Geoghan's "unfortunate traumatic experience" was received by the Church on October 22, 1984.

The description of Geoghan's therapy as "friendly paternal chats" comes from an Institute of Living evaluation dated November 4, 1989.

Information about the referral of clients to Brennan by the late Rev. Fulgence Buonanno comes from confidential interviews.

Bishop Banks's notes of his conversation with Brennan, in which Brennan urged him to "clip" Geoghan's wings, are dated April 28, 1989.

The evaluation by the Institute of Living that Geoghan could be "a high risk-taker" is dated November 4, 1989. Banks wrote that he was "disappointed and disturbed by the report" in a letter dated November 30, 1989.

The Institute of Living's letter to Banks stating it was "quite safe" to return Geoghan to active ministry is dated December 13, 1989.

The account of Geoghan's last years as a priest and his defrocking by Law is taken from newspaper stories in the *Globe*.

Law's statement that he did not have the "powers of incarceration" is taken from a *Globe* newspaper story dated June 7, 1998.

Chapter 3: The Predators

Interviews quoted: Jean Bellow, former Massachusetts Department of Youth Services worker; Lynne M. Cadigan, Tucson attorney; Cornelius Coco, former Alpha Omega staff psychologist; John Isaacson, former Massachusetts Department of Youth Services assistant commissioner; Howard McCabe, father of alleged victim; Michael McCabe, alleged victim; Andrew Menchaca, alleged victim; A. W. Richard Sipe, psychotherapist-author; Frank Taylor, father of alleged victim; Peter Taylor, alleged victim.

Other interviews: Robert Abraham, alleged victim; Arthur Austin, alleged victim; Robert P. Bartlett, alleged victim; Thomas Blanchette, alleged victim; Paul Busa, alleged victim; Rev. James M. Carroll, Massachusetts priest; Paul Cultrera, alleged victim; Kathryn D'Agostino, former parishioner, St. John the Evangelist, Newton, Massachusetts; Carmen Durso, attorney; John J. Facella, father of alleged victim; Gregory Ford, alleged victim; Paula Ford, mother of alleged victim; Rodney Ford, father of alleged victim; Harold F. Francis, father of alleged victim; Sheila Francis, mother of alleged victim; Mitchell Garabedian, attorney; Jacqueline M. Gauvreau, former parishioner, St. John the Evangelist, Newton, Massachusetts; Frederic Halstrom, Boston attorney; Laurence A. Hardoon, Boston attorney;

James Hogan, alleged victim; Olan Horne, alleged victim; Rev. Bernard Lane, Massachusetts priest; David Lyko, alleged victim; Roderick MacLeish Jr., attorney; Marjorie Mahoney, sister of alleged victim; Mary McGee, mother of alleged victim; Patrick McGee, spokesman for Bishop John B. McCormack of Manchester, New Hampshire; Raymond P. McKeon, retired Chelmsford, Massachusetts, police chief; Jeffrey A. Newman, Boston attorney; Kevin O'Toole, brother of alleged victim; Ronald H. Paquin, former Massachusetts priest; William E. Rayno, former head of sexual assault unit, Methuen, Massachusetts, police department; Robert A. Sherman, Boston attorney; Rev. John J. White, Massachusetts priest. Numerous alleged victims and their family members spoke to the *Globe* on condition of anonymity, so while some of their stories appear in this book, their names do not. Many others spoke to the *Globe* on the record, but space constraints prevent their accounts from being included.

Sources quoted: Quotations from letters written by Paul R. Shanley and Cardinal Bernard F. Law are from sixteen hundred pages of previously confidential files released by the Boston archdiocese in April 2002.

Shanley's remarks to a reporter in 1969 were reported in the *Boston Globe*, November 24, 1969.

Other sources: Jason Berry, *Lead Us Not into Temptation: Catholic Priests and the Sexual Abuse of Children* (Urbana and Chicago: University of Illinois Press, 2000).

Information about clergy sex abuse cases in Arizona is from numerous stories that appeared in the *Arizona Daily Star, Los Angeles Times,* and *Tucson Citizen* in 2002.

Some information about allegations made against various priests is culled from civil lawsuits filed by alleged victims and their families.

Chapter 4: The Victims

Interviews quoted: Thomas Blanchette, Patricia Dolan, Frank Doherty, Michael Doherty, Virginia Doherty, Christopher T. Fulchino, Thomas P. Fulchino, Timothy Lambert, Armand Landry, Bryan MacDonald, Kenneth A. MacDonald, Patrick McSorley, Courtney Doherty Oland, and Peter Pollard. All are victims or family members of victims.

Rev. Christopher J. Coyne, a spokesman for the Archdiocese of Boston, confirmed in an interview that the archdiocese was aware that Rev. Peter R. Frost had abused minors.

Chapter 5: Explosion

Interviews quoted: Christopher Dixon; William Donohue, president of the Catholic League for Religious and Civil Rights; Bishop William S. Skylstad, vice president of the U.S. Conference of Catholic Bishops.

Sources quoted: Reports taken from other newspapers, most notably the *St. Louis Post-Dispatch* and the *Hartford Courant,* are attributed directly to them unless otherwise noted here.

Bishop Anthony J. O'Connell's remarks about his "awesome responsibility" during his installation are from the *Palm Beach Post,* January 15, 1999.

Bishop Thomas V. Daily's comments that begin "I am a pastor" are from his deposition of September 15, 2002. It is part of the Geoghan court file.

The remark from Bishop Daily's spokesman that "it's tough to see this happening to him" is from the *New York Times,* January 26, 2002.

The letter from Rev. Timothy J. Lambert's lawyer that describes "the perfect situation for a predator" and other details about his allegations were first reported in the *Globe* on March 14, 2002.

Direct quotation from Daily about his initial plan of "sticking" with the diocesan reporting standards for instances of abuse and that "some of these guys are dead" is from *Newsday,* March 29, 2002.

The quote from the Brooklyn district attorney that begins "If there are any allegations" is from *Newsday,* March 23, 2002.

Details about Rev. John McVernon's warning to Daily about parties at a Queens rectory are from *Newsday,* April 9, 2002.

Daily's pledge to "cooperate with them in any investigation" is from a diocesan news release of April 10, 2002.

Cardinal Law's letter to *The Tablet,* the official newspaper of the Brooklyn diocese, was reported in the January 26, 2002, edition of the *New York Times.*

Cardinal Egan's quotations about returning priests to ministry after an evaluation "if the conclusions were favorable" are from a March 23, 2002, letter from Egan that was made available to parishes in the Archdiocese of New York.

The 1990 memo about a "developing pattern of accusations" against Rev. Charles Carr is contained in court records obtained by the *Hartford Courant,* which first reported about it.

Manhattan District Attorney Robert M. Morgenthau's remarks about "responsible officials in all religious institutions" are from the *Hartford Courant,* March 20, 2002.

Cardinal Egan's pledge to do everything possible so that "abuse by clergy will never happen again" is from a letter from him read at archdiocesan churches on April 21, 2002.

Bishop Sergio Obeso's remark that "dirty laundry is best washed at home" is from the April 17, 2002, edition of the *Washington Post.*

Chapter 6: The Decline of Deference

Interviews quoted: David A. Angier, first assistant district attorney, Franklin and Hampshire Counties; Kevin M. Burke, district attorney, Essex County; Martha Coakley, district attorney, Middlesex County; Daniel F. Conley, district attorney,

Suffolk County; William R. Keating, district attorney, Norfolk County; Jeanine Pirro, district attorney, Westchester County, New York; Thomas F. Reilly, attorney general, Commonwealth of Massachusetts; Marian Walsh, Massachusetts State Senator.

Chapter 7: His Eminence

Interviews quoted: Jack Connors Jr., founder, Hill, Holliday, Connors, Cosmopulos, Inc.; Leonard Florence, friend of Cardinal Law; Paul A. La Camera, president and general manager, WCVB-TV; Carolyn M. Newberger, child psychologist; Thomas H. O'Connor, professor of history, Boston College; Thomas P. O'Neill III, former Massachusetts lieutenant governor and chief executive officer, FH-GPC, Inc.; Patrick J. Purcell, publisher, the *Boston Herald;* David W. Zizik, vice chairman, parish council, St. Theresa's Church, Sherborn, Massachusetts.

Other interviews: James T. Brett, president and chief executive officer, New England Council; William M. Bulger, president, University of Massachusetts; Dr. Michael F. Collins, president and chief executive officer, Caritas Christi Health Care System; David F. D'Allesandro, chairman and chief executive officer, John Hancock Financial Services, Inc.; Neal F. Finnegan, chairman, Citizens Bank of Massachusetts; Donna Latson Gittens, president and chief executive officer, Causemedia, Inc.; Kevin C. Phelan, executive vice president, Meredith & Grew, Inc.; R. Robert Popeo, chairman, Mintz, Levin, Cohn, Ferris, Glovsky and Popeo, PC; Jeffrey B. Rudman, senior partner, Hale and Dorr, LLP; Jack Shaughnessy Sr., chairman, Shaughnessy & Ahern Co.

Sources quoted: The Church's management ethos is examined in Garry Wills, *Bare Ruined Choirs* (New York: Doubleday, 1972), page 24.

A detailed description of the Irish domination of the American Catholic Church is from Maureen Dezell, *Irish America: Coming into Clover* (New York: Anchor Books, 2000), pages 169 and 184.

Other sources: Jack Beatty, *The Rascal King: The Life and Times of James Michael Curley, 1874–1958* (Reading, Mass.: Addison-Wesley, 1992).

Nat Hentoff, *Boston Boy* (New York: Knopf, 1986).

Eugene Cullen Kennedy, "Fall from Grace," *National Catholic Reporter*, March 8, 2002.

J. Anthony Lukas, *Common Ground: A Turbulent Decade in the Lives of Three American Families* (New York: Knopf, 1985).

Charles R. Morris, *American Catholic: The Saints and Sinners Who Built America's Most Powerful Church* (New York: Times Books, 1997).

Thomas H. O'Connor, *The Boston Irish: A Political History* (Boston: Northeastern University Press, 1995) and *Boston Catholics* (Boston: Northeastern University Press, 1998).

James M. O'Toole, *Militant and Triumphant: William Henry O'Connell and the Catholic Church in Boston, 1859–1944* (South Bend, Ind.: Notre Dame University Press, 1992).

Chapter 8: Sex and the Church

Interviews quoted: Dr. Fred S. Berlin of the National Institute for the Study, Prevention and Treatment of Sexual Trauma; Rev. Robert W. Bullock, pastor of Our Lady of Sorrows Church in Sharon, Massachusetts; Rev. Edward J. Burns, executive director of the Secretariat for Vocations and Priestly Formation at the U.S. Conference of Catholic Bishops; Edward Cardoza, former seminarian; David Clohessy, national director of the Survivors Network of those Abused by Priests; Rev. Christopher J. Coyne, professor at St. John's Seminary in Boston; Rev. Donald B. Cozzens, former rector of St. Mary Seminary in Cleveland; Sylvia M. Demarest, attorney; William Donohue, president of the Catholic League for Religious and Civil Rights; Rev. Dr. James J. Gill, founder and director of the Christian Institute for the Study of Human Sexuality at Catholic Theological Union in Chicago; Peter Isely, former seminarian and psychotherapist; Rev. James King, vocations director for the Indiana Province of the College of Holy Cross; Rev. Jay M. Mullin; Rev. Len Plazewski, director of vocations for the diocese of St. Petersburg; Anson D. Shupe, professor of sociology at Indiana University–Purdue University; and A. W. Richard Sipe, author of *Sex, Priests and Power: Anatomy of a Crisis* (New York: Brunner/Mazel, 1995).

Other interviews: Several writers who have spent considerable time examining the sexual behavior of priests have been particularly helpful, including Jason Berry, author of *Lead Us Not into Temptation: Catholic Priests and the Sexual Abuse of Children* (Urbana and Chicago: University of Illinois Press, 2000); and Eugene Kennedy, author of *The Unhealed Wound: The Church and Human Sexuality* (New York: St. Martin's Press, 2001). Other researchers who shared their insights: Dr. David Fassler, professor of psychiatry at the University of Vermont and chairman of the Council on Children, Adolescents and Their Families of the American Psychiatric Association; David Finkelhor, director of the Crimes Against Children Research Center at the University of New Hampshire. Several books were helpful, including *The Changing Face of the Priesthood* by Rev. Donald B. Cozzens (Collegeville, Minnesota: The Liturgical Press, 2000).

Sources quoted: Joaquin Navarro-Valls's comments on the clergy sexual abuse scandal were made in an interview published in the *New York Times* on March 3, 2002.

Mary Louise Cervone's comments on gay priests were made in a news release on March 4, 2002.

The discussion of treatment centers used by the Church over the years is drawn chiefly from a *Globe* story of April 13, 2002, written by Ellen Barry.

Paul Hendrickson's recollection of his experiences in the seminary in Alabama was published in the *New York Times* on April 28, 2002.

Pope John Paul II's apostolic exhortation on priestly formation, *Pastores Dabo Vobis,* was given in Rome on March 25, 1992.

Pope Paul VI's declaration reaffirming the Church's opposition to the ordination of women, *Inter Insignores,* was given in Rome on October 15, 1976.

Chapter 9: The Struggle for Change

Interviews quoted: Paul A. Baier, convocation participant; Mary Jo Bane, public policy and management professor at Harvard University's John F. Kennedy School of Government; Rev. Robert J. Bowers, pastor of St. Catherine of Siena Church in Charlestown, Massachusetts; Rev. Robert W. Bullock, pastor, Our Lady of Sorrows Church in Sharon, Massachusetts; Lisa Sowle Cahill, theology professor at Boston College; Rev. Robert J. Carr, parochial vicar at Cathedral of the Holy Cross in Boston; Patricia Casey, convocation participant; Bonnie Ciambotti, convocation participant; Rev. Walter H. Cuenin, pastor, Our Lady Help of Christians Church in Newton, Massachusetts; Luise Cahill Dittrich, member of Voice of the Faithful; William Donohue, president of Catholic League for Religious and Civil Rights; Thomas H. Groome, theology professor at Boston College; Rev. Paul E. Kilroy, pastor of St. Bernard's Church in Newton, Massachusetts; Ronald P. McArthur, president emeritus of Thomas Aquinas College; Gisela Morales-Barreto, Voice of the Faithful member; Dr. James E. Muller, Voice of the Faithful president; Thomas P. O'Neill III, former Massachusetts lieutenant governor and chief executive officer, FH-GPC, Inc.; Stephen J. Pope, chairman of theology department at Boston College; and Bishop William S. Skylstad, vice president of the U.S. Conference of Catholic Bishops.

Other interviews: R. Scott Appleby, director of the Cushwa Center for the Study of American Catholicism at the University of Notre Dame; Rev. James Coriden, professor of pastoral studies at Washington Theological Union; Ernest J. Corrigan, Voice of the Faithful member; Rev. Donald B. Cozzens, former president-rector of St. Mary Seminary and Graduate School of Theology in Cleveland; William V. D'Antonio, adjunct professor of sociology at Catholic University of America; Rev. Thomas P. Doyle, Air Force chaplain; Chester L. Gillis, associate professor of theology at Georgetown University; Bishop Wilton D. Gregory, president of U.S. Conference of Catholic Bishops; Rev. James F. Keenan, professor of moral theology at Weston Jesuit School of Theology; Rev. Richard P. McBrien, professor of theology at University of Notre Dame; Rev. C. John McCloskey III, director of Catholic Information Center in Washington, D.C.; David J. O'Brien, director of the Center for Religion, Ethics and Culture at the College of the Holy Cross; Rev. Thomas J. Reese, editor of *America* magazine; Richard J. Santagati, president of Merrimack College; and David W. Zizik, parish council vice chairman at St. Theresa's Church in Sherborn, Massachusetts. Numerous other laypeople, priests, members of the hierarchy, and Church staff spoke with the *Globe* in person, by telephone, or by e-mail about the struggle for change.

Sources quoted: Law's comment about "undermining the mission of the Catholic Church" is from remarks he made from the pulpit before the start of Mass on April 21, 2002.

Pope John Paul II's comment about "a purification of the entire Catholic community" is from the pontiff's address to the cardinals of the United States on April 23, 2002.

Mary Jo Bane's op-ed piece was published in the *Globe* on February 3, 2002.

Victor Conlogue corresponded with the *Globe* by e-mail.

Mary Leveck corresponded with the *Globe* by e-mail.

Polling on Catholic attitudes toward Church teachings was conducted by the *Boston Globe* and WBZ-TV on February 4–6, 2002. The *New York Times* and CBS News polled on April 28–May 1, 2002. Those attitudes are also described by William V. D'Antonio, et al., in *American Catholics: Gender, Generation and Commitment* (Lanham, Md.: AltaMira Press, 2001).

The socioeconomic progress of American Catholics is described by Bryan T. Froehle and Mary L. Gautier in *Catholicism USA: A Portrait of the Catholic Church in the United States* (New York: Orbis Books, 2000), pages 14–16.

Lumen Gentium, the dogmatic constitution of the church, was a Vatican II document promulgated in Rome by Pope Paul VI on November 21, 1964.

Helene O'Brien corresponded with the *Globe* by e-mail.

Cardinal Law acknowledged that Catholics felt betrayed by him in his response to lay leaders at Convocation 2002 on March 9, 2002.

Jane Audrey-Neuhauser corresponded with the *Globe* by e-mail.

Cardinal Law's comment that "I have heard you passionately and prayerfully plead for greater openness" was part of the concluding remarks he delivered at the March 9, 2002, convocation.

Cardinal Law outlined his goals for the Vatican gathering of U.S. cardinals in the remarks from the pulpit on April 21, 2002.

Law's opposition to the proposed association of parish councils was described in a letter from the archdiocesan vicar general, Bishop Walter J. Edyvean, faxed to priests on April 25, 2002.

The *Globe* and WBZ-TV polled Boston-area Catholics about their attitudes toward Cardinal Law and toward parish priests on February 4–6 and again on April 12–15, 2002.

Statistics about the changing number of priests in the United States are from the Center for Applied Research in the Apostolate at Georgetown University.

Sociologist Dean Hoge's research was reported in the *Washington Post* on April 27, 2002.

Archbishop Keith O'Brien's comments on celibacy were reported in the *Sunday Herald* of Glasgow, Scotland, on April 21, 2002.

Cardinal Roger M. Mahony's comments on celibacy were reported in the *Los Angeles Times* on March 26, 2002.

Cardinal J. Francis Stafford's comments on celibacy were reported in the *New York Times* on April 19, 2002.

Pope John Paul II's comments on celibacy were made in an address to visiting Nigerian bishops on April 20, 2002.

Ecclesia in America is an apostolic exhortation given by Pope John Paul II in Mexico City on January 22, 1999.

William J. Bennett wrote about the clergy sexual abuse scandal in the *Wall Street Journal* on March 18, 2002.

William F. Buckley Jr. wrote about the clergy sexual abuse crisis in a column syndicated by Universal Press Syndicate on February 13, 2002.

Patrick J. Buchanan wrote about the clergy sexual abuse crisis in a column syndicated by Creators Syndicate, Inc., on March 20, 2002.

The *Wall Street Journal* editorial on the Church and its critics was published on April 26, 2002.

Cardinal J. Francis Stafford's comments on "changing the faith" were reported in the *New York Times* on April 19, 2002.

Cardinal Darió Castrillón Hoyos's news conference on clergy sexual abuse was held at the Vatican on March 21, 2002.

Bishop Charles V. Grahmann's demand that priests get permission before speaking to reporters was reported by the *Dallas Morning News* on April 27, 2002.

Cardinal Law's declaration about secrecy came in a letter to priests on April 12, 2002.

Cardinal Law's assertion that negligence by Gregory Ford and his parents contributed to Ford's abuse came in a legal filing in April 2002.

The Pope's description of "a deep-seated crisis of sexual morality" came in an address to the cardinals of the United States on April 23, 2002.

John L. Allen Jr.'s comments on the next pope are from his book *Conclave: The Politics, Personalities, and Process of the Next Papal Election* (New York: Doubleday, 2002), page 38.

Mary Ann Keyes corresponded with the *Globe* by e-mail.

Richard W. Rohrbacher corresponded with the *Globe* by e-mail.

Other sources: William V. D'Antonio et al., *Laity, American and Catholic: Transforming the Church* (Kansas City, Mo.: Sheed & Ward, 1996).

Richard P. McBrien, editor, *The HarperCollins Encyclopedia of Catholicism* (New York: HarperCollins, 1995).

Thomas J. Reese, *Inside the Vatican: The Politics and Organization of the Catholic Church* (Cambridge: Harvard University Press, 1998).

George Weigel, *Witness to Hope: The Biography of Pope John Paul II* (New York: HarperCollins, 1999).

Acknowledgments

We would like to thank everyone who gave generously of their time to sit for interviews, take our phone calls, or point us toward the latest twist in a story that seems likely to unfold for some time. Some of these people were victims; some were parents. Others were priests, prosecutors, police officers, lawyers, doctors, professors — too many to mention by name. You gave us your time, your experience, and your expertise, and we appreciate it.

There is hardly an editor, reporter, or researcher at the *Globe* who hasn't contributed to the newspaper's coverage of this story, but we would be remiss if we didn't mention at least some of them by name: Ellen Barry, Kathleen Burge, Diego Ribadeneira, Tatsha Robertson, Charles M. Sennott, Farah Stockman, and Jack Thomas. Their enterprising efforts made our work easier.

The *Globe*'s many talented photographers, graphic artists, and designers helped our readers better understand this complex story. Teresa M. Hanafin and her able staff at Boston.com dramatically increased the impact of our work by making it available to millions of Web surfers around the world. Lisa Tuite, her staff at the *Globe* library, and researcher Kathleen Hennrikus helped us sort through a mountain of information.

The *Globe*'s attorneys, Jonathan M. Albano and Anthony E. Fuller of Bingham Dana, with herculean effort and reasoned legal arguments, helped convince three superior court judges, and a justice of the state appeals court, of the public's right to have access to documents that other judges had sealed at the urging of the Archdiocese of Boston.

We are enormously grateful to the folks for whom we do this work: the readers of the *Boston Globe*. Their response to this story has been immediate and intense. In thousands of phone calls, letters, and e-mails they have often lauded and occasionally lambasted us; they have shared their pain and anger, their sorrow and their stories; they have offered us tips and ideas and sources, and they have reminded us of our duty to be both fair and aggressive.

Other journalists dug at this issue before we did, putting it on the map. First and foremost among them is Jason Berry, who put the sexual abuse of children by priests in the national spotlight, first in 1985 by writing about it for papers including the *National Catholic Reporter*, and then in 1992 by writing a major book on this subject, *Lead Us Not into Temptation: Catholic Priests and the Sexual Abuse of Children*. James L. Franklin, the *Globe*'s former religion reporter, wrote many stories about the sexual abuse of minors by clergy over the years, and *Globe* reporters Linda Matchan and Don Aucoin made important contributions to the paper's coverage of the case of James R. Porter starting in 1992. In 2001, Kristen Lombardi of the *Boston Phoenix* wrote a number of articles raising troubling questions about the case of John J. Geoghan that the Archdiocese of Boston refused to address.

Our editors at Little, Brown and Company, Geoff Shandler and Ryan Harbage, helped to focus and tighten our work. Copyediting manager Peggy Freudenthal and her team showed grace under pressure, helping us to hone our language and check our facts.

Martin Baron, the *Globe*'s editor, touched off this investigation by demanding to know, during his first week on the job, why the Geoghan court documents were sealed. He insisted on thorough reporting, rigorous writing, and high editing standards.

This book would not have been possible without the direction of our boss at the *Globe*, Ben Bradlee Jr., deputy managing editor for projects. He oversaw the *Globe*'s reporting and helped conceive the book project, fiercely directing it through its writing and editing phases.

Finally, we acknowledge the victims of clergy sexual abuse, for their dignity and their courage, and for allowing us to tell their stories.

| Matt Carroll | Kevin Cullen | Thomas Farragher | Stephen Kurkjian |
| Michael Paulson | Sacha Pfeiffer | Michael Rezendes | Walter V. Robinson |